I0815060

THE WORST TRICKSTER STORY EVER TOLD

THE WORST TRICKSTER STORY EVER TOLD

Native America, *the* Supreme Court, *and the* U.S. Constitution

KEITH RICHOTTE, JR.

STANFORD UNIVERSITY PRESS
Stanford, California

Stanford University Press
Stanford, California

Printed in the United States of America on acid-free, archival-quality paper.

Library of Congress Cataloging-in-Publication Data
Names: Richotte, Keith, Jr., author.
Title: The worst trickster story ever told : Native America, the Supreme Court, and the U.S. Constitution / Keith Richotte, Jr.
Description: Stanford, California : Stanford University Press, 2025. | Includes bibliographical references and index.
Identifiers: LCCN 2024012421 (print) | LCCN 2024012422 (ebook) | ISBN 9781503641648 (cloth) | ISBN 9781503641655 (ebook)
Subjects: LCSH: United States. Supreme Court—History. | Indians of North America—Legal status, laws, etc.—History. | Indians of North America—Government relations—History. | Constitutional history—United States.
Classification: LCC KF8390 .R53 2025 (print) | LCC KF8390 (ebook) | DDC 342.7308/72—dc23/eng/20240325
LC record available at https://lccn.loc.gov/2024012421
LC ebook record available at https://lccn.loc.gov/2024012422

Cover design: Derek Thornton / Notch Design
Cover art: Michelle Richotte
Text design and typesetting: Elliott Beard
Title page photograph: Christopher Bruno / Creative Commons

For Jenny,
Who should have gotten a chance to read it.

And for Steven,
Who I hope never feels the need to read it
For all of the right reasons.

Contents

Preface ix

ONE *The Mystery* 1

TWO *The Conspiracy* 39

THREE *The Plot Twist* 80

FOUR *The Conundrum* 120

FIVE *The Resolution?* 152

Acknowledgments 185

Notes 191

Bibliography 259

Index 275

Preface

The story they have chosen to tell is wrong. They know it and we know it.
It is time to tell a better story.

One day, Nanaboozhoo realized that he hadn't seen any of his coworkers in a very long time. Since his coworkers were also some of his dearest friends, he decided to throw a party and invite them all. He sent out invitations across the land and built a large campfire in preparation. He also gathered good food to eat and a drum group to make music. It was going to be a real shindig.

All of Nanaboozhoo's coworkers came. There was Iktomi the spider, Nixant, Rabbit, Raven, Coyote, and many more.[1] They were all happy to see each other and thanked and praised Nanaboozhoo for bringing them together (although a few from the south privately grumbled to each other that it was a bit chilly in Nanaboozhoo's part of the world). As was befitting the group, the party was festive, boisterous, full of laughter, and equally full of petty squabbles. They ate and talked and danced and played tricks on each other for a very long time.

As was inevitable, eventually the partygoers found themselves sitting around the campfire swapping old stories. Sometimes the stories were about how they had tricked others, and sometimes they were about how they had been tricked. Sometimes the stories elicited knowing grunts and head nods for the bits of wisdom they imparted or how they explained how the world came to be. Sometimes they were just silly.

"You know who you can have a lot of fun with?" asked Rabbit. "Those bison. They are about as strong as you get, but that's about the only thing they got going for themselves."

Several of the other partygoers thought that bison had at least one more thing going for them—they were pretty tasty. However, they kept their mouths shut because they knew that interrupting or trying to talk over Rabbit was pointless.[2]

Rabbit kept jabbering away. "One day, I saw two bison on opposite sides of the hill. They were completely oblivious to each other. You know how they are. They're just a bunch of big, blind, lumbering oafs."[3] A handful of partygoers thought about disagreeing with Rabbit but thought better of it because they wanted to hear the story. "Anyway, normally I wouldn't bother with them because they can't see where they are stepping, and that can be bad news for someone built as low to the ground as I am. But I was bored and there wasn't much else to do, and when I saw this opportunity, I knew I had to take it."

Rabbit gave a half smile as he started warming up to his own story. "The thing about bison is, as dumb as they are, at least they know they are strong. So I went up to the first one, and I said, 'Hey there, big fella. You look like you have a lot of muscles, but I've never met anyone who is more powerful than me.' He just snorted as if he didn't hear me, but I know he did. So I went to the second bison, and I said the same thing. He also snorted and pretended not to hear me, but I knew that if I kept it up, I would get under their skins. So I kept going back and forth between them several times and saying things like 'You're not so tough' and 'I've never met a creature so scrawny' and 'I've pooped stronger loads than you.' After a while they both would say something back, like 'Get out of here, pipsqueak' or 'I wouldn't waste my time with someone as small as you' or—and this was my favorite—'You don't want to tussle with this muscle.' I wonder who taught them that one."

Rabbit was really starting to laugh at his own story. "So, anyway, I kept going back and forth between these two galoots until I got them real riled up. Finally I got the first bison angry enough that he started stomping his hoofs, and he started yelling at me, 'Fine, let's have a test of strength and see who is the strongest.' I mean seriously, couldn't he think of any other word other than some derivation of the word 'strong'? So I said to this guy, 'Wait right here,' and then I ran to the second bison, and after I needled him a little more, he was finally mad enough to challenge me. So I got a rope and went to the first bison and said, 'We are going to have a tug-of-war to see who is the strongest. When I say go, you pull on your end of the rope, and whoever can drag the other over the hill is the strongest.' Then I went to the second bison and gave him his end of the rope and said the same thing. And then I went to the top of the hill and yelled, 'Three . . . Two . . . One . . . GO!' "

Rabbit could barely contain himself by now. "When I yelled 'GO,' they both thought all they had to do was give one strong tug and I would go flying over the hill. But when they gave that first tug and they both bounced backward, you should have seen the look on their faces! They couldn't believe it! So then they started really pulling on the rope. They kept fighting against each other, still dumbfounded because they thought it was me! What a couple of imbeciles. And then, every once in a while one of them would pull the other about three-fourths up the hill, but then the one that was losing would find some more strength and start pulling the other one up the hill. They kept going and going and going, not having any idea that they were pulling against each other."

Rabbit finished laughing before he started speaking again. "It was hilarious for a very long time. But after this went on for most of the day, I got bored and left. Later I heard that these doofuses went on like this for two days. Finally, at the same time they both dropped their end of the rope and yelled, 'I give up! It's a tie! You're as strong as me, Rabbit!' That's when they realized that the voice on the other end of the rope wasn't mine. They walked around the hill and saw each other and discovered they had been tricked! I suppose it was a good thing that I wasn't there because who knows what they would have tried to do to me if I had been around. But it wouldn't have mattered anyway, because my people are so fast that we could always escape a bison if need be." This raised a few eyebrows because almost everyone around the campfire had seen a few of Rabbit's brethren who had been caught under a bison's hooves.

"Anyway, those silly bison tried to banish me from the watering hole, but I tricked them again . . ." Rabbit tried to continue.

"I have a story to tell," thundered a voice from another part of the campfire. Heads turned and watched Saynday rise. He closed his eyes and paused for a moment to let the gravitas of his impending words sink in before continuing. "I am the greatest warrior of the Kiowa nation, and I have a story of the utmost importance to tell you." All the partygoers looked at the perpetually hungry, oft-defeated Saynday and his pitiful moustache and decided that neither of his boasts was true. Still, they were eager to listen to any story that began that way. Saynday boomed again, "This is the great story of my wardrobe malfunction!"

"I was in need of a belt!" Saynday bellowed. He paused for another moment, caught up in his own words, before more meekly stammering, "Or maybe it was a sash. I don't completely remember. But I needed something like that."[4] Saynday cleared his throat and recovered his momentum. "Anyway, I needed to hold some clothing up. But I didn't have the materials for a belt or a sash or whatever. So I started thinking about how to solve my problem when I realized I did have something that would work!" Saynday grinned. "All I needed was right there with me the whole time! I was in need of a belt so I decided to use . . ."

Saynday briefly paused again, wondering about the sensibilities of his audience. "I suppose I should be a little careful with my language since these are more modest times.[5] Anyway, I decided to use my . . . my thingamabobber. My man rope. You know, my wangdoodle. You know . . ." Saynday said while gesturing toward a portion of himself that you can probably guess.

"We know what you're talking about," Raven yelled with faux exasperation (while trying not to laugh). "Get on with the story."

"Yeah, so anyway, I grabbed my . . ." Saynday was starting to like the nicknames more than the actual name. "My Mr. Pee-Pee and started stretching it out. I mean, it was pretty long already but . . ."

All of a sudden the partygoers heard a huge crash at the edge of the clearing. Everybody got quiet and looked in the direction of the noise. Then many of the partygoers got nervous when they could see a creature of some sort rustling around on the ground, groaning and howling and, so it seemed to the stunned crowd, maybe even . . . swearing?

The creature then jumped to its feet, to the audible gasps of the partygoers. It looked like a man, but unlike any of the ones that the partygoers had ever seen before. It was bedraggled and emaciated and had a very hairy face. But most of all this man was pale. His skin looked like winter, like hard times when there were often few places to go and little to eat.

Everybody was in shock and stood still in silence not knowing what to do, including the pale man. It felt like an eternity passed before someone said anything until . . .

. . . finally, the pale man meekly spoke. “Hey, are you guys Indians?” All the partygoers sighed heavily in unison.

ONE *The Mystery*

When did plenary power become constitutional?

For those of you whose eyes didn't roll so far in the back of your head as to pass out at the deep, scholarly pretentiousness of the previous sentence, I thank you for your perseverance. Please allow me to explain why we need to ask and answer such a question by engaging in a simple trick: Rather than conceptualizing it as a question, let's begin by thinking about it as a mystery—one with two critical clues.

As with many good mysteries, this one begins with a murder. In the early 1880s Crow Dog, a member of the Sicangu Lakota Oyate (or Brulé Lakota or Brulé Sioux in older literature) ambushed and killed Spotted Tail, who was also Sicangu Lakota.[1] The event took place on tribal land, which was increasingly surrounded by colonizers yet still very remote from what then constituted much of the United States. The motivation for the killing was assuredly political in nature—both men vied for leadership authority within the community—but it may have had personal elements as well.[2] Nonetheless, the heinous act created a rift within the community, one that the community sought to repair. Shortly after the killing, a tribal council sent peacemakers who helped the families negotiate a settlement.[3] The issue was resolved within the community to its satisfaction when Crow Dog and his family agreed to pay Spotted Tail's family six hundred dollars, eight horses, and a blanket, an astounding sum that testified to the significance of the family's and community's loss.[4]

As should be clear after only these few, short paragraphs, my career as a mystery writer is not off to an auspicious start. Not only do we know whodunit, but we have a sense of why hedunit, and we have encountered a resolution that did not involve a climactic chase or fight scene or any other details or action that would get the blood pumping. Fortunately for this book (although not so much for Native America), the story does not end here nor is this the mystery with which I am concerned. Rather, the true mystery is furthered by how and why American law developed as a response to Spotted Tail's death.

Although the matter was settled to the community's satisfaction under Sicangu Lakota Oyate law, federal officials seized on what they regarded as an opportunity. At the time, in the 1880s, the federal government was in the early stages of what is regularly referred to as the Allotment Era of federal policy. Over the course of American history, the federal government has decided upon a number of thematically driven methods with which to engage with Native America, which scholars have grouped into eras to better understand and explain them. The Allotment Era, lasting from approximately 1871 to 1934, was defined by attempts by the federal government, philanthropists who believed they were doing right, and those who sought tribal lands and resources to destroy tribal nations and tribalism.[5] The Allotment Era included, among other things, the process of allotment that fundamentally changed and reduced tribal land holdings, boarding schools that sought to eradicate tribal ways of life by forcing Native children into a Western mode of life, and Indian police and Indian courts that enforced Western law and norms in Native spaces.[6] The most famous quotation from the era that best sums it up comes from Richard Henry Pratt, a military man who built a second career as an educator when he opened the first Indian boarding school in Carlisle, Pennsylvania. Pratt stated that his goal for Native people was to "kill the Indian in him, and save the man."[7] It would be difficult to overstate the amount of time, energy, and resources that were directed toward eradicating tribal ways of life during the Allotment Era or the lasting harm that the era's efforts continue to cause.

Law, particularly criminal law, was a major arena in which the federal government (and others) recognized an opportunity to radically transform Native understandings and governance during the Allotment Era. Briefly, criminal law is different from its major counterpart, civil law, in that civil law governs relations between private parties whereas criminal law is perpetuated and enforced by a government.[8] Certainly, federal authorities and others were also interested in civil law but were especially interested in criminal law because of the direct threat of coercion through jail time or other punishments that lie at the heart of Western forms of criminal law. By forbidding tribal behaviors (such as dancing and ceremonies) and otherwise sanctioning or requiring Western behaviors (such as state-recognized marriages) through criminal law, the forces that sought to destroy tribal nations and tribalism could directly further their goal. Shortly after the matter was settled among the Sicangu Lakota Oyate, the federal government arrested Crow Dog under the pretense that a "public outcry" demanded that the killer be brought to justice.[9] The true purpose for arresting Crow Dog, however, had little to do with public opinion. Rather, the federal officials tasked with engaging with Native peoples wanted to develop a test case—a case that ascertained the state of the law.

At the time, federal officials tasked with engaging with Native peoples wanted to exercise criminal jurisdiction over Native peoples on Native lands. Put directly, jurisdiction simply means authority. If a court (or other governmental body) has jurisdiction over certain subject matter, lands, or persons, then that court (or other governmental body) can rightfully act within or upon that subject matter, lands, or persons. If it lacks jurisdiction, then it can't rightfully act. Thus, federal officials were hoping to exercise the authority, or jurisdiction, to employ American criminal law over Native peoples on Native lands. In one respect, the sovereignty and nationhood of Native peoples made this seem absurd—much like it would be absurd if the United States tried to extend its criminal law over peoples living in Canada or Mexico. Yet, tribal nations were increasingly surrounded and imposed upon by the growing colonial force that was the United States. Under these circumstances and within the spirit of the Allotment Era, forcing American criminal law on Native peoples on Native lands felt less like an absurdity to many federal officials and more like a necessity.

Thus, Crow Dog's arrest and trial were intended to produce a test case that would provoke American courts to decide whether the federal government had jurisdiction to exercise American criminal law over Native peoples on Native lands. Had it not been Crow Dog to provide the opportunity for this test case, then it would have been one of the other half-dozen or so cases that federal officials were also working on at the time.[10] The trial was swift, Crow Dog was convicted in a territorial court and sentenced to hang, and federal officials had their test case that was soon to be heard by the Supreme Court.[11] According to legend, Crow Dog managed to convince a federal marshal to let him go free for a period of time to arrange his affairs. The day Crow Dog promised to return was cold and snowy, and few if any expected him to keep his promise. Nonetheless, he showed up on time, making him a local hero.[12]

Before considering Crow Dog's fate at the Supreme Court, it is worth taking some time to consider two aspects of this situation that deserve further attention. First, what were federal officials hoping to accomplish with this test case? The most direct answer is that they were hoping to win the case and receive sanction from American courts to extend American law over Native peoples on Native lands. However, even a loss in the test case held potential for federal officials. The hope was that a loss would provoke Congress to take action to extend American jurisdiction through legislation over Native peoples on Native lands, which federal officials had previously tried, without success, to convince Congress to do.[13]

Second, what do we make of Crow Dog and his divergent fates in two very different legal regimes? This is more difficult than it might seem since assessing the incident with a contemporary perspective is likely to obscure the purpose behind the Sicangu Lakota Oyate's actions.[14] A modern reader—Native or not—might be tempted to dismiss Crow

Dog's substantial payment to Spotted Tail's family as another rich guy seemingly buying his way out of justice (albeit in an unfamiliar circumstance). Yet, the choices and methods employed by the Sicangu Lakota Oyate and the federal government allow us to take a step back and think about criminal law more wholistically. Thus, we might ask, through the prism of Crow Dog, what is the purpose of a criminal justice system?

Put simply, Crow Dog's situation allows us to recognize that the American, or Western, system of justice is focused on punishing the offender. Crow Dog, under this vision of criminal justice, needed to feel a roughly equivalent amount of harm that he caused. Federal officials sought the death penalty and were incensed when he "went free" under tribal law. However, for the Sicangu Lakota, and for many tribal nations, the focus of the criminal justice system was not on punishing the offender but rather on making the victim (or the victim's family) as whole as possible. Restoring a sense of balance and harmony within the community was the foremost goal and best accomplished through restitution rather than punishment.[15] Consequently, under the Sicangu Lakota system, Crow Dog was not buying his way out of or otherwise avoiding justice but fully and meaningfully participating in effectuating it.[16]

Every single court case, from the biggest to the smallest, is just a question that is seeking an answer: Did the accused commit the crime for which she or he is on trial? Did the company breach its contractual obligations? Is a tomato a fruit or a vegetable?[17] Consequently, the key to reading and understanding court opinions is to discern the question that the court is trying to answer. When the test case that emerged from Crow Dog's situation reached the Supreme Court, the question to be considered was blissfully uncomplicated and likely obvious by this point in the chapter: Did the federal government have jurisdiction to enforce American criminal law over Native peoples on Native lands?

The answer, according to the Supreme Court in its 1883 decision *Ex Parte Crow Dog*, was an equally simple "no," even if the methodology for arriving at that answer was somewhat convoluted and the language employed by Justice Stanley Matthews in the majority opinion was replete with the types of rhetorical unnecessities that Strunk and White sought to kill off.[18] Put most simply, the federal government had already given itself jurisdiction over crimes committed in "Indian Country" through two statutes. Yet, in those statutes the federal government specifically exempted from its jurisdiction crimes that were committed by one Native person against another Native person or crimes by Native people that had already been punished by the tribal nation.[19] Since Crow Dog clearly fell within both exceptions, the lawyers for the federal government sought alternative justifications for federal jurisdiction and settled on tribal cessions made in an 1868 treaty and an 1877 agreement.[20] The Supreme Court rejected this line of reasoning, stating among other things, "It is quite clear from the context that this does not cover the present case of an alleged wrong committed by one Indian upon the person of another of the same tribe."[21] Without jurisdiction, the federal government was forced to free Crow Dog, at which point he returned to his community, lived to an old age, and continued to remain a thorn in the side of federal officials.[22]

The Supreme Court's decision in *Crow Dog* was unquestionably a victory for Crow Dog and the Sicangu Lakota Oyate particularly and for tribal sovereignty and Native America more generally. It was an acknowledgment by the courts of the United States that the federal government, in what might be understood as a commitment to its foundational principles, could not simply assert its authority without a basis for that authority. It is rightfully celebrated for that which it stands.

Unfortunately, victories for tribal interests in American courts are rarely complete or without some corresponding aspect or aspects that diminish, limit, or completely negate the positive impact of the case for Native America. This is so with *Crow Dog*. Two distinguishing features significantly dull the shine of this particular outcome. The first is the rationale upon which the decision was made. While the final result of the case supported tribal sovereignty, Justice Matthews's opinion makes clear that this was more an unintended consequence than a purposeful goal or statement of principle. The main focus in Matthews's opinion was on federal claims to authority and their sources, or lack thereof. There is no discussion whatsoever of tribal criminal procedures or that the matter was handled within the community to the community's satisfaction.

The limited discussion of tribal peoples and methods in the opinion centers not on Sicangu Lakota Oyate structures or law but on the supposed deficiencies of Native America. In language that echoed earlier decisions and portended future ones, Matthews described Native peoples as "wards subject to a guardian" and "a dependent community who were in a state of pupilage."[23] Consequently, Matthews would later argue, it was unfair to measure Native peoples against American law. As part of the most famous passage in the case, Matthews wrote that the application of American law to Native peoples "tries them, not by their peers, nor by the customs of their people, nor the law of their land, but by superiors of a different race, according to the law of a social state of which they have an imperfect conception, and which is opposed to the traditions of their history, to the habits of their lives, to the strongest prejudices of their savage nature; one which measures the red man's revenge by the maxims of the white man's morality."[24]

Native peoples, inferior to their American counterparts according to Matthews, were merely the lens to view American jurisdiction and process. Although the opinion happened upon such an end, Matthews clearly did not intend to foster or support tribal sovereignty or methodologies. On the contrary, Matthews's opinion demonstrates a low opinion of Native peoples. Even though it was a win for tribal interests, the case has limited usefulness as a building block or intellectual basis for subsequent arguments in favor of Native rights and authority.

The second prominent feature of *Crow Dog* that mitigated its benefit for Native America—and that is more meaningful for the mystery we are trying to unravel—was how Justice Matthews opened the door to a reconsideration of the result. Near the end of his opinion, Matthews wrote that to find American jurisdiction over Crow Dog's actions on tribal land was "to reverse in this instance the general policy of the government towards the Indians, as declared in many statutes and treaties, and recognized in many decisions of this court, from the beginning to the present time."[25] Had Matthews ended here, he merely would have made the type of general observation that is found in countless court opinions and that may be more or less accurate but is often ephemeral and mostly harmless. However, he did not stop with this bit of fluff. Instead, he continued by stating, "To justify such a departure, in such a case, requires a clear expression of the intention of Congress, and that we have not been able to find."[26]

Particularly at its highest levels, we often conceptualize the three branches of the American government as sometimes "talking" to each other. Since authority is divided between the president, Congress, and the courts, none of the three can exercise its will without limitation. To that end, sometimes when one branch runs against the boundaries of its authority, it will signal through various means to another branch what it would like to see done or propose an alternative path to complete a goal that cannot be accomplished as currently constituted or otherwise offer guidance, advice, or requests.

Understood within this framework, Justice Matthews was very much "talking" to Congress through this opinion. The Court was unable to find American jurisdiction over Crow Dog and tribal lands under the circumstances with which it was presented. Consequently, it is difficult to understand Matthews's assertion it would take a "clear expression of the intention of Congress" for the Supreme Court to find jurisdiction as anything other than an open invitation to Congress to change the circumstances. Matthews offered his brief description of the "general policy of the government towards the Indians" and then explained how Congress might alter that general policy with a "clear expression." Matthews deliberately neutered the opinion's capacity to protect and acknowledge tribal sovereignty by describing to Congress how to overcome the ruling in future cases.

Two years later, Congress accepted Matthews's invitation, passing the Major Crimes Act in 1885.[27] As originally constituted, the new law gave the federal government jurisdiction over seven "major" crimes committed by a Native person against another Native person in Indian Country, including murder.[28] Federal officials and others seeking to radically transform Native peoples and ways of life had another weapon in their arsenal, just as they had hoped when they initiated the action against Crow Dog.

Of course, just because Congress passes a law doesn't mean that it has the authority to do so. As many of us learn in our tenth-grade civics class, our government is one of limited and enumerated powers.[29] Years ago, after I finally looked up the word "enumerated," I better understood the basic premise that the phrase "limited and enumerated powers" is intended to invoke: governmental authority extends only as far as is spelled out in the U.S. Constitution. Put differently, unless the power to act is articulated in the U.S. Constitution, the government doesn't have that power. This is how we assess the constitutionality, or validity, of laws—those laws that are made under demonstrable grants of authority are constitutional and valid, and those laws that lack a demonstrable source of authority are unconstitutional and invalid. When an assessment of the constitutionality of a law occurs in a court, we refer to the process as judicial review.

These are, of course, a few very simple points about some fundamental premises of the American government that you likely already knew and that you take for granted in any discourse you might have about American governance (if you have any at all). As such, I emphasize them not to insult your intelligence but rather to keep us focused on the goal set out early in this chapter. It is vital to bring a few of these concepts we keep in the back of our minds to the forefront of our thinking, as they are necessary to both recognize and engage with the mystery that we seek to confront. Congress passed the Major Crimes Act, but this in and of itself did not settle the question of American jurisdiction over Native individuals on tribal lands. Eventually the constitutionality of the Major Crimes Act would be tested.

People are people, so before long there was another killing. This time the event occurred in California when Kagama and an accomplice, his son Mahawaha, killed another man, Iyouse.[30] In one of the many ironies that populate this area of the law, the dispute centered on the boundaries of Kagama's allotment—one of the tools that the reformers of the day envisioned would civilize Native peoples and lift them up from their erstwhile savage behavior.[31] Furthermore, the dispute did not take place on tribal lands but on state lands, meaning that the federal government should not have been able to assert jurisdiction under the Major Crimes Act. Nonetheless, Kagama and Mahawaha were charged in federal court under the new law, and their case quickly made its way to the Supreme Court.[32]

To be fair, eventually a proper set of circumstances would have risen to test the constitutionality of the Major Crimes Act—again, people are people—and it is difficult to envision much difference in what the Supreme Court would have articulated under slightly different facts than it did in Kagama's situation. Nonetheless, the cavalier disregard with which American officials, including the Supreme Court, had for the facts was indicative of the Allotment Era's disregard for Native America in general.

Once again (and as with any case), the key to understanding *U.S. v. Kagama* is to recognize the question fueling the dispute.[33] Thankfully, as with *Crow Dog*, the question in *Kagama* is relatively straightforward: Is the Major Crimes Act constitutional? Put another way, where in the U.S. Constitution lies the authority for the federal government to pass a criminal law statute that extends jurisdiction over Native peoples—the vast majority of whom were not yet American citizens—on Native lands? What is the source of authority for the Major Crimes Act?

While the question in *Kagama* was fairly simple, finding an answer was much more complicated for the lawyers tasked with defending the American government at the Supreme Court. At a more abstract level, the U.S. Constitution is primarily concerned with limiting the authority of the government—with protections against unreasonable search and seizure, double jeopardy, cruel and unusual punishment, and the like—than it is with extending its jurisdiction. As such, the Major Crimes Act ran counter to the general spirit of the U.S. Constitution (particularly since it sought jurisdiction over peoples who, again, were mostly not U.S. citizens). At a more concrete level, the U.S. Constitution offers precious little textual guidance for the relationship between the United States and Native peoples.

Native peoples or nations are explicitly mentioned only three times in the text of the U.S. Constitution. Twice, in Article I and in the 14th Amendment, the phrase "Indians not taxed" is used when determining apportionment, or the number of representatives each state is able to send to the House of Representatives in Congress.[34] The history and placement of the "Indians not taxed" phrases are telling. The earlier use, in Article I, was part of the original Constitution of 1789 and immediately preceded the infamous three-fifths clause, which tacitly acknowledged and sanctioned slavery. The close placement of "Indians not taxed" to what is assuredly the most onerous and embarrassing part of the document offers a strong sense of how the founders conceptualized Native peoples and their exclusion from the American polity. The 14th Amendment, in which "Indians not taxed" is later used, was one of the Civil War Amendments, which sought to eradicate slavery and its ills from the U.S. Constitution. Consequently, the drafters of the Civil War Amendments sought to undo the effect and legacy of the three-fifths clause while preserving the purpose and meaning of the "Indians not taxed" clause.

The other mention of Native peoples in the U.S. Constitution is in what is commonly referred to as the Commerce Clause. Article I, Section 8, Clause 3 states that Congress shall have the power "to regulate Commerce with foreign Nations, and among the several States, and with the Indian Tribes." The phrase "with Indian Tribes," one of three parts of the Commerce Clause as a whole, is regularly referred to as the Indian Commerce Clause. ***Minor Spoiler Alert:*** The Indian Commerce Clause is going to play a big role in our mystery and the rest of this book—if you plan to continue reading, you would do well to keep it in mind going forward.

Thus, the problem for the lawyers tasked with defending the Major Crimes Act becomes apparent: there is no natural fit between the few times Native peoples and nations are mentioned in the text of the U.S. Constitution and a criminal law statute purporting to extend American criminal jurisdiction over mostly foreign peoples on their own lands. The apportionment, or "Indians not taxed," clauses were of no help whatsoever, as their singular function is to determine representation in Congress. So, the lawyers tasked with defending the Major Crimes Act sought to rely on their only other option: the Commerce Clause. In a desperate attempt to shoehorn a criminal law statute within the ambit of commerce, the lawyers for the federal government essentially argued that the Major Crimes Act was authorized under the Commerce Clause—thus rendering the Major Crimes Act constitutional—because if Indians were allowed to run around and kill each other, then there would be fewer of them with which to engage in commerce.[35] Put another way, unless the United States was authorized to enforce criminal law over Native peoples on Native lands under the Commerce Clause, there would be fewer customers and that would affect commerce.

It was an audacious argument founded on the belief that Native peoples were savages incapable of stopping themselves from killing and unwilling or unable to manage violence within their communities. In the same vein as the federal efforts to criminally prosecute Crow Dog, it demonstrated a willful disregard for tribal capacities and systems of justice in a naked attempt to assert authority. It was also an unconvincing argument before the Supreme Court. Fairly early in his majority opinion, Justice Samuel Freeman Miller noted that the federal government's reliance on the Commerce Clause to justify the Major Crimes Act was "a very strained construction of this clause, that a system of criminal laws for Indians living peaceably in their reservations . . . was authorized by the grant of power to regulate commerce with the Indian tribes."[36] Miller also noted that the apportionment clauses held no bearing on the outcome of the case.[37]

This should have been the end of the case. Congress passed a law for which the Supreme Court could find no constitutional basis. As such, under nearly any other set of circumstances the law would have been declared unconstitutional and void. Because I am something of a ham, when I teach *Kagama* in my courses, I like to make this point theatrically.[38] When we get to the portion of the opinion when Miller announces there is no constitutional basis for the Major Crimes Act, I dramatically slam the textbook shut, breathe an exaggerated sigh of relief, and happily declare that we can all go home because class is over because there is no constitutional basis for the law. What more is there to say?

My students—quite rightfully—never fall for it. Having read the case (well, most of them), they are aware that Miller did not end his opinion once he acknowledged that there is no constitutional basis for the Major Crimes Act. Rather, he continued by first muddying the waters. Like Justice Matthews in *Crow Dog* before him, Miller echoed earlier decisions and portended future ones by claiming, "The relation of the Indian tribes living within the borders of the United States, both before and since the Revolution, to the people of the United States has always been an anomalous one and of a complex character."[39] By making the claim that the relationship between the United States and tribal nations was "anomalous," Miller set the foundation for deviating from the standard practices, procedures, or rules—such as declaring laws with no constitutional basis unconstitutional. After all, if you have an "anomalous" problem, what do you need? An anomalous solution!

By shedding the necessity of following foundational constitutional principles, Miller freed himself to find the federal government's authority to pass the Major Crimes Act beyond the scope of the U.S. Constitution. Yet, this freedom was also a burden, as the opinion as a whole is something of a hodgepodge that meanders without the guideposts of typical constitutional evaluation.[40] The rationale that Miller asserted for upholding the Major Crimes Act, such that it is, began with the questionable claim that "Indians are within the geographical limits of the United States" and that (neglecting tribal governmental structures as Matthews did in *Crow Dog*) there were only two entities that could claim authority over Native peoples: the federal government and the states.[41] Why this claim is questionable and why Miller felt justified in making it are more fully dealt with in the next chapter. Nonetheless, his assertion of American landownership bore the philosophical and legal burden of carrying the authority to pass the Major Crimes Act that the U.S. Constitution could not. Directly quoting famed Chief Justice John Marshall, Miller reiterated: "The right to govern may be the inevitable consequence of the right to acquire Territory. Whichever may be the source whence the power is derived, the possession of it is unquestioned."[42] In short, Indians are on lands that the federal government and states have some right to; thus, either the federal government or the states had authority over Indians. Since Miller described states as the "deadliest enemies" of tribal peoples and nations, governance of Native peoples was best left in the hands of the federal government.[43]

But what about Native peoples themselves? What say do they have in their own governance? Not much, according to Miller. Again making dubious historical claims and citing John Marshall, Miller asserted that Native peoples "are spoken of as 'wards of the nation,' 'pupils,' as local dependent communities. In this spirit the United States has conducted its relations to them from its organization to this time."[44] Later in the opinion, without further elucidation or citation, Miller magically converted Marshall's analogies into fact, stating, "These Indian tribes are wards of the nation."[45]

What is the significance of Miller's sleight of hand that, for legal purposes, changed analogy into fact? Put differently, what is a ward and why does it matter that Miller declared Native peoples and nations as such? In short, a ward is a person deemed to lack a requisite level of capacity. Wards are generally children and/or developmentally disabled persons but can be anyone who society believes lacks the ability to make meaningful decisions for themselves. Importantly, wards do not exist as a category unto themselves but always in relation to guardians—those who do have capacity and are tasked with making the meaningful decisions for the wards who can't make decisions for themselves.

Thus, according to Miller, Native peoples are wards and are therefore incapable of taking care of themselves. But if Native peoples are wards, who is their guardian? Miller's answer is the federal government. Conceding that colonialism and engagement with the United States put Native peoples in their disadvantaged position, Miller once again made a dubious historical assertion: this is the way it has always been. "From their very weakness and helplessness, so largely due to the course of dealing of the Federal Government with them and the treaties in which it has been promised, there arises the duty of protection, and with it the power. This has always been recognized by the Executive and by Congress, and by this court, whenever the question has arisen."[46]

Having built his rickety reasoning on the shaky ground of unsupported and questionable historical generalities, Miller nonetheless ended his opinion by confidently asserting that the federal government had the capacity to pass the Major Crimes Act despite the lack of constitutional authority to do so. Furthermore, it was for the best for Native peoples who were suffering under the effects of colonialism that their guardian has this extraconstitutional authority to save them from themselves and others. "The power of the General Government over these remnants of a race once powerful, now weak and diminished in numbers, is necessary to their protection, as well as to the safety of those among whom they dwell. It must exist in that government, because it never has existed anywhere else, because the theatre of its existence is within the geographical limits of the United States, because it has never been denied, and because it alone can enforce its laws on all the tribes."[47]

Miller's opinion, in short, is that somebody needs to take care of these wards who are living on federal land. Thus, the Supreme Court ruled that the Major Crimes Act is valid even though there is no constitutional basis for the law.

Most scholars point to Miller's opinion in *Kagama* as the first articulation at the Supreme Court of what we call the Plenary Power Doctrine in federal Indian law. We will wrestle more fully with what "plenary power" means a little later in this chapter and the next; right now it suffices to note that Congress's plenary power in Indian affairs consists of the federal government granting itself the expansive authority to pass intrusive legislation like the Major Crimes Act—a criminal law statute that covers tribal peoples on tribal lands originally passed in a time when the vast majority of Native peoples were not American citizens—and to engage in other coercive tactics that reach within Native America. Congressional plenary power over Native peoples only grew in size and capacity in the Allotment Era, providing the legal justification for allotment itself, boarding schools, federally controlled tribal police forces, and other efforts that were intended to eradicate tribes and tribalism.[48] It is a power that extends far beyond what we typically conceive the authority of the federal government to be, and it has been used to radically reshape Native America in many different ways since it was first articulated and judicially sanctioned in *Kagama*.

Therein lies the first critical clue to recognizing and unraveling our mystery. When the Plenary Power Doctrine was first articulated, the Supreme Court openly acknowledged that it had no constitutional basis.[49] The rationale for recognizing congressional authority to pass the Major Crimes Act was a mix of assertions of the status of tribal lands as belonging to the federal government and tribal peoples as wards of the federal government. These assertions, ostensibly regarded as self-evidently true so as to not need any citation or corroborating evidence, were in keeping with the dominant understandings of race and the law of the day.[50] Miller, like Matthews before him (and Marshall before him), assumed so completely as to never question the idea or regard evidence to the contrary in their written opinions that Native peoples were inferior to those who constituted the category of "white" in their time.[51] **Thus, the basis for the Plenary Power Doctrine when it was first announced was not the U.S. Constitution. It was racism.**

The second critical clue for our mystery emerges from a series of cases from the late twentieth and early twenty-first centuries. As with *Crow Dog* and *Kagama,* this newer line of cases considered the Plenary Power Doctrine and the source of congressional authority over Native peoples.

The newer line of cases began in 1973 when a couple of non-Native miscreants were caught causing trouble on a reservation in Washington state. That summer the Suquamish Nation, located on the Port Madison reservation across the Puget Sound from Seattle, was celebrating its annual Chief Seattle Days.[52] During the celebration, Mark David Oliphant got into a drunken fight and was arrested by tribal police for disorderly conduct and resisting arrest.[53] A few months later, Daniel Belgarde was arrested after leading tribal police on a high-speed chase that ended when Belgarde crashed into a tribal police car.[54] Belgarde's passenger on that fateful trip? Mark David Oliphant.[55] The tribal nation sought to try Oliphant and Belgarde in tribal court for their crimes. Oliphant and Belgarde objected and subsequently asked the federal courts to deny that the Suquamish had jurisdiction over them. Thus, the two lines of cases can be understood as opposite sides of the same coin: whereas the older line of cases (*Crow Dog* and *Kagama*) was concerned with American jurisdiction over tribal lands, the newer line of cases (starting with Oliphant and Belgarde's actions) was concerned with tribal jurisdiction over tribal lands.

The Supreme Court majority opinion in *Oliphant v. Suquamish Indian Tribe,* authored by Associate Justice William Rehnquist in 1978, has been the subject of significant scholarly attention, none of which is particularly flattering.[56] It is a watershed decision in the field of federal Indian law and certainly worthy of the attention it has received. If you are not already familiar with the case, I encourage you to engage directly with the opinion and the scholarship that it has produced. For the purpose of our mystery, however, *Oliphant* is important for two reasons. The first is its holding, or the law that the case announced: the Suquamish did not have jurisdiction over Oliphant and Belgarde because tribal nations as a whole do not have criminal jurisdiction over non-Natives. The result of the ruling was to racialize jurisdiction in Native America in a way that does not occur anywhere else in the United States.[57] Under *Oliphant*, tribal nations must ascertain the race of a perpetrator of a crime before criminally prosecuting that perpetrator, which inhibits effective law enforcement on tribal lands.[58] States and the federal government suffer no such burden.

The second reason *Oliphant* is critical to our mystery is the rationale for its holding. According to Rehnquist, tribal nations do not have criminal jurisdiction over non-Natives because that jurisdiction is "inconsistent with their status."[59] This rationale raises significant questions. Primarily, what else is or is not "inconsistent with [the] status" of tribal nations? Subsequently, who gets to decide what else is or is not "inconsistent with [the] status" of tribal nations? What role, if any, do tribal nations have in defining the scope of their sovereignty? Why, after *Oliphant*, does the Supreme Court get to play such an outsized role? Is this the branch of American government best situated to ascertain the scope of tribal sovereignty?

Disturbingly, the only tangible difference between Rehnquist's opinion in *Oliphant* and those of his Allotment Era counterparts is that Rehnquist at least acknowledged that tribal judicial systems exist.[60] Even so, this concession could not overcome the same tenor, rationales, and dubious evidence that fueled *Crow Dog* and *Kagama*.[61] In fact, Rehnquist not only cites those cases positively but quotes directly from them. Most notoriously, Rehnquist's opinion used ellipses (". . .") to cut up the most famous passage in *Crow Dog*—the one with the "superiors of a different race" and "the strongest prejudices of their savage nature" language discussed earlier in this chapter—to remove the most blatantly racist language in the opinion while preserving the spirit behind the passage.[62]

There is more to say about *Oliphant* and, again, others have said plenty (which you should seek out and read if you have not already). For now it suffices to reiterate that the holding of the case—tribal nations do not have criminal jurisdiction over non-Natives—paved a pathway for other considerations or scenarios that the Court might deem "inconsistent" with the status of tribal nations. Decided in 1990, *Duro v. Reina* was the next logical step along that road.[63]

On June 15, 1984, Albert Duro, a citizen of the Torres Martinez Band of Cahuilla Indians of California, was believed to have shot and killed Biscuit Brown, a fourteen-year-old boy who was a citizen of the Gila River Pima Maricopa Indian Community. The alleged crime took place on the Salt River Pima Maricopa Indian Community, which is located in Arizona. The Salt River Pima decided to prosecute Duro after the federal government declined to do so. Duro objected to the prosecution and filed in federal court, leading to the Supreme Court's decision in *Duro*.[64]

The question of the case in *Duro* was whether tribal criminal jurisdiction over non-citizen Natives was consistent with the status of tribal nations. Put differently, does Tribal Nation A have criminal jurisdiction over a Native person who is a citizen of Tribal Nation B? Flowing from the reasoning established in *Crow Dog*, *Kagama*, and *Oliphant*, Justice Anthony Kennedy's opinion in *Duro* answered in the negative. "We hold that the retained sovereignty of the tribe as a political and social organization to govern its own affairs does not include the authority to impose criminal sanctions against a citizen outside its own membership."[65]

On its surface, Kennedy's opinion is little more than the next stop on the newer line of cases. Kennedy did concede that "the tribes are, to be sure, a good deal more than 'private voluntary organizations,' and are aptly described as 'unique aggregations possessing attributes of sovereignty over both their members and their territory.'"[66] Nonetheless, this status could not overcome the basic presumption established by Rehnquist. "For purposes of criminal jurisdiction, petitioner's relations with this Tribe are the same as the non-Indian's in *Oliphant*. We hold that the Tribe's powers over him are subject to the same limitations."[67]

Just barely beneath the surface, Kennedy's regard of tribal judicial systems was in keeping with *Crow Dog*, *Kagama*, and *Oliphant*. The "special nature" of tribal courts, as Kennedy described it, made the Supreme

Court's scrutiny "most appropriate."[68] Perpetuating the foundational understandings that fueled *Crow Dog* and *Kagama*—which *Oliphant* tried to scrub clean while maintaining their import—Kennedy asserted, "While modern tribal courts include many familiar features of the judicial process, they are influenced by the unique customs, languages, and usages of the tribes they serve. Tribal courts are often 'subordinate to the political branches of tribal governments,' and their legal methods may depend on 'unspoken practices and norms.'"[69]

With an intellectual foundation that had changed little since the 1880s, the Supreme Court further limited the scope of tribal criminal jurisdiction in this 1990 case. What had changed, however, in the slightly more than a century between *Crow Dog* and *Duro* were the federal government's policy goals concerning Native America. Whereas *Crow Dog* and *Kagama* were decided in the Allotment Era of federal policy, which was committed to destroying tribal nations and tribalism, *Duro* was decided in what scholars regard as the Self-Determination Era, which has been characterized by congressional efforts to help tribal nations help themselves.[70] Beginning in approximately the mid-1960s, the Self-Determination Era had already seen a number of pieces of legislation passed by Congress that were to the benefit of Native nations and sovereignty by the time *Duro* was decided. Within the Self-Determination Era policy regime, tribal nations were better situated to achieve success in their lobbying efforts to Congress to overturn the result in *Duro*.

Native America mobilized quickly after the decision, and tribal efforts were rewarded a year later in 1991 when Congress passed what is colloquially known as the "*Duro* fix."[71] The "fix" was an amendment to existing legislation that "recognized and affirmed" the authority of tribal nations to criminally prosecute all Native peoples on tribal lands regardless of their tribal affiliation. The authors of the amended legislation were particularly careful with their language because they wanted to avoid a problem that was obvious to the types of legally trained people who write such things for Congress: double jeopardy.

More than just the middle portion of a popular television game show, double jeopardy is a constitutional principle that prohibits the government from trying a citizen twice for the same crime.[72] The Double Jeopardy Clause, found in the 5th Amendment, is in keeping with the U.S. Constitution's general tenor toward circumscribing governmental authority and essentially requires that the government build a strong and legitimate case against a citizen the first time, as it will not get another opportunity to do so for that particular crime or event.[73]

The drafters of the *Duro* fix—led primarily by tribal advocates—faced a dilemma.[74] They needed to write congressional legislation that authorized tribal nations to criminally prosecute non-citizen Natives, but they needed to do it in a way that did not raise double jeopardy concerns. The United States already claimed some jurisdiction on tribal lands through the Major Crimes Act and other statutes, and because Congress was using its authority to expand the scope of tribal criminal prosecutions, the drafters understood that courts might interpret tribal exercises of jurisdiction under the *Duro* fix as merely an extension, or delegation, of the federal authority that already existed in Native America. Under this view, any tribal prosecution of a crime would then prevent any subsequent federal prosecution of that same activity because of the prohibition against double jeopardy.

For example (to be extreme to illustrate the point), imagine that a Native person from Tribal Nation A caused an auto accident that resulted in the death of a pedestrian within the lands of Tribal Nation B. Under the view that the *Duro* fix was an extension, or delegation, of federal authority to tribal nations, if that Native person from Tribal Nation A pled or was found guilty to a simple traffic offense in the courts of Tribal Nation B, then that person could not face any further prosecution from the federal government for, say, vehicular manslaughter because of the prohibition against double jeopardy (and vice versa). Compounding the problem, the legislation that the *Duro* fix amended—the Indian Civil Rights Act—limited the possible punishments that a tribal nation could impose on a criminal defendant to one year in jail and/or a five-thousand-dollar fine.[75] Thus, even if Tribal Nation B did convict the citizen of Tribal Nation A for vehicular manslaughter, the punishment it could impose would not comport with similar sentences for similar crimes in state or federal court.[76] Put simply, if the *Duro* fix was understood to delegate jurisdiction to tribal nations, then the legislation had the potential to curtail federal criminal jurisdiction over Native America and result in significant crimes receiving comparatively paltry sentences.

The drafters of the *Duro* fix, as noted earlier, sought to solve the double jeopardy problem by writing into the amended legislation that Congress "recognized and affirmed" the authority of tribal nations to criminally prosecute citizens of other tribal nations.[77] In their attempt to "talk" to the courts (in the same way that the *Crow Dog* opinion "talked" to Congress), the drafters purposely avoided words like "delegation" or "grant" to describe what the legislation purported to do. Using the "recognized and reaffirmed" language signaled to courts in the inevitable legal challenges that were to come that Congress did not want to be understood as delegating this authority. Rather, Congress wanted to communicate that it was acknowledging the inherent sovereignty of tribal nations to exercise its criminal law over non-citizen Natives. If the source of criminal jurisdiction originated in the tribal nation itself, and not as a delegation from Congress, then the double jeopardy prohibition would not apply when both tribal nations and the federal government criminally prosecuted non-citizen Natives for the same event.

The theory the drafters put forth through the *Duro* fix was bound to be tested, and eventually a case made its way to the Supreme Court in the person of Billy Jo Lara. A citizen of the Turtle Mountain Band of Chippewa Indians, Lara lived with his spouse and children on the Spirit Lake Reservation (both reservations are located in North Dakota). Lara had caused enough trouble at Spirit Lake that the tribal nation issued an order to remove him from the reservation. In defiance of the order, Lara tried to return to Spirit Lake and federal officers tried to stop him. An altercation ensued, and Lara struck one of the federal officers. Shortly thereafter Spirit Lake charged Lara for his actions. He pled guilty in tribal court and spent ninety days in jail. Sometime after that, the federal government also sought to charge Lara for the incident. Lara objected to the federal charges and argued that the Duro fix was unconstitutional. In essence, Lara argued that Congress did not have the authority to "recognize and reaffirm" tribal criminal jurisdiction and could only delegate such authority. Since, according to Lara, the *Duro* fix was a delegation of federal authority to the tribal nation and since he had pled guilty in tribal court and done his time, the federal government could not also charge him for the incident under the double jeopardy prohibition in the U.S. Constitution.[78]

At its simplest, the question in *United States v. Lara* was whether Congress could do what it was purporting to do.[79] Could Congress "recognize" the inherent authority of tribal nations to criminally prosecute non-citizen Natives and avoid double jeopardy? Or was Congress limited to delegating such authority to tribal nations, thus invoking double jeopardy? Put slightly differently, what was the scope of congressional authority concerning tribal nations and peoples? Could Congress just "give back" jurisdiction like this after the Supreme Court had taken it away without any (double jeopardy) consequences?

For the purposes of identifying and unraveling our mystery, it is useful to understand Justice Stephen Breyer's majority opinion as engaging with two issues that were necessary to resolve the question of the case. First, what power or authority was Congress exercising in passing the Duro fix? Second, where did that power come from?

As to the first issue, Congress was acting under its plenary power authority that was first articulated by the Supreme Court in *Kagama*. Echoing the foundational understanding in *Kagama*, Breyer stated that Congress has "broad general powers to legislate in respect to Indian tribes, powers that we have consistently described as 'plenary and exclusive.'"[80] This plenary power, according to Breyer, was both flexible and expansive enough to allow Congress "to enact legislation that both restricts and, in turn, relaxes those restrictions on tribal sovereign authority."[81] In keeping with the tradition of sweeping generalizations of questionable accuracy that have littered the cases in this chapter (and Indian law cases in general), Breyer added, "From the Nation's beginning Congress' need for such legislative power would have seemed obvious."[82] The end result was that the Supreme Court found that Congress could authorize the expansion of tribal powers by "recognizing" the inherent sovereignty of tribal nations as the source of those powers, such recognition was not delegation and did not raise double jeopardy concerns, and Billy Jo Lara could rightfully be tried by the federal government for the same incident for which he pled guilty in tribal court.

Thus, Congress was acting under its plenary power authority in enacting the *Duro* fix. More important for our purposes, however, was the second issue, which reveals the second critical clue in our mystery. Like Justice Miller in *Kagama*, Breyer was compelled to consider the source of congressional plenary power over Native peoples in his *Lara* majority opinion. However, the answers offered by Miller in 1886 and Breyer in 2004 were diametrically opposed. Whereas Miller had rather perfunctorily dismissed it in the *Kagama* opinion, Breyer boldly asserted in *Lara* that "this Court has traditionally identified the Indian Commerce Clause" as the source of congressional plenary power over Native peoples.[83] Moreover, according to Breyer, the Indian Commerce Clause was not simply the basis for plenary power but the primary reason for the existence of the clause. Quoting a previous Supreme Court case, Breyer asserted, "The 'central function of the Indian Commerce Clause,' we have said, 'is to provide Congress with plenary power to legislate in the field of Indian affairs.'"[84] Breyer gestured toward a few other possible sources—which we will consider in greater detail in the next chapter. But he most clearly and forcefully argued that the Indian Commerce Clause was the foundation for congressional plenary power over Native America. **Thus, the basis for the Plenary Power Doctrine as presently understood is the U.S. Constitution.**

We now have the two critical clues that allow us to recognize the mystery before us. The first is in *Kagama*, where the Supreme Court explicitly rejected the Indian Commerce Clause as the basis for congressional plenary power over Native America, stating that such an argument was "a very strained construction of this clause." Rather, the *Kagama* Court relied on the racist assumptions of the day to assert that Congress did have the authority to pass the Major Crimes Act as well as engage in other legislation and practices that intruded on Native America in an attempt to destroy it. In short, the basis for plenary power was not the U.S. Constitution (it was racism). The second is in *Lara*, where the Court not only asserted that the Indian Commerce Clause was the basis for congressional plenary power but further claimed that it had "traditionally identified" the Indian Commerce Clause as so.[85] The expansive scope of congressional authority was not just tied to the Indian Commerce

Clause, but the primary purpose of the clause was to support the plenary power of the United States over Native peoples and nations. In short, the basis for plenary power is the U.S. Constitution.

As is obvious, both statements cannot be true at the same time. The source of plenary power cannot be both absent from the U.S. Constitution and rooted within it. One understanding must give way to the other. So it is in federal Indian law, where the chronology of the cases reveals where we currently stand. As a matter of legal doctrine—or what we consider the law to presently be—the *Lara* perspective prevails. Judges, lawyers, scholars, and others concerned with the legal status of Native America routinely, and often unquestioningly, assert that congressional plenary power over Native America comes from the U.S. Constitution, particularly the Indian Commerce Clause.

Breyer's majority opinion in *Lara* was not the first time the Supreme Court asserted the constitutionality of the congressional plenary power through the Indian Commerce Clause. Nonetheless, Breyer's opinion is helpful because it comes from a relatively modern case that had to directly grapple with the source of federal authority within Native America and because it is indicative of the change that has taken place in the doctrine. At one point (*Kagama*), American law contended that plenary power had no constitutional basis, rejecting the Indian Commerce Clause as a potential source. At present (*Lara*), American law contends that the Indian Commerce Clause is the source of congressional plenary power over Native America. Sometime between 1886 (*Kagama*) and 2004 (*Lara*) this significant shift occurred. All of which gets us to the question that is at the heart of our mystery.

When did plenary power become constitutional?

You see what I did there? You have to admit, that was pretty good, right? But before I fully anoint myself the cleverest Indian law scholar in all the land, it is necessary to take a closer look at the two big components that make up the question at the heart of our mystery.[86] First, what, more precisely, is plenary power? Second, why would anyone care that plenary power became constitutional?

As it concerns plenary power, if this were one of the decidedly uninspired term papers that I am occasionally forced to read, this portion of the chapter might begin as follows: "The dictionary defines 'plenary' as 'unqualified, absolute' when using it as an adjective."[87] In short, this relatively uncommon (and surprisingly difficult to pronounce) word means total or complete or to the exclusion of all else. In a general sense, it is a word that separates the "haves" from the "have-nots" in an all-or-nothing environment.

Of course, the reason term papers that begin this way are so tedious is that dictionary definitions, while certainly helpful, can get you only so far. Dictionary definitions exist in the abstract (which is why most dictionaries use the word in a sentence after its definition[88]). Language, on the other hand, is contextual, and the meaning of words changes or takes new shapes or is reconstituted in different environments. These contextual understandings can take on particular significance in the law, where the meaning of a word can provoke the force of the government for or against someone.

All of which is to make the point that the "plenary" in the Plenary Power Doctrine in federal Indian law has not been bound to a single, inviolable definition. It has shifted and changed depending on the context in which American courts have had to articulate it. At its simplest, federal plenary power in Indian affairs has been understood in two fundamental ways, more or less favoring one definition over the other throughout the course of history.[89] First, as against the states. Second, as over Native America.

The first major articulation at the Supreme Court of the first fundamental definition of federal plenary power occurred in the third of the (in)famous Marshall Trilogy of Indian law cases—*Worcester v. Georgia*.[90] Like *Oliphant*, the Marshall Trilogy (*Johnson v. McIntosh*,[91] *Cherokee Nation v. Georgia*,[92] and *Worcester*) has received significant scholarly attention. Also like *Oliphant*, it is worth your time and attention to become familiar with the Marshall Trilogy, as those cases established the foundation from which we are still operating in the field of Indian law.[93]

We will engage with more of the Marshall Trilogy in other chapters. For the purposes of our mystery, however, we are going to concentrate on John Marshall's explanation of plenary power in *Worcester*. Very briefly, *Worcester* was an 1832 case that was a manifestation of several simmering tensions between tribal interests (the Cherokee in particular), Georgia (and states in general), the presidency (especially the sitting president, Andrew Jackson), and the Supreme Court. Frustrated with what it saw as minimal federal efforts to secure tribal lands within its claimed borders, Georgia began trying to extend its law over tribal lands within those borders. Thus, one way to understand the question in *Worcester* is whether state laws were valid in Indian Country.

The circumstances behind *Worcester* were rife with political intrigue, and Marshall assuredly wrote his opinion much more with American interests than tribal interests in mind. Consequently, much of Marshall's opinion is devoted to the issue of federalism, or the balance of power between states and the federal government. In essence, Marshall reframed the question of the case less as about the state laws unto themselves and more about which American polity, the federal government or the states, had the authority to engage with tribal nations.

On this question, Marshall was unequivocal, stating, "The treaties and laws of the United States contemplate the Indian territory as completely separated from that of the states; and provide that all intercourse with them shall be carried on exclusively by the government of the union."[94] Both the sovereignty of the tribal nation and the division of powers under the federalism system rendered the Georgia laws null. "The Cherokee nation, then, is a distinct community occupying its own territory . . . in which the laws of Georgia can have no force, and which the citizens of Georgia have no right to enter, but with the assent of the Cherokees themselves, or in conformity with treaties, and with the acts of congress."[95] According to Marshall, states had no role to play in the political relationship with Native nations. "The whole intercourse between the United States and [the Cherokee], is, by our constitution and laws, vested in the government of the United States."[96]

Thus, as articulated by Chief Justice John Marshall in one of the earliest and most influential Indian law cases, the plenary power of the federal government in Indian affairs was defined as existing against the states. The federal government alone was authorized to engage with Native America. The states played no role. This version of plenary power made no claims to authority over Native peoples or nations, as those nations were "distinct, independent political communities" whose political status was unaffected by American political authority (with one big exception that we will encounter in the next chapter).[97]

This version of federal plenary power—as against the states—remains an important part of the landscape of federal Indian law, although it has not endured in full.[98] One could say much more about it as it continues to influence questions of jurisdiction in Indian Country and tends to be the definition favored by advocates of tribal sovereignty. For our purposes, however, it suffices to note that this version of plenary power—which is fundamentally entangled with questions of the relationship between the federal government and the states—is not the primary one with which we are concerned. Rather, when engaged with our mystery, we are focused on the second fundamental definition of plenary power in federal Indian law—as over Native America.

From the beginning colonizers in what was to become the United States have regularly made bold claims to their supreme authority over Native lands and peoples, the likes of which were in disproportion to their actual influence and capacity to exercise their wills. Haughty rhetoric about the superiority of European civilization and forces were belied by events on the ground, which were dominated more by trade and other diplomatic relations than by wars or shows of military force. Even as colonizing forces (including earlier generations of Americans) gained a greater foothold on the North American continent, they jealously sought alliances with tribal nations through treaties and other means to protect their own interests. These alliances were necessary, as no single colonizing force could truly claim dominance over any of their neighbors.

By the time *Kagama* was decided, however, the United States was able to exert a substantial amount of influence over the lives and lands of Native peoples. The Allotment Era, in part inaugurated by *Kagama*, was defined by the exercises and excesses of that influence. While the federal government and others were actively trying to destroy tribal nations and tribalism, Native peoples resisted and persisted. Nonetheless, the Allotment Era changed Native America in varied and fundamental ways, including but not limited to significant land loss, the suppression and criminalization of tribal cultural practices and languages, the disruption of families and family practices, oppressive manipulations of tribal resources including sources of food, and other coercive efforts intended to either forcefully assimilate Native peoples into the larger American polity or to allow them to perish under the weight of advancing American "civilization."[99] Within this new power structure the definition of plenary power in federal Indian law began to take a new shape.[100]

The legal basis of the Allotment Era was this second fundamental definition of plenary power—as over Native America. *Kagama,* along with two other Supreme Court cases from the Allotment Era, were instrumental in redefining plenary power from its origins as a question of federalism into an expression of unlimited federal authority over Native peoples and lands. In short, *Kagama* stands for the proposition that the U.S. Constitution does not check, or limit, the plenary power of the federal government over Native America.

Lone Wolf v. Hitchcock, decided in 1903, is the second case of what might be termed the Plenary Power Trilogy of Allotment Era cases. *Lone Wolf* centered around an egregious treaty violation by the United States. Succinctly, the litigation in *Lone Wolf* ensued when tribal members accused the federal government of fraud, coercion, and violation of an older treaty in its efforts to secure a newer treaty.[101] Despite the overwhelming evidence against the federal government, the Supreme Court decided that it had no say in the matter, stating, "Plenary authority over the tribal relations of the Indians has been exercised by Congress from the beginning, and the power has always been deemed a political one, not subject to be controlled by the judicial department of the government."[102] With an obliviousness that seems impossible under the circumstances of the case, the Supreme Court further ruled that Congress needed the authority to abrogate treaties with tribal nations when it saw fit. "When, therefore, treaties were entered into between the United States and a tribe of Indians it was never doubted that the power to abrogate existed in Congress, and that in a contingency such power might be availed of from considerations of governmental policy, particularly if consistent with perfect good faith towards the Indians."[103] In short, *Lone Wolf* stands for the proposition that treaties do not check the plenary power of the federal government over Native America.

The third case of the Plenary Power Trilogy of Allotment Era cases, *U.S. v. Sandoval,* was decided in 1913. Succinctly, during the Allotment Era the federal government enforced several laws, regulations, and other rules against Native peoples that it would not have been authorized to enforce against a typical American citizen. The question in *Sandoval* was whether the federal government could still enforce those laws, regulations, and rules (specifically liquor laws in this case) against tribal members who were also American citizens.[104] The Supreme Court answered in the affirmative, stating, "Citizenship is not in itself an obstacle to the exercise by Congress of its power to enact laws for the benefit and protection of tribal Indians as a dependent people."[105] In short, *Sandoval* stands for the proposition that American citizenship does not check the plenary power of the federal government over Native America.

This definition of plenary power—as over Native America and unconstrained by the U.S. Constitution, treaties, or American citizenship—has long outlived the Allotment Era and remains the primary understanding of the doctrine in American law today. It was founded upon assertions of Native peoples as inferior, incapable, and in need of fundamental change.[106] In the Self-Determination Era, the Supreme Court has ostensibly placed the barest of constraints on this otherwise limitless authority, stating that exercises of plenary power need to be "tied rationally to the fulfillment of Congress' unique obligation toward the Indians."[107] Even so, it is fair to ask if this meek assertion to rationality is any barrier at all, as American courts have never struck down a law on the basis of an overextension of federal plenary power.[108]

It is this fundamental understanding of plenary power—in which the federal government has given itself the authority to reach directly into Native America for whatever purpose it deems necessary—that is at the heart of our mystery. As noted earlier, this version of plenary power has long outlived its Allotment Era origins and is as viable today as it was when it originated. It provided the legal justification not just for the ills of the Allotment Era but for almost all that came after as well, including but not limited to further limitations on sovereignty and jurisdiction, the relocation and termination efforts of the 1950s, continued significant control and destruction of tribal lands and resources, further treaty violations, and more. It is also now generally regarded by the practitioners, scholars, judges, and others who engage with Indian law as a given or otherwise impossible to reconsider.

To be sure, plenary power has sometimes been used to the benefit of Native peoples, most particularly in the Self-Determination Era (a point that we will take up again in Chapter 4). Nonetheless, as eras, politicians, incentives, and moods change, there is no guarantee that this unqualified and ever-present force will continue its current trend of leaning in favor of tribal interests. If for no other reason, that makes a critical examination of the origins, development, and justifications of this definition of plenary power a worthwhile endeavor.

Thus, plenary power itself is the first big component of our mystery. The second is plenary power's constitutional status. Several months before I started on this chapter, while many of the ideas I am presently writing about were more like formless blobs drifting lazily inside my head, I tried explaining this project to my father. I told him about this great mystery that I had yet to solve and that I wanted to find out when plenary power became constitutional. I tried to convince him that this was a critical change that was worthy of further examination. Admittedly, I was having a hard time making the blobs in my head emerge as coherent words from my mouth, but I could not make my father understand why the constitutionalization of plenary power was important. I was able to convey that I thought that plenary power was dangerous and unmoored to any justifiable legal reasoning, and he seemed to agree, but I couldn't get him to take the next step with me. I couldn't get him to understand what role the U.S. Constitution played in this equation. He just kept repeating, "Isn't a lie just a lie?"

Dads: Whaddya gonna do?

I was frustrated with him in the way that sons can get with their fathers, and I have no doubt that he was frustrated with me in the way that fathers can get with their sons. My father and I had reached an impasse in the conversation, and we let the matter drop. Nonetheless, that conversation was important because it made me survey the landscape around our impasse. Because I am a legally trained scholar who has spent his adult life reading, writing, and talking about the law, Native America, and governance, the problem was obvious to me and the U.S. Constitution was central to the issue. My father, on the other hand, didn't see any difference in regarding plenary power as constitutional in origin or not if plenary power remained the method by which the federal government justified its unfettered authority over Native America. What difference could it possibly make as long as plenary power exists? Admittedly, my father, like many old men (and many young men and plenty of women too), can be obstinately allergic to any thing or idea that is new or different, and I was tempted to dismiss his question as the rusty screeching of a brain whose gears did not want to budge. Yet, I knew that the real problem did not lie with him. The real problem was my inability to adequately explain why the constitutionalization of plenary power did matter. After stewing on the conversation for a while, I had to admit to myself that this project would be worthy of the time and attention that I was intending to devote to it only if I could make my father and others like him understand why the constitutionalization of plenary power was critical. This would not be a worthwhile project unless I could make it clear that plenary power's conversion to constitutionality fundamentally changed what was and was not accomplishable for Native peoples in American law and that the present-day general consensus of the constitutionality of plenary power does not allow for a true and full reckoning of the past and justice in the present.

So here I am, trying again because the story they have chosen to tell is wrong. They know it and we know it.

It is time to tell a better story.

The next time I talk to my father about this project, I might start by saying that the U.S. Constitution functions in many ways in a myriad of contexts, including as a symbol that can produce a whole range of discourse about its efficacy or lack thereof.[109] However, we need not wade in those deep and murky waters to make note of what might well be the U.S. Constitution's primary function: to operate as a gatekeeper. In Article VI, the document declares itself to "be the supreme Law of the Land."[110] Thus, it is the center of American law, the standard by which the rest of American law is measured, and the dividing line between that which is permanent and that which is subject to change. Much like the word "plenary" itself, the U.S. Constitution distinguishes between the "haves" and the "have-nots" when it comes to rights or authority. If a right (say against self-incrimination) is "constitutional," then it exists. It cannot be denied or voided by the government. We may argue about how far this right extends, and we may even acknowledge that, on the ground, this right is sometimes violated. But within the ambit of American law, a "constitutional" right is permanent, unalienable, and cannot be taken away. Rights that do not have this "constitutional" protection (say, library privileges), on the other hand, can be temporary, altered, or altogether revoked. They are subject to the whims of the political process and are defined by the political community rather than by the U.S. Constitution itself. As a philosophical matter, it is reasonable to question whether it is appropriate to define them as rights at all instead of privileges or some other word or term that better denotes their ephemerality. In short, the U.S. Constitution creates a border between that which we can question and change and that which we cannot.

A quick example helps summarize the point. In the summer in which I began this project in earnest, the Supreme Court handed down *Dobbs v. Jackson Women's Health Organization*.[111] This 2022 decision overturned the 1973 holding in *Roe v. Wade* that access to abortion was a constitutional right.[112] Whatever your personal feelings about abortion, these cases make clear the difference between that which is constitutional and that which is not. After 1973, various state legislatures could, and did, chip away at access to abortions but could not abolish it entirely (even if, admittedly, access to abortions in some states was severely curtailed). After *Dobbs*, states can cross that final threshold and prohibit access to abortions entirely (although many are finding it difficult to do so in the first months after *Dobbs*). Thus, in a post-*Roe* world, states were unable to abolish access to abortions; in a post-*Dobbs* world, they can. The only difference between those two eras is the perceived constitutionality of abortion.

Having hopefully made my point about the power of constitutionality with my father, I might then ask him to consider what it means to regard federal plenary power over Native America as constitutional. I imagine that my father, an educated man, might now be better able to see that which I had taken for granted as obvious: regarding plenary power as constitutional renders it absolute, authoritative, unquestionable, and unassailable. Deciding that plenary power is part of the U.S. Constitution makes it a natural and permanent part of the organic governing document of the United States. It cannot be changed or challenged or voided. It simply exists, and the rightful authority it permits is beyond debate.

And what are we making permanent and unquestionable by regarding plenary power as constitutional? The Plenary Power Trilogy of the Allotment Era helps us recognize two major consequences. First, as previously noted, the federal government's authority over Native America is barely limited, if at all, by the U.S. Constitution, treaties, or American citizenship.[113] This allows for the exercise of an extensive federal power in Native America that is antithetical to the ostensible purpose of the U.S. Constitution, including (but certainly not limited to) the ability to dissolve, or "terminate," tribal nations as political entities. It also results in the profound irony that the justification for acting outside the scope of the U.S. Constitution is the U.S. Constitution itself.

Second, it places Native peoples and nations in a permanent underclass. Recall that the Court in *Kagama* proclaimed, "These Indian tribes are wards of the nation." The Court in *Lone Wolf* wrote of "Indians and the relation of dependency they bore and continue to bear towards the government of the United States."[114] Writing about a specific tribal grouping but extrapolating it to Native peoples as a whole, the Court in *Sandoval* wrote, "Always living in separate and isolated communities, adhering to primitive modes of life, largely influenced by superstition and fetichism [*sic*], and chiefly governed according to the crude customs inherited from their ancestors, they are essentially a simple, uninformed and inferior people."[115]

In short, the Plenary Power Doctrine circumscribes tribal sovereignty and the rights of Native peoples under an unassailable and limitless federal authority based on racist understandings of Native America established in the law well over a century ago. No amount of carving out of the more explicitly troublesome language by William Rehnquist and his ellipses can cut away that basic fact. Conceptualizing this state of affairs as constitutionally sanctioned makes it impossible to change.

Unfortunately, we have reached a point (with one significant exception and other smaller ones around the margins that are discussed in Chapter 3) where the vast majority of judges, practitioners, scholars, and others engaged with this body of law unquestioningly—perhaps even thoughtlessly—assert the constitutionality of federal plenary power. Perhaps some of us legitimately believe it to be true (although I have my doubts, which are discussed in Chapter 4). Perhaps some of us regard it as a necessary stepping-stone to confront a particular issue in a case or work of scholarship that is more immediately of our concern. Or perhaps some of us have never bothered to question how we ended up in this situation. Whatever the reason, the constitutionality of plenary power has fermented into a generally (although not completely) accepted consensus.[116]

This is where we currently are in the field. Yet, this is not how it started. The genesis of the Plenary Power Doctrine in the Supreme Court—*Kagama*—disavowed any connection to the text of the U.S. Constitution. This assertion that many of us now take for granted, that plenary power is constitutional, was not there in the beginning. It was only at some later point that this idea developed within American law. So . . .

When did plenary power become constitutional?

Engaging with this mystery opens possibilities that are otherwise foreclosed by accepting Breyer's claim that the Supreme Court has "traditionally identified" the U.S. Constitution as the source of federal plenary power over Native America.[117] Rejecting Breyer's blithe assertions opens the space to trace the intellectual and doctrinal history of an idea and a practice forged from racism and colonialism that remains the law of the land today.[118] Recognizing the whitewashing that Rehnquist, Breyer, and others have done (and are doing!)—and that many of us who consider ourselves advocates of Native America uncritically participate in—allows us to see that the constitutionalization of plenary power has been a process, not an inevitability. By denying the deceptively simple and demonstrably false (un)truism that plenary power has always naturally flowed from the text of the U.S. Constitution, it becomes possible to imagine alternatives that are more just, equitable, and better fulfill the text and the spirit of the U.S. Constitution.

And if I still couldn't reach my father after all of that, I would try with one more example that is more suited to his perspective. For the vast majority of my life my father has been a recovering alcoholic. When I was a boy, after my parents divorced, my father would regularly take me to the "open" Alcoholics Anonymous meetings the local chapter would hold at the end of each month.[119] During those meetings I often heard about AA's twelve steps to recovery, the first of which is admitting that you have a problem.

Plenary power is the problem in federal Indian law. Like with the functioning alcoholic, we are presently getting by under the regime of plenary power, but it has already caused plenty of trouble and the next disaster is always right around the corner. Furthermore, it is impossible to imagine a future where things work out well under plenary power. The U.S. Constitution, however, prevents us from admitting that which is obvious. The U.S. Constitution sanctifies everything in its orbit. Thus, regarding plenary power as constitutional makes it not just permissible but authoritative and unassailable. There is no room to think beyond plenary power if it is deemed constitutional. We are incapable of taking the first step. Constitutionalism asserts that there is no problem. Constitutionalism is denial.

We need to take that first step. We can get better only if we admit that plenary power is a problem and that the U.S. Constitution is enabling it. We need to have our moment of clarity. Fortunately, our path (to recovery, if we want to take the analogy a little farther than perhaps it should go) is relatively straightforward. First, we must acknowledge the incongruity that exists: in 1886 the Supreme Court disavowed the U.S. Constitution as the source of plenary power; today the Supreme Court claims that it has "traditionally identified" the U.S. Constitution as the source of plenary power. Next, we must ask a question.

When did plenary power become constitutional?

The partygoers quickly huddled together trying to figure out what to do about the pale man. After a brief yet animated conversation it was decided that, since the author of this book is Anishinaabe, that Nanaboozhoo should talk to him.

Nanaboozhoo ambled toward the pale man, trying to look neither threatening nor suspicious. "Hey there, stranger. Are you doing all right? It kinda sounded like you were shot out of a cannon."

The pale man kept repeating, "I'm fine, I'm fine," as he brushed himself off. His eyes told a different story.

Nanaboozhoo was beginning to take pity on the pale man, who looked hungry and tired and ready to collapse. "I don't mean to be nosy, stranger, but nobody noticed you until we heard a noise. Where did you come from?"

The pale man looked at Nanaboozhoo for a moment. Then he looked off in the distance and gently waved an extended arm as if trying to reach through time and space itself. "I swam across a giant ocean to get here."

Nanaboozhoo hoped that the pale man didn't notice that one of his eyebrows had briefly arched in disbelief. Still unsure of what he was dealing with, Nanaboozhoo resettled his face and calmly asked, "What's your name, stranger?"

The pale man took a couple of very deep breaths. "My name is . . ." He took the biggest breath he could.

"My name is . . .

KingGeorgeWashingtonRedskinsThomasJeffersonLouisanaPurchase JohnMarshallTrilogyJohnsonMcIntoshGeorgiaWorcesterRemovalTrailof TearsBrokenTreatyGrantPeacePolicyAllotmentAssimilationCivilization SandCreekCusterWoundedKneeOklahomaSoonerCarlisleRichardHenry PrattLactoseIntoleranceRacialIntoleranceCulturalIntoleranceReligious IntoleranceKagamaLoneWolfSandovalJohnCollierTerminationRelocationSubjugationReservationChiefWahooIronEyesCodyTomahawkChop MarkDavidOliphantRehnquist . . ."

The pale man heaved a dozen or so times as he caught his breath. ". . . the Third."

"Wow," said Nanaboozhoo, "that's quite a handle. Say, you look like you could use some rest and some food. Why don't you come and sit with us by the campfire for a while?" Nanaboozhoo looked back at the rest of the partygoers. Some seemed to shrug with their eyes. Others closed their eyes in disbelief. No one verbally protested.

"Yeah," said the pale man, seeming to gain a little vigor. "Yeah, that would be great." And before Nanaboozhoo could direct him, the pale man took a seat at the fire.

Everyone else gathered around the fire as well, and after a few awkward moments things began feeling normal again. Somebody else started up another story, and before long all the conversation and laughter and good times started flowing as before. At first the pale man was quiet and reserved, but soon someone gave him a plate of food and something to drink, and immediately he began to take on new life. Before long, the pale man was also intently listening to the stories, laughing and following along with the others (although not always seeming to get the jokes). At one lull in the storytelling the pale man stood up and started handing out gifts to the rest of the partygoers. "Thank you for helping me," he would say when handing someone something. "I don't know what I would have done if I hadn't stumbled upon you all." Nanaboozhoo and the others looked at the gifts and were pleased. These things will be useful they said to each other as they nodded in agreement. As the pale man walked around giving the gifts, he looked much healthier and stronger than when he first arrived. In fact, Nanaboozhoo wondered if his eyes were deceiving him because it looked like the pale man had grown in size. Not much, but just enough to maybe possibly be noticeable. Could that be? Nanaboozhoo wondered.

After giving the gifts, the pale man sat down and the stories started once again. People laughed and joked and teased and had a good time. Everything felt normal. Well, except for one thing—for some reason it felt more crowded than usual around the campfire. There had been enough space before, even after the pale man arrived. Why did it feel a little cramped now?

As host of the party, Nanaboozhoo had waited for everybody else to tell one of their own stories before he was going to tell one of his. But the time had come, and almost all the eyes at the campfire had descended upon him. With an atypical modesty, Nanaboozhoo began to rise. "All right, I guess it's my tu . . ."

Before he could get any further, the pale man jumped to his feet. In a booming voice the partygoers had not heard before, the pale man bellowed, "I want to tell a story."

Two thoughts shot through Nanaboozhoo's mind. The first: "Oh boy, this isn't going to be good." The second: "Has that guy doubled in size?"

TWO *The Conspiracy*

The last chapter introduced our mystery. This chapter details the larger machinations behind our mystery.

Our mystery may not have been a random act.

It could be part of a larger conspiracy.

[Can't you just hear dun, dun, duuuuuuuuuuuuunnnnnnnn music right now?]

OK, fine, I confess that I am really testing the elasticity of this whole "let's think of this as a mystery" concept. And perhaps "conspiracy" is not the ideal word to use.[1] Although there were certainly an intentionality and a deliberateness to what has happened in federal Indian law, it was less the product of back-door dealings between shadowy figures and more an open articulation of the values of the power brokers of the times. Yet, the analogy is still helpful because it demonstrates that the solution to our mystery cannot be fully revealed without placing it in a larger context.

Let's simplify things before we tumble all the way down the slippery slope of overwrought comparisons into the swampy, darkened ditch of academic gobbledygook. We have a question: ***When did plenary power become constitutional?*** This is the mystery we are trying to solve.[2] Yet, to really understand why we even want to bother solving our mystery in the first place, we have to ask the question that stands behind the question: ***How does the United States justify its authority over Native peoples?*** Put another way, what right does the federal government have to exercise power over Native America? Let's call this question behind the question our "meta-question."

In one sense, we already know the answer to the meta-question. At present, the United States justifies its authority over Native peoples most fully through the Indian Commerce Clause of the U.S. Constitution by way of the Plenary Power Doctrine. In other words, the United States gets to exercise this plenary power, as the story goes, because it is authorized to do so under the Indian Commerce Clause of the U.S. Constitution. This is the story that Justice Breyer told us in *Lara* in 2004 when he declared, "This Court has traditionally identified the Indian Commerce Clause" as the source of federal authority over Native peoples.[3]

That Breyer would want to tell this story is unsurprising because it fits our basic understanding of how the law works in the United States. Once again returning to our tenth-grade civics class, we know that the federal government has, for example, the authority to impose taxes or a "taxing power." Yet, we do not regard the federal government's taxing power as inherent or extending merely from its status as a sovereign. Rather, we understand the federal government as having the authority to tax because the U.S. Constitution says it has this power, most specifically at Article I, Section 8, Clause 1 and the 16th Amendment. Thus, our tenth-grade civics class story tells us that the U.S. Constitution defines the scope of federal authority, including its taxing power, and that the document's circumscribed nature protects the citizenry from the tyrannical and arbitrary exercise of governmental force. By connecting federal authority over Native peoples and nations to the Indian Commerce Clause of the U.S. Constitution, Breyer (and others before him) sought to place plenary power into a similar framework as the taxing power.

Yet, Breyer's answer to the meta-question flies in the face of what came before it. As anyone who has read Chapter 1 knows, in 1886 the

Supreme Court in *Kagama* not only rejected the Indian Commerce Clause as the source of federal authority but did not bother to find any textual source at all in the U.S. Constitution.[4] Nonetheless, the Supreme Court in *Kagama* found that the federal government was still justified in its exercise of authority over Native peoples. This strange ruling is a clear deviation from our basic understanding of how the law works in the United States. Consequently, as some rather simple deduction would dictate, the United States has offered more than one justification for its authority over Native peoples over the years and not all of them have been directly connected to the U.S. Constitution. So, what are these other justifications? How closely or not do they adhere to our story about how governmental power operates in the United States? What influence might they continue to hold over our thinking today? What other answers to our meta-question has American law produced?

Furthermore, our meta-question allows us to better understand the concept of plenary power and what it means for Native America. As noted previously, plenary power is like the taxing power in that it is not the source of federal authority unto itself. Rather, it is a shorthand way to describe a bundle of justifications, presuppositions, and common beliefs concerning the nature, scope, and use of federal power. Thus, when lawyers, judges, and others talk and write about the "taxing power," they are making reference to an exercise of authority that is commonly understood as justified under our system of government (in the parts of the U.S. Constitution noted earlier) and that has commonly understood applications and limits (which is the subject of someone else's book).

Breyer in *Lara* would have us believe that the concept of plenary power carries a similar, fairly well-settled set of understandings about federal authority over Native America. Interestingly (as was introduced in Chapter 1 and will be further considered in Chapter 4) many supporters of tribal nations and sovereignty often echo these sentiments. Nonetheless, by this point we know that Breyer's blithe assertion is simply inaccurate. The justifications, presuppositions, and common beliefs that the concept of plenary power contains have been far wider ranging and contested throughout American and Supreme Court history than as asserted by Breyer (and plenty of others), and they reflect a different set of values than simple fidelity to the text of the U.S. Constitution. By asking how the United States justifies its authority over Native peoples—by focusing on power—it becomes that much clearer that the story they have chosen to tell is wrong. They know it and we know it.

It is time to tell a better story.

But before we can consider our meta-question, we have to ask the meta-meta-question:[5] How does the United States justify its authority over its own people? Put another way, by what right can the United States claim any governing authority that its citizenry ought to respect? What makes the United States a legitimate government? Exploring this question allows us to measure the rationale for the general exercise of federal power against the rationale for the exercise of federal power over Native America.

Where should one begin when seeking to identify the theory behind American governance? Why not at the beginning? Fortunately for us, the rabblerousers who started the American Revolution felt the need to justify themselves and the big hullabaloo that they were about to provoke with a Declaration of Independence. In the Declaration they drew broad (yet still helpful) distinctions between the characteristics of the illegitimate governance they understood themselves to be suffering under and the characteristics of a legitimate governing structure they hoped to establish.

Early on, the Declaration states that we all are created equal and that we all have "certain unalienable Rights."[6] And yet, the decidedly affirmative nature of this sentiment does little to cover a darker undertone that the signatories to the Declaration sought to confront: while rights might be unalienable, they are not inviolable. In other words, even though we all have rights that are inherent to us as human beings, those rights might be denied or rejected or otherwise not recognized without the capacity to enforce them. Thus, according to the Declaration, individuals band together as a collective to protect their individual rights. "That to secure these rights, Governments are instituted among Men."[7]

It is through this process of individuals coming together that the legitimacy of a government is established, according to the Declaration. Autonomous individuals with inherent rights cede some of their autonomy to a government to protect those inherent rights. Thus, according to the Declaration, governments "deriv[e] their just powers from the consent of the governed."[8] Often this process is described as a "social contract" because the characteristics of the theory can be made to resemble the process of creating a contract. Free individuals offer some limitations on their freedom to a government in exchange for protection of their rights, property, persons, and so on. The government offers protection and services in exchange for the authority to govern. There is, in keeping with the language of contracts, a meeting of the minds between free individuals and the government.[9] Therefore, according to the theory, the government is legitimate because individuals have, in one way or another, agreed to live under the arrangement or are parties to the social contract.

The U.S. Constitution further echoes this basic philosophy of American governance in the 10th Amendment: "The powers not delegated to the United States by the Constitution, nor prohibited by it to the States, are reserved to the States respectively, or to the people."[10] According to the reasoning, authority originated with the people. The earliest social contracts in North America were between the people and the colonies. When the colonies became states and then came together to form a federal government under the U.S. Constitution, they were ceding some their own authority as derived by the people by engaging in another social contract.[11] Thus, the 10th Amendment acknowledges that power originates with the people, some of this authority passed to the states, the authority given to the federal government by the people and the states was limited, and the power not ceded to the federal government remains with the people and the states. Put simply, the U.S. Constitution identifies as a social contract.[12]

As anyone who has taken a political science class knows, this is a very general description of the theory of American governance, and plenty of others have had plenty more to say about the subject, whether trying to more fully explain it, refine it, critique it, or deny it. Furthermore, the notion of a social contract is what we in the business like to call a "legal fiction." A legal fiction is an idea or understanding that is otherwise false that the law treats as true for the ease of its administration. For example,

American law generally regards corporations as persons so that corporations can sue and be sued like any other person even though corporations are clearly not living, breathing people. The social contract is a legal fiction because no actual human being has agreed to it in any manner that a real person would assent to any other contract. No single individual has negotiated the terms of the social contract with a government or signed a legal document agreeing to abide by it. Recognizing something as a legal fiction inherently admits to the artificiality of the idea.[13]

That all being conceded, this simple explication and the legal fiction that accompanies it are nonetheless critical in moving us closer to solving our mystery and unraveling the conspiracy behind it. Despite the incongruities between the metaphor and lived experience of real people, the concept of the social contract has been at the heart of the justification of American governmental authority over its citizenry from the beginning, and anyone hoping to understand how the United States understands itself must engage with it. Even more important for our purposes, it lays bare the most critical component of the claims to legitimacy by the United States.

Consent.

As the Declaration of Independence notes, the "just powers" of a government emanate from the "consent of the governed."[14] As a matter of basic contract law, a contract is made when willing parties freely consent to take on obligations (such as making payments) to earn a benefit (such as owning a car). Any agreements made without the true consent of one of the parties—such as agreements made under duress or coercion—cannot be enforced under the law as a contract. Consequently, the social contract metaphor lays claim to the understanding that individual citizens have freely consented to be governed by the United States.[15] This consent exists at the state level as well. For example, individual citizens who are discontented with a state's laws or governance are free to move to another state, and individual citizens who are discontented with the laws or governance of the United States are free to move to another country. Furthermore, those who are discontented have the capacity to participate in the political process and change what they don't like. Thus, under a social contract understanding, the United States is justified in its governance over its citizenry because its citizenry has consented to this governance.

Again, many have pointed out that the presumptions upon which the social contract theory is founded are not always in alignment with reality.[16] Nonetheless, the social contract maintains a ubiquitous hold on how we think about power in the United States, to the point that even those who wish to challenge or otherwise refute it must nonetheless engage with it. In fact, many if not most (or even all) of us, whether consciously or not, have internalized the basic reasoning of the social contract. That is why a certain class of very specifically annoying people immediately threaten to move to another country when the person they don't like is elected president. These folks (who, of course, never actually move) are threatening to withdraw their consent to be governed, much in the same way that one might threaten to void a contract if one feels that the other party to the contract is violating the terms of the deal.

In summation, whether we want to or not, we all engage with the social contract theory when conceptualizing how governmental power operates in the United States. Furthermore, the foremost characteristic that defines the social contract is consent. Imagining it as a contractual arrangement makes it easier to conceptualize the theoretical underpinnings. The autonomous citizen has given up some autonomy for the benefit of a government that will protect the citizen's remaining autonomy and the rights that are inherent to humanity. Thus, we have the answer to our meta-meta-question. The United States justifies its authority over its own citizenry because the citizenry has consented to that authority. This is our basis of comparison when considering the relationship between federal power and Native America.

Having answered the meta-meta-question and established this basis of comparison, it is almost time to return to the (only one) meta-question: How does the United States justify its authority over Native peoples? However, three other brief points need to be made before we can tackle the meta-question directly. The first is that the answer to the meta-question cannot simply be "plenary power" because, as described earlier, plenary power is like the taxing power in that it is not a source of authority unto itself but rather is a descriptor that assumes its own justification. Put more simply, it is incomplete and circular to say that the United States justifies its authority over Native peoples because it has plenary power. It would be like arguing that I can take money out of a bank because I have the authority to take money out of a bank. How did I acquire the authority to take money out of the bank? What right to that money can I rightfully claim? What is the nature of my relationship with the bank that I might rightfully make this claim? Furthermore, the original claim tells us nothing of its own boundaries. Even if it is true, what does it mean to have the authority to take money out of a bank? Can I walk into the bank whenever I want, saunter into the vault at my pleasure, and grab whatever I like? As anyone with a bank account knows, claiming that you have the authority to take money out of a bank is not untrue, but it hardly describes why you have that authority and how you can exercise it.

Thus, plenary power cannot be the answer to our meta-question because that term describes only what the United States claims to have, not why it has it in the first place. Rather, the real issue we are trying to resolve is by what means did the United States acquire this plenary power? What justifies plenary power? Consequently, we might refine the meta-question to ask: How has the United States justified its claims to plenary power over Native peoples and nations?

The second point to make before we tackle our (now refined) meta-question directly is that it is hard to deny that the real reason that the United States can claim any authority over Native America is that the United States is significantly more powerful than Native nations.[17] It has been many years since Native nations were a formidable enough military force to give the United States pause. In that sense, it is merely the exercise of raw power that justifies federal authority over Native peoples and nations.

The cynic in me would have stopped the book at that last sentence and left the remaining 150 pages blank to make the argument that the situation that Native America has been living under and continues to live under has more to do with this exercise of raw power than with any high-minded application of political theory.[18] However, the cynic in me will not get his way because there remains significant value in understanding the rationale behind the law and the assertion of power, even if the lofty rhetoric within the chambers of government has not always matched the actions on the ground.[19] This is especially so because colonization has always depended on the law and legal reasoning to justify itself.[20] In asserting a legal claim or argument, colonizing nations could—in theory if less so in practice—make a distinction between their ostensibly rightful actions against other peoples, lands, and nations and naked acts of aggression. The law was and is the key to legitimization. As such, the ideas and understandings that colonizers assert as law remain powerful, even if they are not always aligned with the colonizers' behavior or true motives. Furthermore, as we have already seen, legal fictions are powerful tools in helping explain, understand, and think about the law. Thus, if the "social contract" can help us recognize the claim of the United States to authority over its own citizenry—even though no one in the United States has signed any such contract—then the rationales that the United States asserts over Native America are still helpful objects of analysis even if those rationales are imbued with the same artificiality as the social contract. In summation, don't be a cynic.

Third and finally, the best place to look for answers to our meta-question is in Supreme Court cases, so that is what we will concentrate on in the rest of this chapter. This is not to diminish the role of the other branches in the story about plenary power. Obviously Congress and the president have been foundational to shaping the federal government's relationship with Native America and the scope of American law (which is a point to which we will return in the next chapter). But as our (surprisingly useful in retrospect, even if it didn't feel like it at the time) tenth-grade civics class taught us, the courts have the responsibility of interpreting the law. To that end, even though each of the branches considers plenary power, the courts much more often than the others are tasked with articulating the federal government's claim to authority over Native America. Concentrating on the Supreme Court specifically makes sense because it is not only the most powerful and influential court in the nation but also because it has considered our meta-question much more often than one might expect and has also played an outsized role in not merely interpreting this area of law but of creating it as well.

OK, wow, that was a lot of background stuff to cover just so we can answer the question standing behind the original question we sought to answer (and having answered the question behind the question that is behind the question!). But now here we are, finally ready to consider our refined meta-question: How has the United States justified its claims to plenary power over Native peoples and nations? We know that the United States claims authority over its own citizenry because, under the social contract theory, the citizenry has consented to the exercise of that authority. We also know that the United States presently claims plenary power over Native America under the Indian Commerce Clause of the U.S. Constitution. However, we also know that there have been other justifications for federal authority over Native America because the Supreme Court originally rejected the Indian Commerce Clause as a basis for plenary power yet asserted that the federal government had plenary power over Native America anyway. So, what were these other justifications?

There have been two major answers (other than the Indian Commerce Clause) to our meta-question that we will consider in some depth and a small handful of lesser answers that we will consider more briefly.[21] Both of the major answers—which we are going to label "land" and "protection"—share some important characteristics. Neither is rooted in the U.S. Constitution, and both are founded on an assumption that Native peoples, nations, and their rights are inferior to their colonialist counterparts. Some of the lesser answers do assert a constitutional basis, but without much in the way of traction or lasting authority as a philosophical or conceptual basis for plenary power. More important, these lesser answers also regard Native peoples in the same manner as our major answers.

The fact that land has been one of the major sources of justification for federal authority over Native peoples is unsurprising. Land has always been central to the relationship between the United States and Native America. Furthermore, colonialism is, at its essence, a process of accumulating and maintaining resources. Sometimes the resources that colonizers have sought were meant to be brought home or transported elsewhere, including things like gold, food, and even people. Just as often, however, the resource that colonizers have sought to accumulate and maintain has been land itself. This version of colonialism, in which the land is the object of desire, is central to the origin story the United States tells about itself and has been the subject of countless grade-school plays occurring in November. As the story goes, the Pilgrims sailed across the Atlantic Ocean in the *Mayflower* to find freedom, landed on Plymouth Rock, established the first lasting colony in the United States, and met with the friendly Indians. And that is why we have Thanksgiving today.

Plenty of folks have added much-needed depth and complexity to this overly simplistic and decidedly incomplete version of the Pilgrim story and Thanksgiving.[22] What is less up for debate, however, is that this narrative continues to have a fair amount of resonance and that it reveals how central land is to the American ethos. Variations of this basic story have been told over and over again. The Pilgrims, forebears to Americans, sought to forge a new life on new soil to flee the tyranny of the past and create something better for themselves and their descendants. The hardy pioneers who populated this country headed off west to build a new life on ostensibly readily available lands. In the present day homeownership and owning land are lauded as part of "the American Dream." Land has always been the key to unlock the potential of this transformational development and has fueled the American sense of self from the beginning.

Consequently, land has also played a pivotal role in federal Indian law, eventually serving as a source to the claim of authority over Native America. However, the relationship between Native peoples, power, land, and the law in the United States has evolved significantly over the years, developing along a formulistic line of perverse reasoning. In the earliest stages of development, American law was not yet concerned with how its understanding of land justified its authority over Native peoples. Rather, as befitting the role it played for a colonizing nation, American law was first concerned with justifying its own presence on the lands that it claimed.[23]

Put differently, the United States first had to play defense—by creating a legal framework that legitimized its own existence and claims to the lands originally inhabited by Native peoples—before it could play offense—by creating a legal framework that legitimized federal authority over Native peoples. This was especially so before the creation of the United States and in the earliest days of the republic when tribal nations could and did effectively resist federal overreach through military, diplomatic, economic, and other means.

Most scholars, quite understandably, point to the (in)famous Marshall Trilogy of Indian law cases (mentioned in Chapter 1) as the beginning of the field of federal Indian law as we know it today. We will return our attention to these seminal cases in a couple of paragraphs, but before we do, it is important to note that John Marshall laid his first brick in the groundwork for the justification of federal claims over tribal lands, and thus eventually over tribal peoples, over a dozen years before the Trilogy in another case, *Fletcher v. Peck*.[24] Decided in 1810, *Fletcher v. Peck* is regarded as noteworthy mostly for reasons outside federal Indian law, but a quick aside in Marshall's majority opinion is nonetheless telling. Briefly, in 1795 the state of Georgia sold lands to land speculation companies (these were the "house flippers" of their day) that were claimed by the state but still inhabited and claimed by tribal peoples and nations. Responding to accusations of corruption among the previous body, a newly elected state legislature sought to undo the land sales in 1796.[25]

The status of the land did not hold much sway in the final decision (although it probably should have).[26] Nonetheless, Marshall briefly noted, "The majority of the court is of the opinion" that while Native claims to land needed to be respected, those claims were not incompatible with state claims to the same lands.[27] This short statement, with nothing further in the way of elucidation or support, strongly suggested that the Supreme Court believed that colonial claims to land were on equal footing with tribal claims to land even though tribal nations and peoples were not a party to the case. How the colonizer acquired its claim was left unanswered as were the consequences of this line of reasoning for the parallel tribal land claims.[28]

In the first case of his (in)famous Trilogy, John Marshall answered the questions left behind in *Fletcher v. Peck*. Decided in 1823, that first case, *Johnson v. McIntosh*, may well be the most influential decision about Indigenous rights ever handed down, having established a basic legal framework from which we in the United States still operate today and having significantly shaped the law of other colonizing nations when those other nations confronted Indigenous land claims. Briefly, prior to the American Revolution two tribal nations, the Illinois and the Piankashaw, sold parcels of land to an individual purchaser. After the American Revolution, those tribal nations ceded those same lands to the United States in a treaty. Years later—under highly contrived circumstances that would certainly violate today's ethics rules for lawyers—the folks who inherited the interest in the land from the original individual purchaser manufactured a case that they were able to bring to the Supreme Court in an effort to validate their claim to the disputed land.[29]

At its most basic, the question in *Johnson v. McIntosh* was whether tribal peoples could sell the lands that they claimed as their own. Put a bit more sophisticatedly, the issue was the nature of the claims that Native nations could make to the lands they possessed. To use the parlance of property law, what "title" or right did Native nations have over the land? Could Native nations sell their land to whomever they chose whenever they chose?[30] Or did they lack any title that warranted recognition in American courts?

The very nature of the question demonstrates the disadvantaged position from which tribal nations began in the Supreme Court's analysis. An example will help illustrate the point. Imagine that you owned a house on a lot with a nice, big yard.[31] Now imagine that some recently arrived next-door neighbors walked over to your lawn and began pondering the nature of your ownership of your property and perhaps even hinted that they had their own ownership interest in your lot. Imagine also that these neighbors further pondered openly about your capacity to sell or otherwise make decisions about your property.

Under these circumstances you might ask yourself by what right can your neighbors question your claim to your property? What makes your interest in your property any different from your neighbors' interest in theirs? By what right can your neighbors assert their own interest in your property? By what right are your neighbors able to be on your property in the first place? How might you react in light of your neighbors' behavior? That your neighbors would even entertain such thoughts demonstrates that they could conceptualize your right to your land as less than both their right to the lands they claim and whatever interest they have in your lands as well. Put another way, the question itself presupposes the possibility (perhaps even the inevitability) that your neighbors regard your land claims as inherently inferior to theirs despite living side by side. Even more disturbingly for tribal nations, this question was being considered in a case without any Native participation and thus without any opportunity for Native peoples to argue on their own behalf.

The other side of this conceptual coin was problematic from the U.S. perspective. By the time that *Johnson v. McIntosh* arrived at the Supreme Court, the United States (like other colonizing nations in North America) had a long treaty history with many tribal nations. Most of these treaties involved a cession of tribal land to a colonizing force.[32] Whether tribal nations could sell the lands the United States ostensibly bought in treaties had the potential to significantly alter the U.S. claim to those lands. Thus, under American law what rights tribal nations had to land and what they could sell were important to not just tribal nations themselves but also to what the United States could territorially claim and how the United States conducted its business with tribal nations. Put differently, what did treaties with Native nations accomplish, particularly those that ceded land, if tribal nations did not have the authority to cede land in the first place?

When I teach this case in my course, I begin by asking my students to imagine they are John Marshall trying to decide this case.[33] First, we acknowledge that there would seem to be two answers to the question of whether or not Native nations can sell their land: yes and no. Then we walk through both answers to demonstrate that neither outcome would appeal to John Marshall.[34] Were the Supreme Court to rule that tribal nations were capable of selling their lands to anyone and everyone, then any purchase of tribal lands the United States made in a treaty was valid, but then so was every last purchase by a land speculation company or individual. Since (as *Johnson v. McIntosh* demonstrates) there might be competing claims—and also since (again as *Johnson v. McIntosh* demonstrates) not every party claiming to purchase tribal land was scrupulous—the task of managing these claims would be onerous at best for American courts. However, if the Supreme Court were to rule that tribal nations did not have any claim to land or right to sell that American law was bound to respect, then the consequences might be equally dire if not more so. Not only would such a ruling call the entire history of treaty relations into question; it might further provoke land speculation companies and individuals to make claims to tribal lands irrespective of tribal claims. Both outcomes seemed likely to provoke conflict rather than settle it.

There are many reasons why we engage in this thought experiment in my class, not the least of which is to demonstrate that it would seem that Native interests, if they are in the justices' minds at all, are most often found at the periphery rather than the center of even seminal decisions like *Johnson v. McIntosh*. Along those lines, when the case is viewed with tribal interests at the center, Marshall and his brethren on the Court would seem to be between the proverbial rock and a hard place. Regardless of whether tribal nations could or could not sell or cede their lands, the outcome was likely to produce disadvantageous results from the Court's perspective. However, when the interests of the colonizer are prioritized over those of the colonized, which Marshall ultimately did in his opinion, the conundrum the Supreme Court seemingly faced magically dissipates. Put differently, in a case about the fundamental nature of tribal land rights—can Native nations sell their land?—John Marshall decided to focus his analysis on what the United States could claim—what right does the United States have in tribal lands?

Marshall began his analysis by noting, "On the discovery of this immense continent, the great nations of Europe were eager to appropriate to themselves so much of it as they could respectively acquire."[35] Since these colonizing nations were after the same thing, according to Marshall, "it was necessary, in order to avoid conflicting settlements, and consequent war with each other, to establish a principle, which all should acknowledge as the law by which the right of acquisition, which they all asserted, should be regulated as between themselves."[36] Among the many things that John Marshall was, wordy was definitely one of them. Nonetheless, his fundamental point is clear: colonizing nations decided that they needed a few rules among themselves.

The primary rule of colonization is what we refer to as the Doctrine of Discovery.[37] At its essence, the Doctrine of Discovery (or just Discovery) gave a "discovering nation" certain rights against two different parties. On the one side, the process of "discovery" gave the discovering nation that first entered a new territory rights against other potential discovering (or colonizing) nations. Discovery allowed the discovering nation to exclude all other potential discovering nations from the lands that were "discovered."[38] On the other side, Discovery gave the discovering nation rights against Indigenous peoples as well. As full participants in the colonial project and having inherited England's interests in North America after the American Revolution, Marshall noted, "The United States, then, have unequivocally acceded to that great and broad rule by which its civilized inhabitants now hold this country. . . . They maintain, as all others have maintained, that discovery gave an exclusive right to extinguish the Indian title of occupancy, either by purchase or by conquest."[39] In short, under the Doctrine of Discovery the United States and the United States alone could acquire tribal lands by either buying them or conquering Native peoples.

What consequence did the "great and broad rule" of Discovery hold for Native peoples? According to Marshall, "In the establishment of these relations, the rights of the original inhabitants were, in no instance, entirely disregarded, but were necessarily, to a considerable extent, impaired."[40] Although Marshall conceded that Native peoples "were admitted to be the rightful occupants of the soil, with a legal as well as just claim to retain possession of it, and to use it according to their own discretion," he nonetheless claimed that the process of discovery divested tribal nations of the full authority they held before they were discovered.[41] "Their rights to complete sovereignty, as independent nations, were necessarily diminished, and their power to dispose of the soil at their own will, to whomsoever they pleased, was denied by the original fundamental principle, that discovery gave exclusive title to those who made it."[42]

At its essence, the law of the case is fairly simple. The Doctrine of Discovery gives the United States the sole right to acquire tribal lands, either through purchase or conquest. Having been "discovered," tribal nations' interest in their lands was reduced to occupancy rights (or occupancy or Indian title or Aboriginal title). Under this framework tribal nations are authorized to sell their lands to only one purchaser: the discovering nation (which, as one professor pointed out to me a long time ago, really limits the asking price if there is only one potential buyer). Thus, the original sale to the individual purchaser that precipitated the events in *Johnson v. McIntosh* was not valid, whereas the second sale to the United States in a treaty was valid.[43]

All right, fine. The rule itself is simple enough to understand, but is it fair? The Doctrine of Discovery obviously creates two classes of nations: those that do the discovering and those that can be discovered. What basis is there to make this distinction? Why should the United States be able to make claims to tribal lands that it wouldn't be able to make about the lands of, say, England or Spain or France? What justifies the Doctrine of Discovery, and thus the colonizers' ostensible right to be on the lands it is colonizing?

Interestingly, John Marshall seems to evidence some embarrassment about Discovery, noting, "We will not enter into the controversy, whether agriculturists, merchants, and manufacturers, have a right, on abstract principles, to expel hunters from the territory they possess, or to contract their limits."[44] Yet, whatever embarrassment Marshall may have legitimately held about the Doctrine of Discovery as an abstract concept dissipated quickly within the particular circumstances Marshall described. "Although we do not mean to engage in the defence of those principles which Europeans have applied to Indian title, they may, we think, find some excuse, if not justification, in the character and habits of the people whose rights have been wrested from them."[45] In other words, according to Marshall, whatever else one may think about the Doctrine of Discovery in general, it made sense in its application against Native peoples.

Assuming that Marshall was sincere in his embarrassment at the Doctrine of Discovery in the abstract, why then does it make sense to apply it in this context? Before exploring his reasoning, Marshall offered a short, uncited, deeply euphemistic, and hardly accurate description of the process of colonization. In essence, Marshall argued, typically colonizers treated the colonized humanely and eventually the colonized become one with the colonizers. "The new and old members of the society mingle with each other; the distinction between them is gradually lost, and they make one people."[46] Yet, this allegedly natural progress toward assimilation and acculturation was not possible on the North American continent because, according to Marshall, "the tribes of Indians inhabiting this country were fierce savages, whose occupation was war, and whose subsistence was drawn chiefly from the forest. . . . They were as brave and as high spirited as they were fierce, and were ready to repel by arms every attempt on their independence."[47] Since [*he writes in the hope that you will hear the sarcasm in the sound of his fingertips slapping the keyboard*] Native peoples apparently seemed to hold some crazy objection to others invading their land and trying to alter their way of life, "frequent and bloody wars, in which the whites were not always the aggressors, unavoidably ensued."[48] Thus, according to Marshall, the process of colonization in the United States was atypical because those who were being colonized were atypical: "That law which regulates, and ought to regulate in general, the relations between the conqueror and conquered, was incapable of application to a people under such circumstances."[49]

Stripped of any pretense, Marshall essentially ruled that the Doctrine of Discovery made sense as a principle of American law because Native peoples were too savage to conquer or otherwise "make one people" with. Without the capacity to dominate or assimilate the colonized, the colonizer needed to "resort to some new and different rule, better adapted to the actual state of things."[50] The Doctrine thus allowed the United States to assert title to the entirety of Native America without having to go through the troublesome step of actually having control over the land or the people on the land, ostensibly justifying its own presence and existence in North America and any future acquisitions it might make.[51]

Put differently, a rule that Marshall may not have held in high regard was nonetheless indispensable to the deeply counterintuitive assertion that the colonizer had a superior right to the lands of the "fierce savages" over which the colonizer had no actual possession.[52] Furthermore, by giving the colonizer something it did not actually possess, Discovery necessarily justified both the presence of the colonizer in the "New World" and the process of colonization.[53] Such a backward rule was possible because of the supposedly fearsome, incorrigible nature of the original inhabitants of the lands. In short, racism was the fundamental basis for the illogical American land claims and self-justification upon which the law is still founded today.

As noted in Chapter 1, there is plenty more that can and has been said about *Johnson v. McIntosh*. For our purposes, however, it suffices to note that Marshall's full-fledged adoption of the Doctrine of Discovery into American law had two consequences that are pertinent to our meta-question. First, it established a basis in the law whereby the United States could make claims on the lands of Native peoples irrespective of any actual possession of those lands or any input from Native peoples themselves.[54] In asserting this interest in Native lands—again, merely by declaring it so in a court opinion in a case that had no Native participation—the United States was also asserting the rightfulness of its very existence justified primarily on the basis of the supposedly savage nature of the original inhabitants.

Second, building upon this legal and conceptual groundwork, the United States eventually began asserting authority over Native peoples as a condition of its interest in lands under the Doctrine of Discovery. This shift from defense to offense (if I may harken back to an allusion from a few pages ago that I liked and thought was useful) began at the Supreme Court in earnest with Marshall's successor, Roger Taney.

If John Marshall is the most respected Supreme Court justice in American history, then Roger Taney may well be the most reviled. Taney's reputation, such that it is, is built almost exclusively on his opinion in the 1857 *Dred Scott* case.[55] Regularly regarded as one of if not the worst Supreme Court decision ever, Taney's declaration in *Dred Scott* that individuals of African descent could not become citizens of the United States is understandably considered a major catalyst for the American Civil War.[56]

And what did possibly the worst jurist of all time have to say about the Doctrine of Discovery? Something even worse for Native peoples than what John Marshall originally articulated!

Decided in 1846, eleven years before *Dred Scott*, the facts of *U.S. v. Rogers* offered Taney and his judicial brethren the opportunity to recognize the sovereignty of tribal nations and the political status between those nations and the United States.[57] Taney and his compatriots, instead, chose a different path. Briefly, William S. Rogers was alleged to have killed Jacob Nicholson on Cherokee land. Both men were non-Native by birth, but according to Rogers, both had moved to Cherokee territory, had no intention of returning to the United States, and were recognized as Cherokee citizens by the Cherokee Nation. As such, Rogers argued, it was the Cherokee and not the United States that had jurisdiction over the alleged crime.[58] The sincerity of Rogers's claim to Cherokee citizenry (along with the Cherokee Nation's willingness to claim him as one of their own) may be lost to history, yet it did not matter to the chief justice. As he would eleven years later in his most (in)famous opinion, Taney essentially equated the categories of race and citizenship. According to Taney, the United States held jurisdiction over Rogers because "whatever obligations the prisoner may have taken upon himself by becoming a Cherokee by adoption, his responsibility to the laws of the United States remained unchanged and undiminished. He was still a white man, of the white race."[59]

More pertinent to our meta-question, Taney also opined on the Doctrine of Discovery. He claimed, "The native tribes who were found on this continent at the time of discovery have never been acknowledged or treated as independent nations by the European governments, nor regarded as the owners of the territories they respectively occupied. On the contrary, the whole continent was divided and parcelled out, and granted by the governments of Europe as if it has been vacant and unoccupied land, and the Indians continually held to be, and treated as, subject to their domination and control."[60] Remember those nosy neighbors from a few pages ago that walked over to your lawn and started questioning your rights on your property? Well now they are not only claiming your property as their own, but they are suggesting they have rights over you personally![61]

Interestingly, Taney did slightly temper his articulation of the Doctrine of Discovery in the infamous *Dred Scott* decision, but this was more in service of advocating against the rights of peoples of African descent than in favor of the rights of Native peoples and nations, and it did little to alter what was to come in American law.[62] More important, Taney had allowed this doctrinal horse to escape from the barn in *Rogers*, and, as the United States was expanding and placing more pressures on Native peoples and territory, it began to run wild. Justice John McLean, who participated in the Marshall Trilogy cases as well as *Dred Scott* in his lengthy tenure on the Supreme Court, wrote of Cherokee lands in 1856: "In some respects they bear the same relation to the federal government as a territory. . . . It is not a foreign, but a domestic territory—a territory which originated under our constitution and laws."[63] McLean's claim that tribal lands originated under the U.S. Constitution and laws is bizarre and not necessarily in keeping with the Doctrine of Discovery or how tribal lands were understood then or now. But McLean's larger implication—the federal government had authority over Native peoples because of federal claims to land—was taking hold.[64]

By at least 1870 this basic proposition could be taken as a given at the Supreme Court. Writing in a case about the applicability of federal taxes to crops produced on tribal lands, Justice Noah Haynes Swayne directly quoted from Marshall and Taney's earlier opinions to assert first that tribal lands were considered part of the United States and second that the United States had jurisdiction over those lands, including over Native nations and peoples.[65] Of the groundwork laid by Marshall and Taney, Swayne stated, "Both these propositions are so well settled in our jurisprudence that it would be a waste of time to discuss them or to refer to further authorities in their support."[66] In 1886 in *Kagama*—the very case that started the mystery we are trying to solve!—Justice Miller walked the same path as Swayne (including citing Marshall and Taney) to find federal authority over Native peoples where he could find none in the U.S. Constitution itself. "But these Indians are within the geographical limits of the United States. The soil and the people within these limits are under the political control of the Government of the United States, or of the States of the Union. There exist within the broad domain of sovereignty but these two."[67]

By the twentieth century a casual reader of Supreme Court opinions might be forgiven for being confused about who resided first in what was to become the United States.[68] To be perfectly fair, the Supreme Court did acknowledge and respect the occupancy or Indian title rights of Native nations under the Doctrine of Discovery with perhaps more frequency than one might expect from the institution that legitimized the limitation of those rights in the first place.[69] However, a clear sense that tribal nations and peoples were merely guests in their own ancestral homes had developed. For example, writing in 1937 Justice Benjamin Cardozo stated, "Confusion is likely to result from speaking of the wrong to the Shoshones as a destruction of their title. Title in the strict sense was always in the United States, though the Shoshones had the treaty right of occupancy with all its beneficial incidents."[70] Furthermore, these "guests" were subject to house rules. In 1938, Justice Hugo Black wrote, "The Government retains title to the lands which it permits the Indians to occupy. The Government has authority to enact regulations and protective laws respecting this territory. 'Congress possesses the broad power of legislating for the protection of the Indians wherever they may be within the territory of the United States.'"[71] By the mid-twentieth century, this reversal of positionality within the legal analysis—in which Native peoples seemed to have arrived after their American counterparts—was so complete that the Supreme Court was even willing to deny tribal occupancy rights unless the federal government had first recognized them. In a particularly infamous case from 1955, the Supreme Court essentially ruled that those nosy neighbors standing on your lawn wouldn't need to compensate you for taking your land if they had never acknowledged your right to be on your own property in the first place.[72]

William Rehnquist's notorious 1978 opinion in *Oliphant* (introduced in Chapter 1) offers a useful encapsulation of how land developed into a justification for federal authority over Native peoples. *Oliphant* crystallized the formulistic line of perverse reasoning that commenced in American law with *Fletcher v. Peck* almost 170 years earlier. First, assert that the United States is the true owner of all of the lands it claims. "Indian reservations are 'a part of the territory of the United States.'"[73] Rehnquist's lack of direct reference to Discovery demonstrates how the basic reasoning of the doctrine—again, established so that colonists could claim land over which they had no actual possession and justified under the understanding that Native peoples were too savage to be assimilated—had become so ingrained within the law that it need not even be mentioned, as it was given. Second, describe Native peoples as little more than guests on their ancestral homelands. "Indian tribes 'hold and occupy [the reservations] with the assent of the United States, and under their authority.'"[74] By asserting that the colonized (and thus not the colonizers) were the true interlopers, their displacement and any use of force or law to accomplish this end appear justified. Third, claim a complete or total authority over your land and thus over the miscreants on your land. "Upon incorporation into the territory of the United States, the Indian tribes thereby come under the territorial sovereignty of the United States and their exercise of separate power is constrained so as not to conflict with the interest of this overriding sovereignty."[75] Like many others before him, in his travels down this well-trod path Rehnquist cited and directly quoted Marshall in *Johnson v. McIntosh* and Taney in *Rogers*.

To be clear, this is not to suggest that any and all American claims to land are illegitimate. After all, tribal nations did cede millions of acres to the United States through treaties. Your mileage may vary concerning the righteousness of those treaties and how they came to be, but they are manifestations of something akin to a tangible social contract, and tribal nations tend to hold them in high regard as they are the most prominent acknowledgment of their sovereignty. Furthermore, the federal government did grant itself significant authority on the lands that it did own in the U.S. Constitution in what is known as the Territory Clause or Property Clause (which we will consider in greater detail a little later).[76] That the United States owns land on the North American continent and has control over the land that it owns are not particularly controversial assertions.

That being noted, our mystery and the conspiracy behind it are not really about land—they are about power. Thus, it is one thing to say that the United States owns land in North America and has control over the land it owns (as would any other landowner). It is quite another thing to say that the United States has plenary authority over the original inhabitants of the land simply because it says it has an interest in the land regardless of any actual possession of it or cession to it. Making this leap in illogic requires following the formulistic line of perverse reasoning we have traced in this chapter. First, your nosy neighbors who stepped on your lawn have to assert an interest in your property for themselves—an interest that they justify to themselves because they believe you to be too savage and bloodthirsty to dominate and/or produce children with. Next, as more of their kind move into the neighborhood, your neighbors have to act as if they were here first and are doing you a favor by letting you live in the place you lived in before they got here. Finally, after treating you like a guest on your own land, your neighbors have to assert not only that they are the true owners of everything that you have claimed as yours but that this ownership allows them to make any and all rules that you have to follow. This includes rules for not only the land upon which you have always lived but also for yourself as a person. As is obvious, this formulistic line of perverse reasoning bears no relationship to the understanding of consent that is fundamental to other exertions and justifications of federal power.[77]

Hey, do you know what's crazy? You're totally not going to believe this, but our second major answer to our meta-question—protection—also originated with John Marshall and his (in)famous Trilogy! I know, crazy, right?

Anyway, let's be clear about what we mean by "protection" before we give Marshall his due. Truth be told, although the Supreme Court has made many references to the ongoing relationship between the federal government and tribal nations, it has only sporadically used the word "protection" to describe what we are trying to understand. Nonetheless, the Supreme Court has determined that the federal government has assumed an obligation to Native peoples and nations to act in their best interests. This is in large part because many times it was expressed explicitly in treaties.[78] However, a generalized understanding that the federal government has this obligation to all tribal peoples and nations has developed in the law.[79] As we have already encountered in Chapter 1, the Supreme Court originally likened the obligation the United States assumed to a guardian and a ward. In more recent times, the Supreme Court has described it as a trust relationship whereby the United States is the trustee tasked with operating in the best interests of tribal nations who are the beneficiaries.

Quite often, the purpose of describing or defining the federal government's duty to Native America has been to articulate why it has authority over Native peoples and nations.[80] Thus, we are going to use the word "protection" as a catchall for the differing words and terms that the Supreme Court has used to explain how a generalized obligation to Native America has been regarded as a basis for the exercise of authority over Native America. By using the word "protection" to describe this aspect of the law, we can maintain our focus on the conspiracy standing behind our mystery—how has the United States justified its claims to plenary power over Native peoples and nations? In short, the Supreme Court has often found that the United States has plenary power over Native America because it has decided it is obligated to protect Native America.

Now, we probably should be fair to John Marshall by taking a quick step back to consider his function in our conspiracy. Too often those of us who are legally trained tend to invest too much authority in Marshall and what he wrote during his time on the Court. This is at least somewhat understandable because Marshall really did raise the Supreme Court's level of prominence and authority in the American governmental structure. However, he is not the origin of all American legal thinking—an impression that some might have with the way that lawyers and legal historians sometimes talk and write about Marshall. He was a man who was operating within the marketplace of ideas of his time (including some that held Native peoples and sovereignty in higher regard than the law would come to).

To that end, it is worth acknowledging that John Marshall did not invent the idea of protection in the relationship between the United States and Native nations.[81] But what he did accomplish—with his outsized influence and platform—was to open a pathway that allowed the Supreme Court to use the idea of protection as a justification for federal authority over Native America (much in the same way he had with land). While others would further refine and shape it, Marshall forged the idea into a doctrine of American law.[82] To put it into the words of our ongoing metaphor, John Marshall was not the original mastermind of our conspiracy, but he was certainly a key operative in perpetuating it.

So what did Marshall do? It begins, as with many things in this area of law, with *Johnson v. McIntosh*. During his defense of the Doctrine of Discovery, Marshall sought to (very loosely) describe the scope of tribal occupancy rights. First claiming that Discovery "cannot be questioned," he then hinted that the colonizer nonetheless held an obligation to the colonized.[83] "So, too, with respect to the concomitant principle, that the Indian inhabitants are to be considered merely as occupants, *to be protected*, indeed, while in peace, in the possession of their lands."[84] (I decided to add a little emphasis there just to make sure you caught it.) Eight years later, in the second case of his Trilogy, *Cherokee Nation v. Georgia*, Marshall further elucidated on the colonizer's obligation. Building on the same understanding of tribal inferiority that guided his reasoning about land, Marshall stated that Native peoples were "in a state of pupilage" and that "their relation to the United States resembles that of a ward to his guardian."[85] This analogy, among other things, implied that the "guardian" had an obligation to the "ward." Painting with his typically broad brush, Marshall continued, "*They look to our government for protection*; rely upon its kindness and its power; appeal to it for relief to their wants; and address the president as their great father."[86] (I did it again with the extra emphasis.) Thus, the state of the law was such, according to Marshall, in no small part based on the Indians' need for protection. Furthermore, the brief reference to a familial relationship was in keeping with the language of diplomacy between Native nations and the United States, yet it also assuredly implied a type of hierarchical, patriarchal relationship and legal status that would have been familiar to Marshall in his time in which a father was expected to care for his children yet had almost limitless rights over them.[87]

Again, to be perfectly fair, Marshall did seek to temper some of the worst excesses of the Doctrine of Discovery and its consequences—although while still adhering to it—in the third case of his Trilogy, *Worcester v. Georgia*.[88] Pointedly (for our purposes), Marshall noted in *Worcester*, "Protection does not imply the destruction of the protected," and "a weaker power does not surrender its independence—its right to self government, by associating with a stronger, and taking its protection. A weak state, in order to provide for its safety, may place itself under the protection of one more powerful, without stripping itself of the right of government, and ceasing to be a state."[89]

Nonetheless, as with land, this doctrinal horse had also escaped from the barn and also quickly began to run wild. The understanding that Native peoples were underdeveloped and that the United States had a duty to them took hold in short order. Writing about a specific tribal nation in 1851, Justice Robert Cooper Grier stated that they were "in a state of pupilage, under the guardianship of the United States."[90] Three years later, Justice James Moore Wayne wrote, "The Indians . . . were considered in a state of tutelage. . . . Again: Indians, although of age, continue to enjoy the rights of minors. . . . Indians are considered as persons under legal disability, and their protectors stand in the light of guardians."[91]

As it did with land, the tenure and writings of Chief Justice Roger Taney marked a shift in the thinking about protection as a justification for federal authority over Native peoples. In *Dred Scott* (which, again, is regularly regarded as the worst Supreme Court opinion ever handed down) Taney nudged the general understanding of a duty to protect into the more concrete realm of tangible action. "It is true that the course of events has brought the Indian tribes within the limits of the United States under subjection to the white race; and it has been found necessary, for their sake as well as our own, to regard them as in a state of pupilage, and to legislate to a certain extent over them and the territory they occupy."[92] After the Civil War, this sense that the United States needed to be proactive in the maintenance of its duty only grew. Writing in 1866 Justice David Davis stated, "The only efficient way of dealing with the Indian tribes was to place them under the protection of the general government."[93]

Even more disturbingly, the Supreme Court began signaling that it would not tolerate any challenge in the courts to the scope and boundaries of the federal government's self-proclaimed duty to protect. An 1877 opinion written by Stephen Johnson Field aptly traced the genealogy of the understanding of protection to that point. Reminiscent of *Johnson v.*

McIntosh, the case itself, *Beecher v. Wetherby*, concerned a land (or, more correctly, resources on the land) dispute between two non-Native persons on what had fairly recently been tribal land.[94] Consequently, Field's opinion outlined the rights of Native nations under the Doctrine of Discovery, stating that "the right which the Indians held was only of occupancy. The fee was in the United States, subject to that right, and could be transferred by them whenever they chose."[95] Having reiterated this overarching authority, Field then presumed benevolence while rejecting oversight. "It is to be presumed that in this matter the United States would be governed by such considerations of justice as would control a Christian people in their treatment of an ignorant and dependent race. Be that as it may, the propriety or justice of their action towards the Indians with respect to their lands is a question of governmental policy, and is not a matter open to discussion in a controversy between third parties."[96]

Not even Native peoples themselves, according to the Court, could challenge the growing understanding of protection that was based on the inferiority of Native peoples. John Elk had been born among the Winnebago, but, according to the Court, by at least the 1880s he had "severed his tribal relation to the Indian tribes."[97] He had been living in Omaha, Nebraska, for about a year when he tried to register to vote and was denied on the basis of his race.[98] Reiterating the basic understanding of Native people under American law, Justice Horace Gray's opinion echoed a common refrain. "They were in a dependent condition, a state of pupilage, resembling that of a ward to his guardian."[99] As a consequence, according to Gray, John Elk was incapable of deciding for himself whether he had the capacity to vote. Rather, it was the federal government's decision. "The national legislation has tended more and more towards the education and civilization of the Indians, and fitting them to be citizens. But the question whether any Indian tribes, or any members thereof, have become so far advanced in civilization, that they should be let out of the state of pupilage, and admitted to the privileges and responsibilities of citizenship, is a question to be decided by the nation whose wards they are and whose citizens they seek to become, and not by each Indian for himself."[100]

Protection as the basis for federal plenary power over Native peoples reached its apex in the Plenary Power Trilogy of cases (introduced in Chapter 1).[101] Our old friend, Justice Samuel Miller, in the case we just can't quit—*Kagama*—took prior rationales to another level. Whereas John Marshall had described the relationship between the United States and tribal nations as "resembl[ing]" that of a guardian and ward, Miller made it a reality. "These Indian tribes are wards of the nation."[102] This rhetorical shift left no doubt about the federal government's claim of authority over Native peoples under the guise of protection.[103] According to Miller, "The power of the General Government over these remnants of a race once powerful, now weak and diminished in numbers, is necessary to their protection."[104]

As noted in Chapter 1, the second case in the Plenary Power Trilogy, *Lone Wolf v. Hitchcock*, concerned an egregious treaty violation on the part of the United States. Nonetheless, Justice Edward Douglass White, writing in 1903, reasoned that the duty to protect not only authorized treaty violations; it practically necessitated them. "To uphold the claim would be to adjudge that the indirect operation of the treaty was to materially limit and qualify the controlling authority of Congress in respect to the care and protection of the Indians, and to deprive Congress, in a possible emergency, when the necessity might be urgent for a partition and disposal of the tribal lands, of the power to act, if the assent of the Indians could not be obtained."[105] In short, the words of a treaty were meaningless if the federal government decided to act under its self-appointed duty to protect.[106] Furthermore, in a case where it was clearly lacking, the Supreme Court deepened its commitment to not questioning the actions of the other branches acting out of this obligation by assuming a "perfect good faith" on their part.[107]

Decided in 1913, the third case of the Plenary Power Trilogy, *U.S. v. Sandoval*, also embraced protection as the basis for its ruling, with Justice Willis Van Devanter writing, "Long continued legislative and executive usage and an unbroken current of judicial decisions have attributed to the United States as a superior and civilized nation the power and the duty of exercising a fostering care and protection over all dependent Indian communities within its borders."[108] One question that the parties to *San-*

doval thought was significant was whether or not the tribal members that were part of the dispute were American citizens. However, Van Devanter brushed this question away in support of the federal government's expansive authority under its self-appointed obligation. "Whether they are citizens is an open question, and we need not determine it now, because citizenship is not in itself an obstacle to the exercise by Congress of its power to enact laws for the benefit and protection of tribal Indians as a dependent people."[109]

The Plenary Power Trilogy of cases not only embraced and enhanced protection as a legitimate claim to federal authority over Native peoples in American law; it effectively denied any limitation on the federal government's claims to power under this duty. Neither the U.S. Constitution nor treaties, or American citizenship, placed a check against it according to the Plenary Power Trilogy. Moreover, it reinforced the foundational presumption that justified protection in the first place: the Americans were superior and therefore guardians, and Native peoples were inferior and therefore wards. The Supreme Court would reference this foundational presumption again and again in the late nineteenth century and well into the mid-twentieth century. I mean, seriously, they wouldn't quit with it. Don't believe me? Well, why don't you just look at the next end note I give you and see for yourself. Go on, here it is.[110]

From the mid-twentieth century forward the guardian/ward and dependency descriptions of the relationship between the United States and tribal nations lingered and still make an occasional appearance in modern cases.[111] But they were gradually more or less replaced with assertations about a trust responsibility and other, softer language.

We should pause for a moment because in the back of my head I can hear what my dad would say if we ever got to this part of the conversation: "Does it really matter if they call it guardian/ward or trust or anything else? Isn't a lie just a lie?" To which I might reply to him that in one sense he is right. If this were another area of law, the difference between a ward and a beneficiary or a guardian and a trustee would be meaningful.[112] In Indian law, however, the distinctiveness of the words carries less meaning because any language is still based on the foundational presumption of Native inferiority and American superiority that is used to justify an essentially unlimited federal authority over Native America. Whatever the words, they all support federal plenary power over Native America.

But in another sense I would argue (to the made-up question that I have put in my father's mouth without his knowledge or blessing) that it is important to pay attention to these rhetorical shifts. It is easy to see (and apply) the pejorative connotation that a word like "ward" carries. It readily reflects the foundational presumption of Native underdevelopment. On the other hand, the softer the language, the more difficult it is to see this foundational presumption. The language of trust implies a more strictly financial arrangement that is less inherently imbued with pejorative connotations than the language of wardship. It removes the rhetoric of federal power further from the presumption of Native inferiority without making much in the way of practical change in the presumption itself.

I suppose you can decide for yourself the extent to which this shift was deliberate, but it is pretty clear that it fits into a pattern. For example, we noted in Chapter 1 that William Rehnquist used ellipses to remove the most blatantly racist language from an 1883 decision yet maintained that opinion's spirit in the 1978 *Oliphant* decision. Moreover, the mystery we are trying to solve—when did plenary power become constitutional?—evidences a similar change. The Supreme Court used to describe things one way. Now the Supreme Court is describing them another way. What, if anything, has actually changed for Native America? What is being perpetuated and maintained, and what has become hidden and inaccessible? To that end, it is important to trace the change from wardship language to trust language because not doing so risks losing sight of the fact that whatever the language, it has the same origin and offers essentially the same answer to our conspiracy—the federal government has authority over Native America because Native America needs to be protected.

Perhaps the earliest and most prominent example of the Supreme Court describing the relationship between the United States and Native America in trust terms is the 1942 decision *Seminole Nation v. United States*, written by Justice Frank Murphy.[113] However, a case from a year later, *Creek Nation v. United States*, better describes the jumbled interconnectedness of the language of protection and federal claims to authority over Native America. This time writing in dissent, Murphy nonetheless noted, "We have held that the Government in its relations with the Indian tribes occupies the position of a fiduciary, that the relationship is similar to that of guardian and ward, and that the duties and responsibilities of the United States toward its wards require a generous interpretation."[114]

Around the same time that Rehnquist was scrubbing the most racist language from precedential cases to craft his argument in *Oliphant*, the Supreme Court began more fully utilizing the language of trust to identify protection as the source of federal authority.[115] Writing in 1983, Thurgood Marshall noted about laws pertaining to Native peoples, "Our construction of these statutes and regulations is reinforced by the undisputed existence of a general trust relationship between the United States and the Indian people. This Court has previously emphasized 'the distinctive obligation of trust incumbent upon the Government in its dealings with these dependent and sometimes exploited people.'"[116] Writing in 1985, Justice Lewis F. Powell Jr. took note of "the unique trust relationship between the United States and the Indians."[117] Also writing in 1985, Justice William Brennan noted, "Since the 19th century the cornerstone of Congress' policy has been to impose strict restraints on alienation of Indian title—a policy grounded on the federal trust responsibility toward Indian tribes."[118] Again, you can determine for yourself the extent to which the Supreme Court's shift to trust language in a moment when it was altering its precedential language in other cases was deliberate. Regardless, today the language of trust predominates.

There is more that can and has been said about the scope and contours of what we now tend to refer as the Trust Doctrine (and we will say more in Chapter 4!).[119] However, for the purposes of our meta-question—How has the United States justified its claims to plenary power over Native peoples and nations?—it suffices to note that "trust" is the most recent articulation of the bigger category of "protection." While protection has a conceptually more direct connection to power than our previous major answer—land—it still requires the same sort of leap of illogic to find justification for federal authority over Native peoples. To be sure, Native peoples did agree to come under the "protection" of the United

States in various treaties, and the United States has committed itself to the betterment of Native America through legislation and other means. Furthermore, one might argue that, if nothing else than a matter of justice and humanity, the colonizer does bear a responsibility to the colonized. However, it is one thing to say that the United States bears some responsibility to Native America. It is quite another thing to say that this responsibility authorizes essentially limitless control over Native peoples, nations, and lands.

Let's put the issue in what is likely to be more familiar terrain. Perhaps you are an older sibling. Now let's imagine that, for whatever reason, you came to the conclusion that your younger sibling needed your protection. Under those circumstances you might decide that you have an obligation to your sibling. Furthermore, you might feel that your sibling is obliged to you as well. Maybe you would expect some reciprocation the next time you needed some help, or at least some loyalty. Is this unreasonable? I suspect most would say "probably not." I further suspect that many of us have found ourselves in such an arrangement, whether as the older sibling, the younger sibling, or, depending on the size of your family and the predilections of your siblings, in either position.

But let's take it a step further. If you decided to "protect" your younger sibling, would your obligation give you the right to fully and totally control her or him from that point forward? From the moment you decided that you had an obligation—perhaps even without consulting your sibling—could you then pick her or his friends, choose where she or he hung out, and make choices about any and all other aspects of her or his life? How does your obligation to protect connect to an unfettered authority over your sibling? Now put yourself in the shoes of the younger sibling. To what extent does accepting the protection of your older sibling mean that you are under the authority of your older sibling? If you ask for help with your homework, should that mean that your older sibling gets to pick your classes for you or decide where you go to college or what religion you practice? Who would ever agree to this version of protection? Why would one assume, as the Supreme Court has done so often, that Native peoples would agree to such an arrangement? To connect an obligation to protect to plenary power requires just such a leap in illogic, one that, as noted previously, even John Marshall rejected. It also denies the traditional process developed by American courts to read treaties with Native nations in a way that accounts for various language and social barriers.[120]

Furthermore, as the lineage of these cases make clear, the duty to protect as a justification for plenary power is built upon an understanding of Native peoples as inferior and underdeveloped. While a transition to trust language obscures these origins, it hardly rectifies them or their consequences.[121] And, as with land, the reasoning behind protection bears no relationship to the understanding of consent that is fundamental to other exertions and justifications of federal power.

So, land and protection are the big ones (besides the Indian Commerce Clause). But as noted earlier, there are a handful of other, lesser justifications for federal authority over Native America that the Supreme Court has offered over the years. While none of them are as prominent as land and protection, they are still worthy of mention because they fit the pattern of our conspiracy. These less prominent justifications require similar leaps in illogic that are fundamentally premised on conceptions of Native inferiority.

On occasion, the Supreme Court has pointed to the Territory or Property Clause as a source of authority.[122] However, this argument has been mostly subsumed by larger arguments about land and suffers from the same basic flaw: just because your nosy neighbors can claim dominion over their land does not mean that they can claim dominion over your land and you by stepping on your lawn.[123] Even with some measure of textual basis in the U.S. Constitution this argument is nothing more than a rearticulation of the Doctrine of Discovery and its distinctly colonial reasoning. As such, it is difficult to see any distance between the foundational rationale of Property Clause arguments and that of Doctrine of Discovery arguments that presumes the inherent savagery Native peoples.[124]

A slightly more popular rationale for plenary power over Native peoples at the Supreme Court has been the Treaty Clause, which states that the president "shall have Power . . . to make treaties."[125] The Treaty Clause is similar to the Property Clause in that both are perfectly reasonable on their own, yet both require a leap in illogic to justify plenary power over Native America. For example, no one disputes that the United States can make and has made treaties with, say, Canada. Yet no reasonable person argues that the Treaty Clause gives the United States unfettered authority over Canada, its territory, and its citizens. To be sure, there are a lot of factors that can complicate how we read treaties and think about the treaty power in general.[126] But it does not follow that just because the federal government has the capacity to make treaties with tribal nations—and did so on many occasions—that it thus has plenary power over them.[127]

At this point it is fair to note that Native nations are generally not similarly situated to Canada militarily, economically, or in several other respects. We will more deeply consider the size and scope of Native nations in relation to the Treaty Clause in Chapter 5. But for now, it is also fair to note that Canada is also not similarly situated to the United States militarily, economically, or in several other respects.[128] Consequently, Canada IS similarly situated to tribal nations in that it has a treaty history with the United States, shares borders with the United States, and is presumably ultimately equally incapable of resisting American military force. So why does the United States (sometimes) claim plenary power over tribal nations through the Treaty Clause but not over Canada? The most obvious answer should feel familiar by this part of the chapter: there is a class of sovereigns that do the discovering and a class that can be discovered, and there are different rules for each. Thus, the leap in illogic that allows for federal plenary power under the Treaty Clause over Native America but not over Canada makes sense in the colonial mind-set.

In addition, on occasion the Supreme Court has asserted that the United States has plenary power over Native America because Native America has been conquered.[129] Frustratingly, this assertion is always lightly sprinkled in without any further comment from the Supreme Court on the many challenging questions that it raises. For example, at what point is a people or nation conquered? As we have noted more than once, Native peoples are no longer a military threat to the United States, but does it necessarily follow that they have been conquered? To what extent does the long treaty history between Native America and the United States refute the application of conquest as a conceptual category to tribal nations and peoples? In other words, shouldn't the relationship between Native nations and the United States be dictated by the terms of a treaty when there is a treaty rather than some ill-defined notion of conquest? Furthermore, even if one conceptualizes Native peoples as conquered, why would it follow that the United States can exercise plenary power? After all, even "conquered" peoples and territories are understood to have rights that otherwise contradict the all-encompassing nature of plenary power.[130] Along those same lines, if the legitimacy of the federal government is based on the consent of the people to be governed, then how can the federal government assert any legitimacy without that consent? Aren't consent and conquest irreconcilable bases for claims to power? To what extent does a conquest-based argument in favor of plenary power over Native America run contrary to any other argument in favor of federal power elsewhere? The Supreme Court has not addressed any of these questions, making it difficult to imagine that the true basis for conquest-based arguments for plenary power is anything more than the open racism that has fueled the rest of the rationales we have explored in this chapter.

Finally, every now and then the Supreme Court has stated that the federal government's plenary power over Native America stems not from the U.S. Constitution itself but is part of the natural and inherent authority that any sovereign has. In fact, both cases that bookend our mystery—*Kagama* and *Lara*—make a version of this claim.[131] However, the general proposition that the United States has any authority beyond what is enumerated in the U.S. Constitution is controversial.[132] Furthermore, even if there are federal powers beyond those enumerated in the U.S. Constitution, it is difficult to understand why plenary power over Native America would be among them. Arguments in favor of an inherent sovereign authority tend to be most concerned with foreign affairs, particularly military actions and the scope of presidential power. Admittedly, tribal nations were once a military concern for the United States but are no longer and are no longer regarded as fully foreign either. And even if we understood federal authority over Native America as a vestige of a previous state of military and foreign affairs, is there any legitimate version of sovereignty that allows for this sort of extensive control over individuals and political entities? In essence, this argument posits that an unlimited authority (plenary power) is justified by an indeterminate and thus unlimited source (inherent authority). All of which is much more in keeping with a totalitarian regime rather than a government of the people expressed in a written document based on consent. Perhaps we do (or do not; I leave it up to you to decide) need to preserve the authority of the president to act in times of military emergency in ways that the U.S. Constitution does not fully articulate, but it is difficult to see how that logic can be extended to plenary power over Native America.

So there you have it. We've spent another chapter together, sharing laughs, shedding tears, learning and growing and generally living our best lives. Were we in the same room together—and if it wasn't too creepy—I would give you a hug right now and promise that we would always keep in touch.

And yet, even as we feel all the feels, perhaps you are still left with a question: Why did we bother? What were we trying to accomplish? Emotionally enriching as it clearly was, why did we trace the major (and a few minor) lines of justification that the Supreme Court has offered for federal authority over Native peoples and nations? What was the point again? What are we even doing here?

This is where the metaphors we've been dragging through two chapters get to really shine. We have traced the history and basic understandings for a couple of major, and a few minor, rationales that the Supreme Court has articulated in favor of federal plenary power over Native America. And yet, regardless of which rationale one chooses—and whether it has a direct textual tie to the U.S. Constitution or not—the foundational reasoning of each rationale understands Native peoples and nations as savage, inferior, underdeveloped, and/or lesser than the colonists who are crafting the law. This is our conspiracy. No matter what guise the arguments are dressed up in, they all originate in racism. They all come from the same place no matter what they look like on the outside, and they all perpetuate the lesser status of Native peoples under the law. Furthermore, any understanding of consent—which is so critical to other articulations of federal power—in these rationales is either completely lacking or so far removed from the true claims to authority to be meaningless.

This is why we need to solve our mystery. At present, the Supreme

Court (and others) asserts that the Indian Commerce Clause is the source of federal plenary power over Native America. Yet, we know that this has not always been the case. By figuring out when the Supreme Court changed its mind about the Indian Commerce Clause—when the Court decided that plenary power did have this basis in the U.S. Constitution—we will learn if today's accepted rationale is a break from our conspiracy or yet another extension of it. Does the Indian Commerce Clause offer a legitimate basis for federal power over Native America that is in alignment with constitutional values and that is more closely hued to consent-based articulations of federal authority in other areas? Or does the Indian Commerce Clause merely offer the latest and greatest shield—one that is impossible to pierce because of its place in the U.S. Constitution—to cover the racism that has been the true root of previous claims to power over Native America? We can only figure this out by finding out when, and thus why, this change happened.

So let's get to it.

The pale man cleared his throat. The gesture seemed to make him grow even more.

"I have a story to tell," he spoke with an increasingly thunderous voice. "It is the great and important and completely true story of how I conquered this land upon which I stand that was always mine to begin with anyway."

Nanaboozhoo could feel a murmur ripple through the rest of the partygoers. He overheard one whisper to another, "Is he trying to be funny?" The other responded, "He doesn't really give off a stand-up comedian type of vibe, if you know what I'm saying. But we listened to everybody else, so I suppose we should hear what he has to say."

The pale man continued. "This is a story of how the world came to be. It is a story of triumph and truth and righteousness. It is a story of destiny." The pale man nodded at his own point. "One might even say it was manifest."

Nanaboozhoo's mouth opened but no words came out. The pale man continued. "A long time ago my ancestors—we called them Pilgrims—

left their homelands to come to these shores. They landed on Plymouth Rock, which, to this day, is still a rock. After landing on the rock, they got off of the rock and spread out. Then they had a party that was a lot like this one. They decided to throw the party because they realized that they liked all of this new land beyond the rock and all the other stuff that was theirs that God had given to them. A collection of your kind was at the party, but then you all ran off and the Pilgrims never saw you again, which is why I was surprised to see you. Anyway, the Pilgrims were really cool and totally not at all weirdos. I mean, yeah, they did wear buckles on their hats, but . . ."

Nanaboozhoo could hear the hushed consternation among the rest of the partygoers increasing. He didn't want to be rude, but he knew that the situation was moving in an inopportune direction, and, as the host, he felt an obligation to say something. "I'm sorry, but this story doesn't make any sense."

"Well, where do wear your buckles, big shot?" the pale man retorted.

"No, I don't mean that," Nanaboozhoo paused for a moment as he tried to sort out the pale man's words that were jumbling his thoughts.

"I mean . . ."

". . ."

"OK . . ."

". . ."

"I'm just saying that . . ."

". . ."

Nanaboozhoo took a deep breath and gathered himself. "Earlier you said something about how you conquered this land and now you just said something about how these Pilgrims owned the land or something like that. Anyway, that's the thing that doesn't make sense. You just fell out of a tree in the forest like two hours ago. So what are you talking about?"

The pale man, who was now at least four times his original size, smiled broadly. "Ah yes, I should have realized that you wouldn't understand. That's on me. I mean, look at you. Look at where you live. I feel so bad for you." The pale man shook his head before continuing. "Even so, I really believe that you have the capacity to learn, and someday I will teach you the ways of civilization. You are going to be so grateful!"

Nanaboozhoo was annoyed, but he brushed aside the condescension because he was more focused on his question. "Fine. Whatever. We like learning and we are happy to share knowledge with you, but that's not what I was getting at. What do you mean this land is yours?"

"Oh, that's easy," the pale man replied. "I discovered this place."

The rumblings among the partygoers became louder as the disbelief and resentment rose. Nanaboozhoo kept pressing with his questions. "What do you mean you discovered this place? I mean seriously, how hard did you hit your head when you fell out of that tree? You literally emerged from the forest not more than two hours ago."

"That's right," said the pale man. "I discovered this place."

"How can you claim to discover this place? "Nanaboozhoo continued. "All of us were here first."

The pale man, who was now at least ten times his original size, slowly nodded. "Ah, yes. Now I see the issue. But don't worry about it. I am totally going to let you all stay where you are," said the pale man, before adding after half a beat, "for as long as I want." He started to trail off. "I mean, it is my land and all . . ."

The pale man was now large enough that Nanaboozhoo felt that he needed to shout to be heard. "Wait a minute. We are willing to share. We have always been willing to share. You have already benefited from our largesse. We are happy to sit with you at the fire and figure out how to coexist. But this is crazy. You didn't discover anything. We were here first. You can't possibly really believe that you own everything that you see just because you found your way out of the trees a couple of hours ago."

The pale man grew visibly agitated and roared with a sound so loud that it was almost impossible to make out the words.

"I DISCOVERED THIS PLACE!"

The pale man huffed a few times, still agitated but no longer shouting. "You are the ones who are benefiting from my largesse." After a few more moments' pause he spoke with an unnerving calmness. "Besides, you need my protection."

Nanaboozhoo was scared and confused, but he knew he needed to persist. “Why do we need protection? Who are you going to protect us from?”

The pale man’s eyes narrowed. “I am going to protect you from others like me.”

The partygoers looked around at each other. Their expressions ranged from baffled to dubious to exasperated.

The pale man continued. The depth of sincerity in his tone left many of the partygoers with the sense that he was either putting on a show or that he was a little off his rocker. “I have a solemn duty to protect you. It is my burden because you happened to be on the land that I discovered. But I accept this awesome responsibility, and I do not take it lightly. Fortunately, I know what is best for you. I will guide you to where I know you need to go. I will use my strength for good, and I will make you see that I am right. You are lucky that I am here to protect you and to show you the light.”

Pieces of paper started falling from the sky. “So if you’ll just sign these treaties . . .”

The pale man, whose size had grown too large to calculate, cupped his hands into a dome and started lowering them over the partygoers.

“Oh, &%$@,” Nanaboozhoo thought to himself. “This is not going to be good . . .”

THREE *The Plot Twist*

All right, let's get to it. Let's figure out when plenary power became constitutional! Let's go!

. . .

• • •

• • •

All right, fine. Here's the deal. I promise that we will tackle our mystery head-on in this chapter. I mean it. You only have to have a little more patience with me. But there really are a couple of other things that we need to do. First, we need to figure out when the concept of plenary power shifted from primarily concerning federalism—or the balance of federal authority compared to state authority—to primarily concerning expansive federal authority over Native America. Second, we need to think about the words of the Indian Commerce Clause and the simplest, most natural way to read them.

Before we go any further, I want you to know that I understand why you might be rolling your eyes at me right now. After all, didn't we just spend two chapters laying this sort of groundwork so that we could finally solve our mystery? Why do we need to do more? But please hear (or read) me out. It is critical to ask these questions because they further help place the solution of our mystery into the context of the conspiracy that we have also been tracing. They also help us see that the story they have chosen to tell is wrong. They know it and we know it.

It is time to tell a better story.

Besides, it's only going to take five pages.[1]

As we noted in Chapter 1, there have been two major definitions of plenary power in American law. The first one to make its presence felt in American law involves federal authority against the states. Our old friend John Marshall most forcefully articulated this version of plenary power in his (in)famous Trilogy in *Worcester v. Georgia*, writing that state laws "can have no force" within tribal lands and that "the whole intercourse between the United States and [the Cherokee], is, by our constitution and laws, vested in the government of the United States."[2] In other words, it was the federal government, not the states, that was tasked with engaging with Native nations. Moreover, there was a border between tribal and state lands that the states could not cross.

Definitive as it might have seemed to be, Marshall's statement in *Worcester* hardly kept states from trying to exercise various forms of jurisdiction over Native lands and peoples. Thus, a tug-of-war commenced that is still being waged today. For a number of decades after Marshall's pronouncement states kept trying to gain greater control over tribal lands and peoples, and the Supreme Court mostly kept reasserting federal authority against those efforts. Unsurprisingly, taxes were a regular source of conflict in these types of disputes. For example, in an 1867 case in which a state was trying to tax tribal lands, Justice David Davis wrote, "As long as the United States recognizes [the] national character [of tribal nations] they are under the protection of treaties and the laws of Congress, and their property is withdrawn from the operation of State laws."[3] Another case from 1903 in which a state was trying to tax tribal lands demonstrates how issues of land, protection, and federalism were often deeply intertwined. "These Indians are yet wards of the Nation, in a condition of pupilage or dependency, and have not been discharged from that condition. They occupy these lands with the consent and authority of the United States. . . . To tax these lands is to tax an instrumentality employed by the United States for the benefit and control of this dependent race."[4] Even our other old friend Justice Samuel Miller in—you guessed it!—*Kagama* got into the act, justifying his ruling in part on federalism grounds. Having earlier in the opinion asserted that either the federal government or the states had to have jurisdiction over Native peoples (and consequently disavowing tribal jurisdiction by omission), Miller reasoned that it had to be the federal government exclusively.[5] "Because of the local ill feeling, the people of the States where they are found are often their deadliest enemies. From their very weakness and helplessness, so largely due to the course of dealing of the Federal Government with them and the treaties in which it has been promised, there arises the duty of protection, and with it the power."[6]

As noted in the last paragraph, the tug-of-war between the states, the federal government, and tribal nations in any given set of circumstances remains a critical issue to this day. However, the federal government's commitment to preserving its exclusive authority to engage with Native America began to wane during the Allotment Era (introduced in Chapter 1) of the late nineteenth and early twentieth centuries. The Allotment Act itself—which was passed in 1887 and obviously was instrumental in defining the Allotment Era—intended that Native peoples and their allotments eventually be subjected to state law.[7] Writing in 1939 Justice Hugo Black perhaps best summed up the shift that had occurred in the recently ended Allotment Era. "Congress has traditionally treated the Indian wards of the Nation with particular solicitude, but has also gradually evolved a policy looking to their eventual absorption into the general body of citizenry. This policy has progressively subjected Indians to the laws under which all other citizens must live in the Indians' States of residence, if not in conflict with specific protective measures of Congress."[8] By 1959 in *Williams v. Lee*, a case that many scholars regard as the beginning of the modern era of federal Indian law, the Supreme Court was openly breaking with John Marshall's assertion in *Worcester* to rule that state laws could sometimes extend into tribal territory.[9] This trend has continued into the present, much to the chagrin of advocates for Native America.[10]

The general erosion of both the prominence and efficacy of the original definition of plenary power in Indian law coincided with the growing importance of the second definition—federal authority over Native peoples. Since we've mentioned it in both of the previous chapters, my bet is that you can guess that the rise to prominence of the second definition occurred in earnest at the Supreme Court with the Plenary Power Trilogy of cases—*Kagama, Lone Wolf,* and *Sandoval.* Other cases from the period that span the life of the Plenary Power Trilogy further testify to the Supreme Court's developing sense of the enormity and scope of this second definition.[11] For example, writing in an 1898 case—twelve years after *Kagama* and five years before *Lone Wolf*—Justice George Shiras Jr. stated, "The unlimited power of Congress to deal with the Indians, their property and commercial transactions, so long as they keep up their tribal organizations, may be conceded."[12] A year later in *Stephens v. Cherokee Nation,* Chief Justice Melville Fuller made note of the "paramount authority of Congress over the Indian tribes."[13] Building the reasoning and rulings of these cases upon themselves, in 1902—just one year before he would author the majority opinion in *Lone Wolf*—Justice Edward Douglass White noted about *Stephens,* "The plenary power of control by Congress over the Indian tribes and its undoubted power to legislate . . . was in that case reaffirmed."[14] In 1914—a year after the final case of the Plenary Power Trilogy, *Sandoval,* was decided—Justice Willis Van Devanter, who also authored *Sandoval,* succinctly summarized this era of the Supreme Court's rulings and the basic understanding of the newer, ascendant definition of plenary power. Writing about the Creek specifically but extrapolating it to Native America as a whole, Van Devanter wrote, "Like other tribal Indians, the Creeks were wards of the United States, which possessed full power, if it deemed such a course wise, to assume full control over them and their affairs, to ascertain who were members of the tribe, to distribute the lands and funds among them, and to terminate the tribal government."[15]

Consequently, we are forced to conclude that the second definition of plenary power—federal authority over Native America—found its footing in American law during the development of the Plenary Power Trilogy in the Supreme Court in the Allotment Era of the late nineteenth and early twentieth centuries. All of which leads to another perfectly reasonable query: Why did we bother with a handful of pages about a question with an obvious answer? After all, we've been calling it the "Plenary Power Trilogy" for a reason, haven't we?[16] Why did we waste all of that time? Why can't professors ever just get to the point?

Well, yes, professors can seem to drone on a bit, but you see that's just because we have a lot of enthusiasm for the things that we study and we just want to share the knowledge that we've acqu . . .

No, no, no, let's stay on task. It is important to locate when this second definition of plenary power developed—when the version of plenary power that Justice Breyer sought to justify under the Indian Commerce Clause in *Lara* became a thing—because it helps us recognize that it was part of a larger pattern. Put in the parlance of our metaphors, our conspiracy was part of an even larger conspiracy.

The focus of this book is on Native America. Yet, we would not be telling the full story if we did not acknowledge that this version of plenary power—in which the federal government claims essentially unlimited authority—also exists in other areas of American law, most particularly in the fields of the territories and immigration. Moreover, by examining the origins of this version of plenary power in Indian law and similar versions elsewhere, it becomes clear that each articulation in the various fields are of the same era of Supreme Court history, each evidences a common set of (mis)understandings about who is being acted upon, and the versions of plenary power in other areas of American law are continuations of what Justice Miller started in *Kagama*.

Plenary power in the law of the territories commenced in earnest with what is known as the *Insular Cases*. Briefly, by the late nineteenth century Spain's influence as a colonial power had significantly faded while at the same time the United States was increasingly seeking to expand its own territorial acquisitions. In 1898 the United States entered into a conflict with Spain known in the United States as the Spanish-American War. The hostilities were relatively short-lived and ended the same year they started with the Treaty of Paris.[17] In the Treaty of Paris, Spain ceded the authority it claimed over Cuba, Puerto Rico, Guam, and the Philippines to the United States.[18] The question thereafter for the United States became how to think about these new territorial acquisitions and the (mostly non-white) people in them.

Put a bit more sophisticatedly, the Supreme Court was asked to answer a series of questions about these newly acquired territories that resulted in the decisions that make up the *Insular Cases*. Generally, the questions concerned how to regard the territories and what rights under the U.S. Constitution, if any, the people of the territories had. To what extent were the territories akin to foreign nations? To what extent were the people in the territories akin to U.S. citizens? What rights needed to be respected in these newly acquired spaces?

Again, in brief, the Supreme Court essentially ruled in the *Insular Cases* that the federal government had greater authority to set its own rules in the newly acquired territories than in other lands recognized as part of the United States. In *Downes v. Bidwell*, perhaps the most prominent of the *Insular Cases*, Justice Henry B. Brown harkened to John Marshall in writing, "We are also of [the] opinion that the power to acquire territory by treaty implies not only the power to govern such territory, but to prescribe upon what terms the United States will receive its inhabitants, and what their status shall be in what Chief Justice Marshall termed the 'American Empire.'"[19] To that end—without any textual basis in the U.S. Constitution, just like in *Kagama*—the Supreme Court developed a distinction between "incorporated" territories, which more or less enjoyed full constitutional protection, and "unincorporated" territories, which did not. According to the Supreme Court, the territories that were rapidly becoming states in the western half of North America were incorporated. On the other hand, the territories acquired in the wake of the Spanish-American War were unincorporated.[20]

And what was the basis for making the distinction between incorporated and unincorporated territories? Justice Brown in *Downes* left little to the imagination. He openly worried about automatically ascribing American citizenship to the peoples, "whether civilized or savage," on the acquisition of a territory.[21] He further opined, "If such be their status, the consequences will be extremely serious. Indeed, it is doubtful if Congress would ever assent to the annexation of territory upon the condition that its inhabitants, however foreign they may be to our habits, traditions and modes of life, shall become at once citizens of the United States."[22] In short, according to Brown, having to regard a vastly non-white population as full-fledged American citizens might disincentivize the United States from its growing colonial ambitions.[23] Echoing the reasonings and rationales that were developing in Indian law as well, Brown argued that the federal government needed this extensive oversight and that it should not be questioned.[24] Also as in Indian law, the underlying basis propping up the doctrine was the supposed inferiority of the people over whom the United States sought to exercise power.[25] And yet again also as in Indian law, this version of plenary power over the territories has remained relatively unchanged since its inception.[26]

OK, so that's a bit of a downer, isn't it? Racism is pretty clearly at the heart of the doctrine of plenary power in both Indian law and the law concerning the territories. But hey, maybe things will start looking up when we look at plenary power in immigration law![27]

The development of the Plenary Power Doctrine in immigration law is in response to Chinese immigration in the mid- to late nineteenth century. Briefly, in 1868 the United States and China signed the Burlingame Treaty, which recognized "the inherent and inalienable right of man to change his home and allegiance" and "the mutual advantage of the free migration and emigration of their citizens and subjects, respectively, from the one country to the other, for purposes of curiosity, of trade, or as permanent residents."[28] The biggest benefit of the Burlingame Treaty for the United States was to provide a significant source of labor, most particularly for the railroads, on the West Coast. However, after the completion of the transcontinental railroad in 1869 many Chinese immigrants were left unemployed and many politicians of the day regarded them as an easy target, including Supreme Court Justice Stephen Field, who harbored ambitions for the White House.[29] In 1880 the United States and China amended the Burlingame Treaty to allow the United States to regulate, but not to prohibit, the immigration of Chinese citizens.[30] Beginning in 1882 Congress passed the first law, known as the Chinese Exclusion Act, of a series of laws that effectively prohibited any further immigration from China.[31]

Decided in 1889, *Chae Chan Ping v. United States* is perhaps the most prominent case in immigration from this era.[32] The issue arose when a Chinese laborer challenged the exclusionary laws that Congress was passing in contravention of the Burlingame Treaty. The question of the case was whether Congress had the authority to pass legislation that ran against the terms of the treaties signed between the United States and China.[33]

My guess is that, as an astute reader, you've already recognized that we've seen this same question in the previous two chapters.[34] Fourteen years after *Chae Chan Ping* the Court confronted a very similar issue in *Lone Wolf.* In fact, the *Lone Wolf* decision affirmatively cited *Chae Chan Ping.*[35] All of which means that, as an astute reader, you probably know where this is headed.[36] The Court in *Chae Chan Ping* ruled that treaties and congressional legislation were on equal footing.[37] As equals, according to the Court, congressional legislation and treaties could supersede each other, and when in conflict the one that is in force is the one that was most recently passed.[38] With a logic that it would later echo in *Lone Wolf,* the Court in *Chae Chan Ping* reasoned that the federal government needed to not be so constrained by a treaty as to be incapable of acting under an emergency or changed circumstances.[39] Thus, the exclusionary legislation was valid, both because it came after the treaty and because it was an expression of federal plenary authority over immigration. "Those laborers are not citizens of the United States; they are aliens. That the government of the United States, through the action of the legislative department, can exclude aliens from its territory is a proposition which we do not think open to controversy. Jurisdiction over its own territory to that extent is an incident of every independent nation. It is a part of its independence."[40]

In the abstract, the basic principles of *Chae Chan Ping* may not necessarily strike one as outrageous or pernicious. After all, don't all countries police their borders? And shouldn't countries be able to respond to emergencies? However, a closer look at the opinion makes clear that the Supreme Court was less concerned with high-minded questions of national security and more concerned with keeping certain people out. The laws in question were not simply ministerial directives to be applied to anyone at the border but rather prohibitions directed specifically at Chinese citizens. They were clearly and unambiguously intended to keep people of a certain race out of the country.

The author of the opinion in *Chae Chan Ping* was none other than Justice Stephen Field who, as noted earlier, had previously offered his public support for exclusionary legislation. Field briefly recounted the economic history that incurred significant immigration and that, according to him, led to resentment among non-immigrants.[41] Leaving no doubt as to where he saw the true origins of the friction, he continued, "The differences of race added greatly to the difficulties of the situation."[42] As the Court would do time and time again with Native peoples, Field placed the blame on those he sought to displace. "[Chinese immigrants] remained strangers in the land, residing apart by themselves, and adhering to the customs and usages of their own country. It seemed impossible for them to assimilate with our people or to make any change in their habits or modes of living."[43]

Hey, do you remember in Chapter 2 that we went over how John Marshall justified the Doctrine of Discovery in *Johnson v. McIntosh*? Remember that Marshall cooked up some questionable sociological analysis to claim that racial conflict—"in which the whites were not always the aggressors"—was inevitable and thus Discovery was necessary? Well, Field must have learned from the master because Field's ruling was also laced with underlying threats of violence and militarism. Summarizing a petition from California politicians, Field described Chinese immigration as an "Oriental invasion" that was a "menace to our civilization."[44] In justifying plenary power in this area Field continued in this vein, claiming that it was the "highest duty of every nation" to "give security against foreign aggression and encroachment."[45] To that end, Chinese immigration was, according to Field, akin to an act of war that necessitated the more expansive wartime authority of the federal government.[46] That there was no actual war between the United States and China—to the contrary, there was a treaty between the two nations that authorized immigration!—was of no practical concern to Field. In fact, according to him, it proved his point. "The existence of war would render the necessity of the proceeding only more obvious and pressing. The same necessity, in a less pressing degree, may arise when war does not exist, and the same authority which adjudges the necessity in one case must also determine it in the other."[47] This assertion is, without question, just plain silly.[48] It is like arguing that I should have the right to shoot people who are walking on the sidewalk in front of my house because their presence on my sidewalk is a war-like invasion of my property and that if those people on the sidewalk ever did break into my house, it would only further demonstrate that I was right to shoot them before they further invaded my property. This leap in illogic is no different from the ones we witnessed in Chapter 2 in that it reveals the racism at the heart of the law that was created. Another case four years later paralleled what was happening in Indian law and the law of the territories when the Supreme Court decided it would not question the federal government's decisions or authority in immigration law.[49] Also in keeping with these other areas of law, this version of plenary power remains relatively unchanged to this day.[50]

As with other subject matter that we have engaged with, there is more that can and has been said about the concept of plenary power in American law broadly, and I encourage you to seek out the scholarship in this area.[51] For our present purposes it suffices to note that the all-encompassing versions of plenary power that dominate the fields of Indian law, the law of the territories, and immigration law share some significant characteristics that demonstrate the true nature of the doctrine wherever it resides. First, they all come from the same historical moment in American law.[52] Put another way, the version of plenary power that is at the heart of our mystery has siblings that were all born around the same time: the late nineteenth and early twentieth centuries. It is also worthy of note that this is the same legal era of the rise of Jim Crow laws that effectively kept African Americans in subjugation in the wake of the American Civil War. This was not a coincidence; it was a pattern. Second, each version of plenary power is founded on an understanding that the people being acted upon were inferior or lesser than or underdeveloped compared to the people doing the acting. In *Kagama* Native peoples were "dependent on the United States";[53] in *Downes v. Bidwell* the people of the territories were "foreign . . . to our habits, traditions and modes of life";[54] in *Chae Chan Ping* Chinese people were a "menace to our civilization."[55] Third, each version of plenary power remains in effect and relatively unchanged in the present day.

All right, that was a lot, so a brief summation is probably in order. Luckily, our metaphors are once again here to help. Tracing this history allows us to see the "conspiracy" that we unraveled in Chapter 2 was part of a larger effort within American law in the late nineteenth and early twentieth centuries. The racism that fueled the expansive version of plenary power in Indian law fueled plenary power in other areas of American law as well as Jim Crow laws that developed during that time. Consequently, it is impossible to dismiss plenary power in Indian law (and elsewhere for that matter) as a historical anomaly or isolated aberration. Nor is it merely an embarrassing relic of the past. It is appropriate to think of this version of plenary power through the metaphor of a conspiracy because it was part of a larger attempt in this era of American law to subjugate non-white peoples. This was not a mistake; it was a movement. Moreover, it is a "conspiracy" because the true motivations stand to the side of a veneer of respectability. Thus, *Kagama* becomes about protecting Native peoples from their "deadliest enemies": the states;[56] *Downes v. Bidwell,* concerning the acquisition of territory;[57] *Chae Chan Ping,* about national security.[58] Not to mention that the various rationales for plenary power have connections to the U.S. Constitution and the underlying theory of consent that are tenuous at best (and nonexistent as concerns *Kagama*). Understanding it as a conspiracy allows us to see the deliberateness with which plenary power originated and has been maintained. It also reinforces why we need to solve our mystery. The Supreme Court currently articulates that plenary power in Indian law is justified under the Indian Commerce Clause. Has the Supreme Court found a legitimate basis for the exercise of this extensive federal power over Native America under the U.S. Constitution and its underlying theory of consent? Or it is just the next iteration of the conspiracy? We can figure this out only by finding out when (and thus how) the Indian Commerce Clause became the basis for plenary power.

And yes, we will do that.

Shortly.

But there's just one more thing we need to clear up before we get there. After all, in the U.S. Constitution it does say that Congress "shall have the power . . . to regulate commerce with foreign nations, and among the several states, and with the Indian tribes." So how should we think about the Indian Commerce Clause? The version of plenary power that is central to our mystery, which the Supreme Court currently declares is justified under the Indian Commerce Clause, is boundless and not in keeping with the concept of consent that is foundational to the theoretical underpinnings of American governance. Consequently—and forgive me if I am getting a little too technical here—that version of plenary power doesn't really **FEEL** constitutional, does it? It's certainly not about protecting rights or limiting the government or the types of things that we typically ascribe to the U.S. Constitution. But the words in the document have to mean something, don't they? So what would be a more natural and reasonable reading of the Indian Commerce Clause?

When considering what could and should be the scope of the Indian Commerce Clause, perhaps the most logical place to start is with its neighbors. Article I, Section 8, Clause 3 authorizes Congress to "regulate commerce . . . [not only] with the Indian tribes" but also "with foreign nations, and among the several states." Thus, the Commerce Clause is less a singular thing unto itself and more a collection of three parts that share a common bond. The folks coming up with the U.S. Constitution believed that the regulation of commerce with the three aforementioned entities was better handled in a more uniform manner at the federal level than much more haphazardly and inconsistently among the individual states.[59]

Admittedly, making any statement about the intent of the founding fathers is like stepping onto a minefield, particularly because debates about the "intent" of the founding fathers—if we want to get real about it—tend to be less than high-minded, objective pursuits of the truth and more defenses for one's political preferences in the present. Furthermore, how American law and the American political system have regarded the Commerce Clause has changed over the years (a point to which we will return later in this chapter), and while all three parts do share a bond, they have also all followed different trajectories. Along those same lines, Congress has had a tendency to keep trying to increase its reach under the Commerce Clause, which has further provoked heated debates about what the founders intended the U.S. Constitution to accomplish.[60]

Fortunately, we don't have to dive too deeply into the minds of Alexander Hamilton, James Madison, or any of their brethren to make our point. The states ceded some of their authority to a federal government through the U.S. Constitution. That constitution authorizes Congress to regulate commerce with or among three political entities: states, foreign nations, and Indian tribes. Thus, the U.S. Constitution took authority to engage with these political entities from the states and gave it to the federal government.[61]

One can debate just how much was taken from the states and given to the federal government and to what extent states can still engage with these other political entities.[62] But those questions are about federalism, or the balance of power between the federal government and the states. They much more resemble the original definition of plenary power in Indian law that John Marshall articulated in his Trilogy. Conversely, they are not about some limitless authority the federal government holds over states or foreign nations. In fact, the very suggestion of the federal government exercising the version of plenary power at the heart of our mystery in these other arenas comes across as absurd. Our constitutional model was built to preserve a measure of sovereignty among the states, not completely subsume it under the federal government. And claiming paramount authority over another nation is closer to an act of unjust war than an act of legitimate governance.[63] Thus, the placement of the Indian Commerce Clause as part of a whole strongly suggests that a more natural reading of the text allows for the federal government—rather than the states—to engage with tribal nations rather than dictate over them. It is more in line with the original definition of plenary power in Indian law than what subsequently developed in *Kagama*, *Lone Wolf*, and *Sandoval*.

A brief glimpse into the legal history also strongly suggests that the folks who were building a government under the U.S. Constitution when it was new and fresh understood the Indian Commerce Clause as operating within this more natural reading of the text.[64] For example, one of the most critical sets of legislation not just in Indian law but in the early republic were the Trade and Intercourse Acts (also sometimes referred to as the Non-Intercourse Acts).[65] The first of these meaningful laws was passed in 1790 with a "sunset provision," which set a date at which it expired.[66] The law proved important enough that Congress kept tweaking and renewing it before finally making it permanent in 1834.[67] The purpose of the Trade and Intercourse Acts was to further reinforce treaty promises to Native nations and to quell unrest caused by settlers who acted in disregard of treaties and tribal rights.[68] To that end, the first iteration of the law required, among other things, that anyone seeking to trade with tribal nations first obtain a license from the federal government,[69] it prohibited any purchase of land by "any person or persons, or to any state" directly from tribal nations,[70] and it instituted criminal penalties for "any citizen or inhabitant of the United States" who committed crimes in Indian Country.[71]

The most striking characteristic of the first Trade and Intercourse Act and its subsequent iterations is their focus. The acts do not purport to regulate the internal affairs of tribal nations or otherwise impinge upon tribal sovereignty directly.[72] Rather, the targets of the acts are American citizens and others under American jurisdiction.[73] As the acts expanded in coverage and specificity over the years, they maintained their focus on the American side of things. Even when they sought to address alleged wrongs committed by Native peoples against non-Natives, it was by diplomatic means as filtered through the federal government. For example, Article 17 of the 1834 Act addresses allegations of wrongdoing by Native peoples. The recourse for any "citizen or inhabitant of the United States" who felt wronged by a Native person was to "make application to the proper superintendent, agent, or sub-agent" of the federal government.[74] Upon being "furnished with the necessary documents and proofs," that representative of the federal government then went to the appropriate tribal nation to seek recourse.[75] If the tribal nation "refuse[d] to make satisfaction, in a reasonable time," it became a diplomatic matter with the United States guaranteeing to compensate the victim for her or his loss.[76] Furthermore, if the alleged victim were to contravene the purpose of the act "by seeking or attempting to obtain private satisfaction or revenge," then that person "shall forfeit all claim upon the United States" for her or his loss.[77] Article 17 does not claim to extend American jurisdiction over Native America even when it is alleged that a Native person or people have done wrong. Rather, it creates a mechanism with which to engage with Native America should a harm be alleged. It does not impose any direct sanction on an offending tribal nation or person. In fact, the only parties that can be punished under Article 17 are those under American jurisdiction who attempt to take the law into their own hands.

This brief example is illustrative of the larger point. The words of the U.S. Constitution have meaning. The most natural reading of the Commerce Clause is that it invests the federal government, rather than the states, with the authority to engage with Native nations (and with foreign nations and among the states). Perhaps the most prominent congressional legislation dealing with Native America of the early era of American constitutional law—the Trade and Intercourse Acts—reflects this understanding of the Indian Commerce Clause. These laws operated directly upon American citizens and those under American jurisdiction—those who have consented to this authority under the social contract theory—rather than directly upon Native nations and peoples, who cannot be said to have consented to constitutional authority in general.[78] Thus, John Marshall was hardly on an island when he articulated his definition of plenary power, most prominently in *Worcester*. Rather, he was firmly in the mainstream on this point in his time. Marshall's colleague Justice John McLean may have even better summarized the understanding of the time in his concurrence in *Worcester*. "In the regulation of commerce with the Indians, congress have exercised a more limited power than has been exercised in reference to foreign countries. The law acts upon our own citizens, and not upon the Indians, the same as the laws referred to act upon our own citizens in their foreign commercial intercourse."[79] Nearly a half century later this version of plenary power was still prevalent at the Supreme Court. Writing in 1876 Justice David Davis stated that "Congress now has the exclusive and absolute power to regulate commerce with the Indian tribes,—a power as broad and as free from restrictions as that to regulate commerce with foreign nations. . . . Treaties have been made and laws passed separating Indian territory from that of the States, and providing that intercourse and trade with the Indians should be carried on solely under the authority of the United States."[80]

All of which is to note that there seems to be a fairly straightforward and obvious way to read the Indian Commerce Clause—as a restraint not on tribal nations but on those under federal jurisdiction (including the states). Such a reading is much more in line with the social contract theory that justifies federal authority in other areas more generally and in how it was understood in the beginning. Conversely, the way the Supreme Court currently reads the Indian Commerce Clause—as the basis for an all-encompassing grant of plenary power over Native America—is not the most natural reading of the text nor is it as traditional as Breyer's opinion in *Lara* would have you believe.[81]

To be fair, circumstances do change. Things that seemed obvious and natural at one time might seem outrageous or bizarre in a later time, and we should always be mindful about how much we allow the proverbial dead hand of the past to control our actions in the present. Certainly much is dramatically different for Native America and the United States since the U.S. Constitution was first drafted and when John Marshall articulated his understanding of plenary power. For example, today Native peoples are regarded as American citizens, whereas when the U.S. Constitution was drafted, next to none were. Admittedly, the 1924 Indian Citizenship Act that blanketed Native peoples with American citizenship was a product of the Allotment Era, it was an exercise of the type of plenary power that is at the heart of our mystery, and at least some Native peoples were against it at the time.[82] Yet, while there are still plenty of Native people who challenge and raise questions about American citizenship, most folks, Native or otherwise, seem to take this status as a given.[83] So does a major change like this force us to think differently about plenary power and the Indian Commerce Clause? How should we account for the differences between now and when John Marshall wrote *Worcester* in 1832?

We will consider the issue of changed circumstances in greater detail in Chapter 5. But for now, it is useful to consider specifically the citizenship question as we think about how to think about the Indian Commerce Clause. In one sense, regarding Native peoples as American citizens would seem to complicate the issue. After all, we just spent a bunch of pages demonstrating that the most natural and historical reading of the Indian Commerce Clause is as granting the federal government (rather than the states) authority over those within its jurisdiction in regard to engagements with Native America (and as opposed to unfettered power over Native America). Thus, it makes sense that the federal government could require a license before permitting someone to trade with Native nations or buy land from them. But if Native peoples are now American citizens, aren't they also now under the jurisdiction of the federal government? Does this mean that the version of plenary power at the heart of our mystery is justified under the Indian Commerce Clause under these changed circumstances?

And now I am going to do another annoying professor-type thing and answer a question with a question: Why would that be? How does American citizenship justify the expansive version of plenary power? Sure, it is true that it undoubtedly strikes some people as odd that Native peoples can and do claim rights as both American citizens and tribal citizens. And if you listen to those who are rooted in this perspective, they will argue that it is unfair that Native peoples get "special" or "extra" rights just because they are also tribal citizens. Engaging with folks with this viewpoint might leave one with the impression that this is some bizarre anomaly that is outside the bounds of reasonableness.

[I'm going to do it again.] Is it an anomaly? After all, citizenship is merely a political classification, isn't it? And it is hardly outrageous or unusual for an individual to have more than one political classification. For example, there are plenty of people with dual (or more) citizenship. And should a person be a citizen of, say, both the United States and Canada, we generally do not regard it as beyond the pale or so far outside order and reasonableness that we should react strongly against it.[84] So why do some react this way when it concerns American and tribal citizenship?

Further to our point, viewing the question through the framework of dual citizenship much more detracts from the expansive version of plenary power at the heart of our mystery than it supports it. After all, if a person has dual citizenship, then that person can claim a set of rights (and has corresponding obligations) within two countries that do not negate each other. Put differently, let's imagine a person who is a citizen of, again say, both the United States and Canada. That person's rights as an American must still be respected by the United States and are not limited or revoked merely by the person's other status as a Canadian citizen. So why should it be any different for an individual who is both an American citizen and a tribal citizen? Why shouldn't Native peoples have rights as both American and tribal citizens?

There is more to say on this subject. As noted earlier, we will take up the issue of changed circumstances in more detail in Chapter 5 and will more fully consider why tribal advocates seem reluctant to rock the plenary power boat in Chapter 4. For now, it suffices to note that even though the world has changed quite drastically since the U.S. Constitution was written, those changes more fully support the more limited understanding of plenary power that John Marshall articulated than the unbounded version that the Supreme Court currently claims is supported by the Indian Commerce Clause. In short, changed circumstances, even one as critical as the citizenship status of Native peoples, do not change the most natural and obvious reading of the Indian Commerce Clause.

OK fine, I lied. That took waaaaaaaaaay longer than five pages.

But now here we are. After all of that groundwork we are finally ready to tackle our mystery head on. We know (from Chapter 2) that the prominent and lesser rationales for plenary power other than the Indian Commerce Clause are all rooted in racist understandings of Native peoples and their capacities. We also know that the version of plenary power that we are concerned with developed as part of a larger pattern in the late nineteenth and early twentieth centuries in which the Supreme Court opened a path for the federal government to exercise greater control over non-white populations without constitutional restriction yet under the guise of the law. And we also know that attaching this version of plenary power to the Indian Commerce Clause runs contrary to a natural reading of the text and of original understandings of the constitutional text. With that all in mind, we can finally get back to where we all started with this.

When did plenary power become constitutional?

As you have probably figured out—since we are halfway through this book and are only now firmly focused on the question that we started with—finding an answer to this question is more difficult than it would appear at first glance.[85] There are three major obstacles standing between us and the answer that we are looking for. Each one poses its own challenge, but we can overcome them by acknowledging and confronting them. Taking the little bit of time we need to address these obstacles will give us the capacity to move forward and finally solve this mystery. Besides—and I really mean it this time—it's only going to take a few pages.

The first major obstacle is that we don't have that seminal, easily identifiable moment in which the law perceptibly and dramatically changed. For example, the one case that everybody has heard of, *Brown v. Board of Education*, is famous precisely because it was a moment in which the Supreme Court declared that the law had changed.[86] *Brown*, of course, overturned *Plessy v. Ferguson*, which allowed for segregation along racial lines under a premise that has been shorthanded to the phrase "separate but equal."[87] *Brown* rejected this premise, stating among other things that "we conclude that in the field of public education the doctrine of 'separate but equal' has no place. Separate educational facilities are inherently unequal."[88]

If there is a consensus among the people in my line of work (and to be fair I'm not sure there is one), it is that the moment of change that we are looking for occurred in a footnote to a 1973 case.[89] Justice Thurgood Marshall authored the majority opinion in *McClanahan v. Arizona Tax Commission* in which he wrote in footnote 7 that "the source of federal authority over Indian matters has been the subject of some confusion, but it is now generally recognized that the power derives from federal responsibility for regulating commerce with Indian tribes and for treaty making."[90] With nothing but respect to the folks who have pointed to this footnote—especially since none of them appear to be writing for the purpose of solving our mystery—this is a pivotal moment but not a seminal one.[91] Rather, we have to accept that we don't have that one definitive pronouncement like in *Brown*.[92] The solution to our mystery is messier than can be explained with a singular event, as will become apparent later in the chapter.

The second major obstacle goes hand in hand with the first. As we have seen, the Supreme Court has been, shall we say, less than rigorous in identifying a specific constitutional source of federal authority over Native America. To that end, on a number of occasions the Supreme Court has simply asserted that the U.S. Constitution as a whole is the source of federal authority with little if any reference to specific provisions within the document. For example, writing in 1856 about the Cherokee Nation, Justice John McLean stated, "A question has been suggested whether the Cherokee people should be considered or treated as a foreign State or territory. *The fact that they are under the constitution of the Union*, and subject to acts of congress regulating trade, is a sufficient answer to the suggestion."[93] (I put a little emphasis in there to make sure you caught it.) We have already noted in Chapter 2 that McLean's opinion in this case is a little unhinged.[94] So we are not engaging with this language to gain insight into the status of the law but rather to focus on the trend to which it is a part. While McLean gestures obliquely toward the Indian Commerce Clause, his assertion is much broader. According to McLean, it is the U.S. Constitution as a whole unto itself that authorizes federal authority over Native America. This is why, as we noted in Chapter 2, later in the opinion he would further claim that Cherokee lands "originated under our constitution and laws."[95]

It might be tempting to dismiss McLean's opinion as an outlier, especially as it was not really in keeping with how we understand the law either then or now. But it is nonetheless helpful because it is evidence of a pattern: on a number of occasions the Supreme Court has asserted that the authority being claimed over Native America is authorized under the U.S. Constitution as a self-evident truism. For example, writing in 1886, Justice Stanley Matthews stated about the Choctaw Nation that it stood "in a peculiar relation to the United States. It was capable under the terms of the Constitution of entering into treaty relations with the government of the United States, although, from the nature of the case, subject to the power and authority of the laws of the United States when Congress should choose."[96] Matthews did not cite or otherwise make claim to any portion of the U.S. Constitution that made the Choctaw "subject to the power and authority" of the federal government. Rather, in a demonstration of how these types of unsubstantiated assertions become solidified under the weight of layers of precedent, Matthews turned to *Kagama*, decided just six months prior, to support his claim.

These unabashed assumptions of constitutional authority have been indiscriminate in that they have appeared in both victories and losses for tribal nations. Decided in 1896, *Talton v. Mayes* was a rare win for tribal interests in the Allotment Era. The question of the case was essentially about the source of tribal sovereignty. As Justice White (who, as you will remember, would go on to author *Lone Wolf*) put it, the issue to consider was whether "the powers of local government exercised by the Cherokee nation are Federal powers created by and springing from the Constitution of the United States . . . or whether they are local powers not created by the Constitution, *although subject to its general provisions and the paramount authority of Congress*."[97] (Once again I put the emphasis in there.) Where the "paramount authority of Congress" over Native America is located in the U.S. Constitution is left unsaid by White, although in keeping with how such doctrines become self-fulfilling, he did make reference to cases from the Marshall Trilogy and *Kagama*.

This phenomenon has hardly been confined to the nineteenth century. In a 1930 case about perpetuating trust restrictions on an individual Native person's parcel of land, Chief Justice (and former president) William Howard Taft stated, "Congress has authorized the Executive, in his discretion, to continue the restrictions for such period as he may deem best. That this is within the constitutional power of Congress must be considered as concluded by" not a citation to the U.S. Constitution but by citations to previous Supreme Court cases.[98] Writing in 1943, Justice Frank Murphy was perhaps a little too honest. "From almost the beginning, the existence of federal power to regulate and protect the Indians and their property against interference even by a state has been recognized. This power is not expressly granted in so many words by the Constitution, except with respect to regulating commerce with the Indian tribes, but its existence cannot be doubted."[99] To be completely fair, Murphy did make note of the war and treaty powers under the U.S. Constitution, but it was in reference to acquiring tribal lands that then led to a manifestation of the notion of protection that we examined in Chapter 2 as a source for plenary power. In the end, as with the other cases we have considered in this part of the chapter, Murphy cited *Kagama*.[100] Writing in 1977, Chief Justice Warren Burger stated, "Congress has undoubted constitutional power to prescribe a criminal code applicable in Indian country."[101] Hey, you're never going to believe this, but guess what Burger cited for this proposition? No, not the U.S. Constitution, you silly goose! He cited *Kagama*![102] Crazy, right! Now, lest you think that all of these cases are middle-aged at best, let me direct your attention to *Oklahoma v. Castro-Huerta*, a case from 2022. Writing for the majority, Justice Brett Kavanaugh stated, "To begin with, the Constitution allows a State to exercise jurisdiction in Indian country."[103] To be fair, Kavanaugh did cite to the 10th Amendment, which reserves the authority not granted to the federal government in the U.S. Constitution to the states and the people.[104] Yet, it is hard to connect the dots between Kavanaugh's assertion and the 10th Amendment, which does not mention Native nations or peoples or in any other way indicates that either the federal government or states can exercise any degree of plenary power over Native America. Consequently, Kavanaugh's assertion rings as hollow and facile as the others we have regarded in the last handful of paragraphs, a point that has been made elsewhere, including in the dissent in the case.[105]

Thus, one of the obstacles to answering our question is that the Supreme Court has not always been interested in finding a constitutional basis for plenary power, nor has it been particularly precise when it has asserted constitutional authority. That being noted, the third major obstacle we face is that our question itself is not as sharp as it needs to be to cut through the morass of imprecision left behind by the Supreme Court. It is less helpful to ask when plenary power became constitutional than one might think because the Supreme Court has shown remarkably little real interest in the question.

Wait a minute. Am I really saying that the question that has fueled this whole book to this point is essentially useless? Then what are we even doing here?

OK, I can understand why you might be a little upset, but this accusation is unfair, so let me try to explain what we are doing here.[106] I haven't written and you haven't read half a book for no point at all.[107] The question that we began with was a necessary starting point, but it can't take us all the way that we need to go because the Supreme Court has never taken the question all that seriously (which is an understanding to which we will return later in this chapter—foreshadowing![108]). Luckily for us, however, the Supreme Court does seem invested in perpetuating the story that Breyer tried to tell us in *Lara*: that the Supreme Court "has traditionally identified the Indian Commerce Clause" as the constitutional authority for the version of plenary power that developed out of *Kagama*, *Lone Wolf*, and *Sandoval* and other cases of their ilk. This is convenient for people like Supreme Court justices because this story ostensibly lacks the obvious baggage of some of the other justifications for plenary power—like land and protection—that we looked at in Chapter 2, and it fits neatly into how we understand how American law is supposed to operate.

But as the first half of this book demonstrates, this story is not so neat and tidy. The Supreme Court originally rejected the Indian Commerce Clause as the basis for the all-encompassing version of plenary power in *Kagama*. Since that seminal moment it has offered a handful of rationales for federal authority over Native America, all of which are rooted in the type of racist understandings that allowed plenary power to develop not just in Indian law but elsewhere in American law in a particular historical moment. Since the doctrine of plenary power has this history and since the Supreme Court seems committed to the story that it is presently trying to tell—best exemplified by Breyer in *Lara*—what we really want to know is if anything has changed. Did the Supreme Court figure something out? Does the Indian Commerce Clause offer a legitimate basis for federal authority over Native America that is in keeping with the theoretical underpinning of consent? Or is this new rationale simply a more stealthy, less perceptibly onerous upgrade over the same old ones? We can only make this determination by ascertaining when, and thus how, this new story came to be. So we need a more precise question.

> When did the Indian Commerce Clause become the basis for the all-encompassing version of plenary power?

This works, right? This question much better describes the true mystery that we are trying to solve. And yet, now with more than a half of a book of insight, you can see why we couldn't start there. It's a little wordy and full of stuff that doesn't make a lot of sense without the necessary background. We had to walk before we could run.

But now that we are armed with this more effective question, we are finally able to see that two phenomena contributed to where we presently stand with plenary power and the Indian Commerce Clause. The first is that the Supreme Court couldn't hold its liquor. Put a bit more sophisticatedly (and with less snark), in the late nineteenth and early twentieth centuries—the Allotment Era of federal policy—the Supreme Court started haphazardly conflating the two versions of plenary power—against the states and over Native America—in a series of cases about alcohol and Indian Country.

The relationship between alcohol and Native America is long and convoluted and has resulted in, among other things, unsubstantiated stereotypes and beliefs about Native peoples' propensity toward alcoholism.[109] Fortunately, we don't have to dig too far down into that history to engage with our mystery. For our purposes, we need only acknowledge that alcohol was a tool of colonialism, one that the federal government has sought to control in Indian Country from its earliest days.[110] Stating that he was acting on the request of tribal nations, President Thomas Jefferson requested that Congress regulate the trade of liquor with Native America.[111] Congress obliged, and Section 21 the 1802 version of the Trade and Intercourse Act stated "that the President of the United States be authorized to take such measures, from time to time, as to him may appear expedient to prevent or restrain the vending or distribution of spirituous liquors among all or any of the said Indian tribes."[112] Today there are still several "Indian liquor laws" like this on the books.[113]

The most striking characteristic of Section 21 is the same as the most striking characteristic of the Trade and Intercourse Acts in general: it is a regulation of those under American jurisdiction, not of Native peoples and nations directly. After Section 21 was passed, the secretary of war—who at the time was tasked with engaging with tribal nations on behalf of the federal government—sent a letter to various other governmental officials informing them that those who traded with Native peoples would have their licenses revoked if they provided liquor to Native peoples.[114] Thus, Section 21 was very much in keeping with the first definition of plenary power that focused federal authority against states and on those under its jurisdiction. It easily fell under the most natural reading of the Indian Commerce Clause.

And yet, Indian liquor laws were very much predicated on the stereotype of the drunken Indian. Consequently, in the Allotment Era when the Supreme Court began more widely embracing the second definition of plenary power—all-encompassing authority over Native America—the nature of the Indian liquor laws became confused within the Court's reasoning. The Indian Commerce Clause, which offered seemingly ample justification for such laws directed against American citizens and others under federal jurisdiction, was forced to stand alongside protection-based rationales for extensive federal authority over Native America. An 1876 case—a precursor to the Plenary Power Trilogy—in which a white man was accused of introducing liquor into Indian Country offered an early glimpse into what would become an uneasy trend. Writing about the change from the Articles of Confederation to the U.S. Constitution, Justice David Davis noted that "Congress now has the exclusive and absolute power to regulate commerce with the Indian tribes,—a power as broad and as free from restrictions as that to regulate commerce with foreign nations."[115] Such a statement clearly references federal authority as against the states and falls neatly into the original definition of plenary power that John Marshall articulated in *Worcester*. However, in the very next sentence, the soon-to-explode second definition of plenary power was offered as justification as well. "The only efficient way of dealing with the Indian tribes was to place them under the protection of the general government."[116]

A number of cases with similar facts followed this same pattern of forcing together the Indian Commerce Clause and constitutionally unhinged, protection-based rationales for federal authority as if they were one. The most prominent example is none other than one of our Plenary Power Trilogy cases—*Sandoval*. The Sandoval in *Sandoval* was Filipe

Sandoval, a non-Native person accused of bringing liquor into Indian Country. This time, in asserting federal jurisdiction over Filipe, Justice Willis Van Devanter didn't even bother breaking the rationales into two sentences. "Not only does the Constitution expressly authorize Congress to regulate commerce with the Indian tribes, but long continued legislative and executive usage and an unbroken current of judicial decisions have attributed to the United States as a superior and civilized nation the power and the duty of exercising a fostering care and protection over all dependent Indian communities within its borders, whether within its original territory or territory subsequently acquired, and whether within or without the limits of a State."[117] Unsurprisingly, Van Devanter used *Kagama* to support his claim.

Van Devanter is perhaps best known for consistently voting against New Deal legislation and for not being particularly prolific during his twenty-six years on the Supreme Court.[118] However, he became something of a specialist in Indian law during his time as the chief justice of the Wyoming Supreme Court and as an assistant attorney general in the Department of the Interior, where he argued on behalf of the federal government in *Lone Wolf*.[119] Thus, he was a leader in these cases. A mere four months after *Sandoval* he essentially repeated himself. "The power of Congress to prohibit the introduction of intoxicating liquors into an Indian reservation, wheresoever situate, and to prohibit traffic in such liquors with tribal Indians, whether upon or off a reservation and whether within or without the limits of a State, does not admit of any doubt. It arises in part from the clause in the Constitution investing Congress with authority 'to regulate commerce with foreign nations, and among the several States, and with the Indian tribes,' and in part from the recognized relation of tribal Indians to the Federal Government."[120] Two years later he was at it again. With the type of self-confidence only a Supreme Court justice can have when saying the same thing over and over, Van Devanter claimed that the law in these types of cases "is well settled. It has long been exercised and has repeatedly been sustained by this court."[121] Making the point once again, Van Devanter stated, "Its source is two-fold; first the clause in the Constitution expressly investing Congress with authority 'to regulate commerce . . . with the Indian tribes,' and, second, the dependent relation of such tribes to the United States."[122]

This conflation of the two different versions of plenary power into a singular, indistinguishable whole took root. Writing in 1959 Justice Hugo Black, citing both *Kagama* and Van Devanter, stated, "The federal Government's power over Indians is derived from [the Indian Commerce Clause] and from the necessity of giving uniform protection to a dependent people."[123] Writing in 1975 in yet another Indian liquor law case, Associate Justice William Rehnquist noted, "This court has repeatedly held" that the Indian Commerce Clause "affords Congress the power to prohibit or regulate the sale of alcoholic beverages to tribal Indians, wherever situated, and to prohibit or regulate the introduction of alcoholic beverages into Indian country."[124] Were this where Rehnquist stopped, it might be possible to see how it would fit under the first definition of plenary power. However, Rehnquist did not stop there. He went on to directly quote Van Devanter to assert the much broader, second definition of plenary power.[125] In a 1977 case about the imposition of federal criminal law on a reservation, Chief Justice Warren Burger cited the Indian Commerce Clause in a footnote when writing that "classifications expressly singling out Indian tribes as subjects of legislation are expressly provided for in the Constitution and supported by the ensuing history of the Federal Government's relations with Indians."[126] The most significant consequence of this process of conflation of the different versions of plenary power was that the rationales behind the different versions also became indistinguishable. Thus, the justification for the original, more limited version of plenary power—the Indian Commerce Clause—could and did stand in for the later, much broader version.

The other phenomenon that helped us get to where we are was the exponential growth in importance of the Commerce Clause in American law more generally. As noted earlier, the Commerce Clause is less a singular thing unto itself and more a collection of parts that share a common bond. Consequently, it is difficult to make proclamations about it as a whole. That being noted, the part of the Commerce Clause that tends to receive the most attention in the legal academy and law schools is the part about regulating among the several states. The influence of what is known as the Interstate Commerce Clause has fluctuated over the years, but it is reasonable to argue that it has become the most important and impactful basis for federal authority in general at present.[127]

As with many things we have touched upon in this book, there is a lot that can and has been said about the Commerce Clause. For our purposes, however, it suffices to note that by the mid-twentieth century the Commerce Clause had become the easiest and most accessible tool by which Congress wielded its authority and by which the Supreme Court justified exertions of federal authority. In fact, the extent to which the federal government could rely on the Commerce Clause to exercise power for the bulk of the twentieth century and even today is hard to overstate. From 1937 to 1995 the Supreme Court upheld every piece of congressional legislation passed under the Commerce Clause that came before it.[128] Whether this is good or bad thing is the subject of someone else's (actually many, many, MANY other peoples') scholarship, but it was definitely a thing. This included the realm of civil rights legislation, most notably the Civil Rights Act of 1964.[129]

Boy, this is confusing, isn't it? I mean, where exactly has all of this gotten us? We don't have an easy-to-identify moment when everything changed. Instead, we have some trends that are pointing us in a certain direction without saying much more. And, some pages ago, I told you that the one place where some of the folks in my field think this all started—a footnote in the 1973 *McClanahan* decision—isn't exactly wrong, but it isn't exactly right either. So are we any closer to our destination than when we started? Have we made any real progress, or are we just sitting here holding a bunch of loose ends?

Well, yes, we do have a bunch of loose ends. But we finally have everything we need to weave them together into something useful. So, let's start by more closely looking at the day *McClanhan* was decided. According to Thurgood Marshall's footnote, there was "some confusion" about the source of federal authority over Native America but that "it is now generally recognized that the power derives from federal responsibility for regulating commerce with Indian tribes and for treaty making." However, the Supreme Court's true understanding of the source of federal authority—or at least the more traditional one to that point—was better summed up by Justice William O. Douglas in another case decided on the very same day as *McClanhan*. In *Mescalero Apache Tribe v. Jones* Douglas wrote, "The power of Congress granted by [the Commerce Clause] is an exceedingly broad one. In the liquor cases the Court held that it reached acts even off Indian reservations in areas normally subject to the police power of the States. The power gained breadth by reason of historic experiences that induced Congress to treat Indians as wards of the Nation."[130] The mashup of the rationales that allowed for the Indian Commerce Clause to replace the other foundations for the all-encompassing version of plenary power is in full display in Douglas's words.

Yet, Douglas, who had been appointed to the Supreme Court by Franklin D. Roosevelt in 1939, wrote this statement during the second term of the Richard Nixon administration. Times were changing, both societally and in the law. The civil rights legislation of this era offers a useful look at the transformation that was occurring and how the plenary power doctrine was affected.

The Civil Rights Act of 1964, possibly the most famous piece of legislation ever passed by Congress, was built in large part on the back of the Commerce Clause.[131] Shortly after it was passed, the new law and its reliance on the commerce clause survived challenges at the Supreme Court.[132] Thus, by the time Congress passed the much less famous Civil Rights Act of 1968 four years later, the authority of Congress to enact such legislation and the growing importance of the Commerce Clause had taken firm root.

Titles II through VII of the 1968 act consisted of what is commonly referred to as the Indian Civil Rights Act. Among other things, the Indian Civil Rights Act imposed most of the standards of the U.S. Constitution on tribal governments, such as the prohibition against double jeopardy and the right to a speedy trial.[133] This direct imposition on tribal nations was a clear exercise of the second, all-encompassing version of plenary power. So under what authority did Congress pass the Indian Civil Rights Act? Well, there you go again, being a silly goose asking a silly question! The perfunctory assertions in the few times the question seemed to come up during the nearly decade that the Indian Civil Rights

Act was being considered in Congress strongly suggest that the powers that be thought that the answer was so obvious and/or so immaterial that it hardly merited any consideration at all. For example, North Carolina senator Sam Ervin, the driving force behind the legislation, stated without any further citation or elaboration that "the sovereignty of an Indian tribe can be limited by act of the Congress."[134] Along those same lines, a Senate report accompanying an early version of the bill, also without any further citation or elaboration, stated, "Several sections of the Constitution have been used to establish restraints on Indian self-government although Congress has exercised its power to legislate such restraints on numerous occasions."[135] Additionally, Marvin J. Sonosky, an extremely well-known and prominent practitioner of Indian law, stated in a congressional committee hearing about the bill that "Congress can do anything with respect to Indians" and "Congress has plenary authority under our Constitution over Indians, under our Constitution."[136]

Thus, the dominant discourse of the times claimed that Congress just simply had the authority to legislate in this area. However, a rare signal of contemplation on this issue does offer some unease with what the powers that be allegedly agreed upon. A 1966 committee report about the Indian Civil Rights Act stated, "Deriving authority to limit Indian self-government from several sections of the Constitution, Congress has exercised its power on numerous occasions."[137] The report footnoted to the Commerce Clause as well as four other parts of the U.S. Constitution.[138]

The statement and footnote in the 1966 committee report hint at a moment of difficulty and change that much of the rest of the governmental material about the Indian Civil Rights Act tried to ignore or pretend had already been settled. Whereas the more famous 1964 Civil Rights Act laid claim and found sanction under the Commerce Clause (and other parts of the U.S. Constitution), the hodgepodge of otherwise unsupported constitutional clauses that Congress meekly recited in a footnote on behalf of the Indian Civil Rights Act suggests that the federal government was less than convinced of the constitutional source of the plenary power over Native America even though it was sure that it could exercise plenary power. To slightly amend an old saying to suit my purposes, it was like throwing everything against the wall with the assumption that something would stick. The Indian Civil Rights Act was eventually passed into law, but not because the federal government found any clarity over the source of plenary power. Rather, it was because it had become embroiled in the larger Civil Rights Act of 1968, which was quickly passed when the federal government sought to make a meaningful statement in the wake of the assassination of Martin Luther King Jr.[139]

Moreover, the tenor and policy around Native America was changing at this time as well. Perhaps best understood as one of many overreactions to the Cold War, the Termination Era of federal Indian policy lasted from approximately 1953 to the mid-1960s.[140] Much like its older cousin, the Allotment Era, the Termination Era was defined by federal efforts to destroy tribes and tribalism through means like ending the political relationship with tribal nations, relocating Native peoples to urban centers (without adequate support once they got there), and shunting criminal justice responsibilities to states that were indifferent at best.[141]

The Termination Era was mostly unsuccessful in its stated goals and had the unintended consequence of increasing Native resistance and activism rather than further assimilating Native peoples and dismantling tribal governments.[142] By the mid-1960s, as civil rights and the treatment of disadvantaged groups were a major part of the public discourse in American life, the purpose and rationale that fueled the Termination Era seemed increasingly outdated. In 1966, partially in support of the Indian Civil Rights Act, President Lyndon Johnson sent a special message to Congress concerning Native America, seeking to reverse the course of the Termination Era. "I propose, in short, a policy of maximum choice for the American Indian: a policy expressed in programs of self-help, self-development, self-determination."[143] Four years later, in 1970, President Richard Nixon delivered a similar message. "The time has come to break decisively with the past and to create the conditions for a new era in which the Indian future is determined by Indian acts and Indian decisions."[144]

The Self-Determination Era of federal policy, ushered in by Johnson, Nixon, and others, is best characterized as the federal government seeking to help tribal nations help themselves.[145] The full level of success of these efforts, particularly with the Supreme Court often moving in the opposite direction, can be debated. Nonetheless, it was (and continues to be as most agree that we are still in the Self-Determination Era) a significant break from the spirit and purpose of the Termination Era and has resulted in a significant reinvigoration of tribal governing structures.

More to our purposes, the Self-Determination Era, as part of the Civil Rights Era in American history more generally, altered the discourse about plenary power. Returning to March, 27, 1973—the day that *McClanahan* and *Mescalero Apache Tribe* were decided—helps us see the transition taking place. In *Mescalero Apache Tribe* Justice William O. Douglas was still willing to describe Native peoples as "wards." Yet, as noted in Chapter 2, by this point the language of trust—which gestured toward the relationship between the federal government and tribal nations—was beginning to replace the language of wardship—which gestured toward the supposedly diminished capacity of tribal peoples. While Justice Thurgood Marshall's opinion in *McClanahan* does use the word "wards" once, it is in the context of a direct quotation from a 1930 case. His noteworthy footnote, on the other hand, seems to implicitly reject any wardship rationale as the basis of plenary power, claiming that there has been "some confusion" on the matter before stating that it was "now generally recognized" that the Indian Commerce Clause (and the Treaty Clause, whose mention we will wrestle with soon) was the real source of authority.

Put more directly, at the onset of the Self-Determination Era, which coincided with a major Civil Rights Era, the Supreme Court both seemed to grow increasingly embarrassed and bothered with a wardship rationale as a basis for plenary power and was nudged by the other branches to rearticulate its reasonings. Whereas in previous generations the Supreme Court could openly assert the ostensible superiority of the United States and the inferiority of tribal nations as a rational justification for an all-encompassing federal authority, such arguments ran contrary to the development of American law and society in the mid-twentieth century. This is not to suggest that the language of wardship and dependency completely disappeared (after all, Supreme Court justices are rarely accused of being on the cutting edge of societal development).[146] However, the necessity of moving beyond the older language and tying plenary power to the U.S. Constitution became increasingly apparent and important to the Supreme Court.[147] Furthermore, the footnote in the 1966 congressional committee report about the Indian Civil Rights Act—which pointed to the Indian Commerce Clause as well as four other clauses in the U.S. Constitution for the source of federal authority to pass the legislation—as well as the statements from Presidents Johnson and Nixon make clear that the Supreme Court was not the only branch of the federal government rethinking and reshaping its understanding of plenary power, nor was it the leader in this movement.

As the Self-Determination Era progressed, the language the Supreme Court used concerning plenary power both softened and became more focused on the Indian Commerce Clause. For example, consider a quotation that we already looked at a handful of pages ago. In 1977 Chief Justice Warren Burger, footnoting to the Indian Commerce Clause, wrote that "classifications expressly singling out Indian tribes as subjects of legislation are expressly provided for in the Constitution and supported by the ensuing history of the Federal Government's relations with Indians."[148] While this statement partially clings to a wardship model of federal authority, it does so with muted language that obscures the history of the rationale. Before long, the Indian Commerce Clause could stand alone for assertions of the all-encompassing version of plenary power. Writing in 1978, Justice Harry Blackmun made note of the "continued federal supervision" of Native peoples "under the Commerce Clause."[149] Writing in 1980, Justice Thurgood Marshall claimed that "Congress has broad power to regulate tribal affairs under the Indian Commerce Clause."[150] Writing in 1985, Justice Lewis F. Powell Jr. cited the Indian Commerce Clause in first stating that "the Constitution vests the Federal Government with exclusive authority over relations with Indian tribes" and then "in keeping with its plenary authority over Indian affairs, Congress can authorize the imposition of state taxes on Indian tribes and individual Indians."[151]

All of which is to note that when we ask our more refined question—When did the Indian Commerce Clause become the basis for the all-encompassing version of plenary power?—we can finally see an answer. In a time of significant change in the mid-twentieth century, in which the more obviously racist rationales for plenary power were not as feasible as they once were, the Supreme Court further leaned on the most useful and accessible tool at its disposal: the Commerce Clause. The Indian Commerce Clause was available as a basis for the all-encompassing version of plenary power because its more natural, limited reading had become conflated with other rationales that presumed the inferiority of Native peoples, most particularly in the liquor cases of the late nineteenth and early twentieth centuries. Furthermore, the Indian Commerce Clause gained a particular prominence because it is the only place in the U.S. Constitution where Native peoples are explicitly mentioned.[152] Although we don't have the singular, seminal moment to which we can definitively state that the law became what it is today, we can see the patterns of change that made the Indian Commerce Clause the most important source of plenary power by the latter part of the twentieth century.

So, there you have it. We have finally solved our mystery. Admittedly, it is not as tidy as your average detective TV show where a single culprit is definitively identified by the end of the episode. But at least now we know where the all-encompassing version of plenary power came from, how it got entangled with the Indian Commerce Clause, and why the Supreme Court justifies exercises of the all-encompassing version of plenary power under the Indian Commerce Clause today. And we were able to do it in a neat, concise three chapters—which I think we can all agree is typically the exact number of chapters that every great book has. So anyway, this was fun. Thanks for reading!

. . .

. . .

. . .

OK, fine. We actually have a couple of serious problems on our hands that we need to address. One problem is that all of this is crazy. The all-encompassing version of plenary power was born out of racism. It is out of sync with the principle of consent that justifies American governance more generally. Its ties to the Indian Commerce Clause reflect that racist history and reject a more natural reading of the document. Around the mid-twentieth century the Indian Commerce Clause became the crutch to prop up plenary power when it was no longer acceptable to trot out the obviously racist tropes that had previously been available to the Supreme Court. There is nothing in this history to suggest that the Supreme Court has found a logical or meaningful tie between the all-encompassing version of plenary power and the U.S. Constitution that is consistent with the underlying theory of consent. Rather, the Indian Commerce Clause has become the constitutional shield to protect the overarching authority that the federal government claimed for itself in an era when it was trying to destroy tribes and tribalism.[153] The racism is hiding behind the U.S. Constitution.

Again, this is crazy. So what can be done about it? Trust me when I note that I recognize that I am testing the limits of your patience when I write that we will have to wait for a bit before coming back around to this question. I promise we tackle it head-on in Chapter 5, but there are a few other things we need to do first.

The second serious problem is related to the first: the Supreme Court doesn't actually believe the story that it is telling. It is no more convinced that there is a justifiable connection between the all-encompassing version of plenary power and the Indian Commerce Clause that is in line with American theories of governance than you should be at this point. Yet, it is willing to tell a story it doesn't believe because that story is simple, useful, and fits comfortably among the types of stories that it regularly tells.

A closer look at Justice Stephen Breyer's opinion in *Lara* helps illustrate the point. Breyer actually offered six reasons for why the congressional exercise of plenary power in that case was valid. We are already familiar with the first one: "This Court has traditionally identified the Indian Commerce Clause" as the source of congressional plenary power over Native peoples.[154] However, Breyer did not stop there, stating that the Indian Commerce Clause "and the Treaty Clause" were the "sources of that power."[155]

The bundling of constitutional clauses, led by the Indian Commerce Clause, to justify plenary power has been a common tactic of the Supreme Court. Remember Justice Thurgood Marshall's footnote in *McClanahan*?[156] It also referenced both the Indian Commerce Clause and the Treaty Clause as being "generally recognized" as the source of plenary power. More recently, Justice Amy Coney Barrett offered four sources of authority, beginning, of course, with the Indian Commerce Clause as well as the Treaty Clause, "preconstitutional powers necessarily inherent in any federal government," and the trust responsibility.[157]

Yet, as noted in Chapter 2, these and other alternative rationales for plenary power are even more empty and troubling than the Indian Commerce Clause. Furthermore, their collective force is no greater than any one individually. The net result of adding zeroes to zeroes is still zero, no matter how many you put together. To bend an old saying back closer to its original shape, this feels like throwing everything against the wall and hoping that something will stick.

Hey, speaking of throwing everything against the wall, you should check out the other five reasons Breyer gives us in *Lara* for why the exercise of plenary power in that case was constitutionally sound. They are, in essence, that plenary power lets Congress both relax and restrict tribal sovereignty,[158] this exercise of plenary power isn't anything too crazy,[159] nobody said Congress couldn't do it,[160] this isn't a big deal,[161] and we've let this kind of stuff go before.[162] This list doesn't exactly inspire a sense of scholarly gravitas, does it?[163] It feels more like the desperate attempt of a teenager trying to convince a parent to let her or him do something they both know the teenager shouldn't do rather than a rigorous accounting of the language of the U.S. Constitution and the scope of the powers it permits to the federal government. Consequently, it is hard to believe that Breyer believed in what he wrote. Barrett's more recent opinion is at least more honest with its readers. "Admittedly, our precedent is unwieldy, because it rarely ties a challenged statute to a specific source of constitutional authority."[164]

All of which is to point out that the justices of the Supreme Court don't seem particularly confident in or convinced of their own claims to the constitutionality of the all-encompassing version of plenary power. And yet they still keep making these claims. Making matters even more perplexing, one of their own has spent nearly twenty years yelling at the top of his lungs (as much as one can yell at the top of one's lungs in Supreme Court opinions) about the lack of constitutional support for the all-encompassing version of plenary power.

A polarizing figure even before he was confirmed, Justice Clarence Thomas has hardly tempered the feelings surrounding him in his over three decades on the Supreme Court.[165] My purpose in introducing Thomas into the conversation is not to change your mind about him one way or the other but rather to note that he is the only justice to clearly identify the situation for what it is. In his concurrence in *Lara*—which was obviously a response to Breyer's wishy-washy majority opinion—he stated, "As this case should make clear, the time has come to reexamine the premises and logic of our tribal sovereignty cases," before further noting that "this case raises important constitutional questions that the Court does not begin to answer. The Court utterly fails to find any provision of the Constitution that gives Congress enumerated power to alter tribal sovereignty. The Court cites the Indian Commerce Clause and the treaty power. I cannot agree that the Indian Commerce Clause 'provide[s] Congress with plenary power to legislate in the field of Indian affairs.' "[166] Quite bluntly he added, "The Court should admit that it has failed in its quest to find a source of congressional power to adjust tribal sovereignty."[167]

At every opportunity since *Lara,* Thomas has reminded the Court of the disconnect between the Indian Commerce Clause and the all-encompassing version of plenary power. Nine years after *Lara,* in another concurrence Thomas stated, "The assertion of plenary authority must . . . stand or fall on Congress' power under the Indian Commerce Clause. Although this Court has said that the 'central function of the Indian Commerce Clause is to provide Congress with plenary power to legislate in the field of Indian affairs,' neither the text nor the original understanding of the Clause supports Congress' claim to such 'plenary' power."[168] Three years later he directly called out the decision in *Kagama.* "No enumerated power—not Congress' power to 'regulate Commerce . . . with Indian Tribes,' not the Senate's role in approving treaties, nor anything else—gives Congress such sweeping authority. Indeed, the Court created this new power because it was unable to find an enumerated power justifying the federal Major Crimes Act, which for the first time punished crimes committed by Indians against Indians on Indian land."[169] In a rare dissent to a Supreme Court decision not to hear a case, he stated, "We should have [heard the case] to reexamine our Indian Commerce Clause precedents, instead of standing idly by as Congress, the Executive, and the lower courts stray further and further from the Constitution."[170] Six years later the message was still the same. "Although our cases have at times suggested a broader power with respect to Indians, there is no evidence for such a free-floating authority anywhere in the text or original understanding of the Constitution."[171]

Consequently it is impossible to dismiss the Supreme Court's continual justification of the all-encompassing version of plenary power under the Indian Commerce Clause as simple ignorance (or even the general indifference that most justices seem to hold for Indian law cases[172]). This isn't happening because the justices just don't know any better.[173] Whatever you might think of any particular justice or the Supreme Court as a whole, these are not unintelligent people and this has not been a minor oversight. This has been a choice.[174] The Supreme Court is using the Indian Commerce Clause because it is convenient, not because it is convincing. And yet, even though they don't believe their own story, they keep on telling it.

So there you have it. We have more or less figured out when the Indian Commerce Clause became the primary source for the all-encompassing version of federal plenary power over Native America. Yet, our journey has left us with a couple of troubling realizations. First, the Indian Commerce Clause offers less of a logical connection to a legitimate exercise of an enumerated federal power and more of a constitutionally adjacent alibi for the continuing existence of a racist overreach of authority. Second, the Supreme Court doesn't believe its own story even though it keeps asserting it.

All of which leads us to one final conclusion for this chapter: this is not a mystery that we have been trying to solve . . .

This is a trickster story.

Nanaboozhoo and the others kept looking up as the pale man's gigantic hands were slowly but steadily lowering upon them. Nanaboozhoo could hear someone in the group say, "Well, this party took a sharp right turn into poopsville." A few tepidly laughed at the comment. Some others tried to make some jokes of their own, but the normally jovial crowd could not stem the growing sense of discomfort among themselves.

Shortly thereafter the jokes died off as the gravity of the situation—as well as the gigantic hands—continued to descend on the partygoers. Soon, a number of the partygoers started to grumble. Then others started to openly worry. Before long a few were panicking. Some shouted insults at the pale man. They beat their chests and challenged him to a fight. They looked defiantly at the large hands yet silently and secretly worried for their lives. A few charged the pale man's hands, determined to live or die as a hero. Many were crushed.

Others, hoping to escape, tried to run. They strapped the absolute minimum number of things they needed on the fastest horses they had, and they took off. But the pale man's hands were growing too large to run from under. A few managed to make it to the far edges of where the hands were descending, but most were too late. Most were trapped. Others were also crushed. A few others were never heard of again. Perhaps they had escaped. Perhaps they became somebody else.

Still others tried other tactics. Some sought to acquiesce to the pale man. They began proclaiming their love for him. They promised to behave just like him. They sat quietly on hard wooden benches to show that they worshipped just like he did. Despite their efforts there was no indication that the pale man was listening, and their actions did not seem to make much of a difference. And yet others kept trying to further reason with the pale man. They kept trying to explain to the pale man how he should behave. They kept offering to show him their ways. They kept trying to get him to see their logic. Again there was no indication that the pale man was listening, and their actions did not seem to make much of a difference.

The giant hands landed on the ground with a deafening thud, and the whole world changed. The cupped hands were pressed together so tightly that no sunlight entered. It was frighteningly dark, and the air became humid and stuffy. It was hard to breathe. Even though the hands were large, they did not leave enough space for all of the partygoers trapped under them. When cramped together, the already anxious partygoers got even more testy. Old rivalries flared; new ones began.

Many days passed like this. Or maybe it was months or even years. It was impossible to tell for sure in all of the darkness. Nanaboozhoo had been stupefied as he watched the pale man's hands lower over him and the others and had been dumbstruck and unable to move when they landed on the ground and left everyone in the dark. But he had finally gathered enough of his wits, and he decided he needed to walk around and survey the situation. As he got up and started to move, he could hear the snide remarks that the others pretended they didn't want him to hear but that they really did. "That was the worst party ever," someone hissed. "Why did I accept Nanaboozhoo's invitation?" another lamented. "Nanaboozhoo has never been any good," another one spat.

Nanaboozhoo did his best to let the hurtful comments slide off of his back, but he could not ignore what he was able to see even in the dark. There was not enough to eat and too much to drink. Children and words and land vanished. Many were dead; many others wished they were. The end of one fight was quickly replaced with the start of another. Abuse had become commonplace. There were certainly those who tried to lift everyone's spirits. There were those still willing to fight and hold out hope. These people gave Nanaboozhoo the strength to keep walking. Even so, as he made his way all the way around the enclosed space, it was impossible to tell if the dominant mood among the crowd was anger or fear. Did it even matter?

Nanaboozhoo returned to his small, cramped corner of the enclosed space. He sat on the ground and rubbed his face with his hands to keep himself from crying. He sighed heavily, hoping the mournful cries he kept hearing would end so that he could have a moment of silence to think. But they didn't stop. So he put his hands over his ears and put his head between his legs. "What are we going to do?" he whispered to himself.

"What are we going to do?"

FOUR *The Conundrum*

Yep, this is a trickster story. But it's a really bad one. It's the worst, actually. And yet, we all keep retelling it as if it were authentic and authoritative and real.

If you are somewhat confused (and maybe even a little bit wary of where I am going with this), I don't blame you. It is difficult to explain—let alone connect it to American legal doctrine—because tricksters and trickster stories defy easy explanation or compartmentalization (which sort of proves their point—but we will get to that shortly). In fact, there has been some debate as to whether it is feasible to think of the trickster as an archetype and the trickster story as a genre.[1] Put a bit more simply, asking "what is a trickster story?" is a lot like asking "what is a movie?" While there is something that connects the various things that we might describe as a movie, there can be lots of different answers depending on who is making the movie and what the moviemaker is trying to convey. A Hollywood blockbuster is different from a documentary, which is different from a home movie meant just for the family, which is different from a TikTok video (if those still exist by the time you read this), which is different from a training video you might have watched at your job.

Yet, they all can make a claim to being a movie. All of which is to note a couple of critical points that demonstrate the challenge before us. First, tricksters and trickster stories are flexible and adaptable and can suit many purposes depending on what the teller wants to say and what the audience needs to hear. Sometimes these stories are meant to teach and sometimes they are meant to explain and sometimes they are meant to be funny; often they are more than one of these things at once. Consequently, and second, they are hard to define with any precision or with a universal applicability to all versions or tellings. The trickster and his story, as you might guess, are awfully tricky.[2]

Nonetheless, if I am going to be bold enough to title this book *The Worst Trickster Story Ever Told*, then I at least need to try, right? Thus, the first thing that we need to acknowledge is that trickster stories and trickster figures are incredibly common throughout various world cultures and histories.[3] While they are definitely associated with and part of Native cultures, they are not exclusively of them, and their near ubiquitous presence among peoples across the globe helps demonstrate their influence and authority. In today's modern world, there is a tendency to treat the trickster as both a relic of the past and most suitable for juvenile literature, trapped in the long ago and the realm of childhood by words like "folklore," "mythology," and "legends." And yet, the trickster remains with all of us, at the very least having shaped how many peoples have and continue to see the world. The trickster has been fundamental to our understandings of the cultures in which we live and thus continues to exert influence over our own perceptions of life, nature, and ourselves, whether we are aware of it or not.[4]

Tricksters are also difficult to pin down yet are ideally suited to their role because they maintain all of the characteristics, flaws, and abilities that are exhibited by both humanity and other spiritual or supernatural beings. They are regularly weak and foolish and apt to make bad judgments. Yet, they are also able to use their magic to shape-shift, create new things the world has never seen before, and even resurrect themselves.[5] They are always clever, but often too clever for their own good, especially when they are driven by the various hungers that a person can experience—for food, flesh, or otherwise.[6] This wide range of possibilities thus creates a wide range of outcomes for trickster stories. Consequently, tricksters give us someone to relate to, laugh at, and learn from. They can be like us, but their distance from us allows us to examine them with a more critical eye.

The Anishinaabe trickster figure, Nanaboozhoo, helps us see the varied roles that he and others like him play:[7]

> One day Nanaboozhoo was walking near his home, which at that time happened to be near a body of water.[8] Absolutely famished as usual, he was surveying the landscape, looking for food. All of a sudden, he saw the biggest, juiciest, ripest berries he had ever seen in his life just underneath the surface of the water. "Oh man," Nanaboozhoo thought to himself. "Those look sooooooooooo good. I better get them before someone else does." Immediately Nanaboozhoo dashed as quickly as he could over to the edge of the water and plunged his hand in to grab the berries. But when he pulled his hand out of the water, it was both empty and soaked. "What the heck . . ." he thought to himself as he was confused by what just happened. So, he decided to try again. And again he was unable to grab the berries and was left with an empty, soaking hand. Nanaboozhoo was getting frustrated, and he decided that he absolutely had to have those berries. So, he tried again, this time plunging both hands into the water. Once again, he had no berries, and now both hands were soaking wet. His teeth grinding and his brow furrowing, Nanaboozhoo was getting really mad. "I MUST HAVE THOSE BERRIES!!!" he shouted as he repeatedly plunged both hands into the water over and over trying to grab them. But it was all to no avail as he could not grab them no matter how hard he tried. Finally, at his wits' end, Nanaboozhoo said to himself, "If I can't grab the berries and eat them above the water, I will go to them and eat them under the water!" So, with all of his strength, Nanaboozhoo lifted his head up in the air and plunged it into the water. But the water was shallow and Nanaboozhoo ended up slamming his forehead into the rocks on the bed of the body of water. Nanaboozhoo pulled his head—which was now also soaking from the water and from the blood on the gash

> he had opened on his forehead—out of the water and fell backward onto the shore. He laid there, groaning for a long time before he finally opened his eyes and saw the berries again. But now he realized that the berries had been hanging from a tree the whole time, and he had only been seeing their reflection in the water. Angry that it had deceived him, Nanaboozhoo gave the tree a swift kick, but the tree was unmoved. Vowing never to eat that tree's berries, Nanaboozhoo hobbled off with his sore forehead and now also a sore foot, just as hungry as ever.

If we acknowledge that it is perhaps only fulfilling a portion of its potential on the printed (or e-reader) page, it becomes easy to imagine how this story could entertain an audience. Much like a seasoned stand-up comedian can wring every last bit of humor out of nearly any situation, a talented storyteller could truly bring this tale to life with gestures and changes in voice tone and other goofy details. The story is, to put it succinctly, a crowd pleaser. However, there is also something of substance there for those willing to take the time to think a bit more closely about the story. It is a lesson about impetuousness as well as, as they say, throwing good money after bad. If Nanaboozhoo hadn't been in such a hurry and had considered his situation, he would have realized what he would have needed to do to get the berries. Have you ever been in such a rush that your own impatience kept you from what you truly wanted? Furthermore, the ill effects of the situation were compounded by kicking the tree. It was not the tree's fault that Nanaboozhoo had acted rashly, and by casting the blame where it didn't belong, Nanaboozhoo only injured himself further. Nanaboozhoo let his emotions get the better of him more than once, and he ended up with a sore head and a sore foot to go along with his empty stomach.

Another tale in which Nanaboozhoo plays a less central but still critical role demonstrates some of the other dimensions to the trickster figure and story:[9]

> For a long time, roses flourished across the land. They were plentiful and multicolored and aromatic. They were both pleasant and

common, which also meant that nobody gave them all that much thought.

However, after a while the roses became less plentiful. At first, nobody noticed because there had been so many of them and there were still lots of them all around everywhere. But the rose population continued to steadily thin. Not so coincidentally, the rabbit population began to expand and fatten.

After another while a few of the animals finally started to notice that the roses were not nearly as abundant as they once were. In addition, the roses that remained were not as colorful or tall or strong as they had been in the past. This started to concern the hummingbirds and the bees, who depended on the nectar from the flowers. Before long, it also started to concern the bears, who depended on the honey produced by the bees. The three species would occasionally privately grumble to each other about the situation, mostly to confirm their own suspicions—"Hey have you noticed that . . ." "Does this seem strange to you?" "It kind of seems like something weird is going on . . ."—but they kept it among themselves.

Eventually humans also started to feel like something was amiss, but nobody could explain why. Things just seemed a little off. The landscape looked different, but nobody could explain how. It took more time and effort to find honey, which was not as plentiful or potent when it could be found. There was less noise from the bees. There were fewer hummingbirds dashing about from place to place. The bears were noticeably thinner, and their flesh was less sweet and more gamey. Despite all of this, humans brushed their concerns aside. They had seen cycles of decline before and regeneration always followed. Nobody seemed to think it was a big deal.

That is until one summer when there were no roses.

The bees and hummingbirds grew desperate and panicked. The bears became enraged. A big meeting was called, which everyone attended. After days of intense discussion it was decided to dispatch the swiftest of the animals to the furthest reaches of the land to see if they could locate any remaining roses. After several days of searching, there was one weak, pitiful rose found clinging desperately to the side of a mountain. A hummingbird carried the delicate, suffering flower back to the meeting, where the animals asked the rose what happened. With a pale, halting cadence the rose told the group that the rabbits had eaten all of his kind.

In unison, the heads of all the other animals turned to look at the rabbits. The pudgy rabbits gave a quick, wry smile and a shrug before they shot off, trying to escape. But the other animals caught the rabbits and thrashed at them. In so doing they stretched open their mouths and split their lips, which is why the mouths of rabbits look the way they do today. Still, the other animals were angry and were going to leave other permanent marks and perhaps even kill the rabbits when they all overheard the hoarse voice of the rose shouting as loud as it could. "Stop what you are doing! Yes, the rabbits are at fault but so are you! If you had tended to us and cared for us, none of us would be in this situation right now! Leave the rabbits alone!" Recognizing that the rose was correct, the angry mob around the rabbits slowly dissipated.

Nanaboozhoo had been sitting at the back of the meeting the whole time and had not participated in the angry mob. He had kept quiet during the proceedings because he felt that others were more invested in the situation than he was. But now he realized that he had to do something. So Nanaboozhoo stood up, which gained everyone's attention, and he walked over to the rose. "I want you to have these, my brother," he said, giving the rose thorns. "They will help you protect yourself from those who would thoughtlessly do you harm."

Then Nanaboozhoo turned to the rest of the group and addressed them. "It is easy for any of you to take a life. But not one of you can give it back." Then Nanaboozhoo departed the meeting, leaving the rest of the animals to ponder his words.

This story is more obviously didactic than the first. One need not dig too deeply to recognize the theme of ecological interconnectedness.[10] Thus, between the two we are able to see how trickster stories can be meant to entertain or teach or both. Moreover, these differing stories demonstrate the range of capacities for the trickster. In the first story Nanaboozhoo is a hapless fool driven by base human emotions and desires. In the second story it is Nanaboozhoo's wisdom and supernatural abilities that lead to a resolution. Nanaboozhoo can be as silly and ignorant and emotional as any one of us, but he also has an authority and capacity far beyond that of any human. He can make magic, change his form and that of others, and even cheat death. Yet, he can also suffer the indignities of everyday human foibles, leaving him to explain why he has a scar on his forehead from trying to eat berries.

Nanaboozhoo (and other trickster figures) can exhibit characteristics of both the human realm and the divine realm because Nanaboozhoo is both human and divine.[11] His mother was human and his father was a spiritual being.[12] As a product of this union, Nanaboozhoo exists on every degree of the spectrum between mere mortals and the gods. He lives both on our plane of existence and theirs and operates as the bridge between them. Consequently, he has the capacity to change both our world and theirs and regularly does so.[13] For example, Nanaboozhoo (like many other tricksters in many other cultures around the world) brought fire from the heavens to the people of the earth.[14] His supernatural exploits, often acts of theft, trickery, or bravery, have also netted humans canoes for travel, tobacco and ceremonies for religious purposes, and various foods for nourishment.[15] He is a nuisance and a troublemaker, and you should be wary of him if you cross his path because he is undoubtedly up to something. But he is also a teacher and a giver, and he makes our lives possible. Without Nanaboozhoo we simply could not exist. Nanaboozhoo, with all of his faults, abilities, and contradictions, is the essence of life.[16]

All of which gets us to the most significant point we need to make in relation to our understanding of the Supreme Court's treatment of plenary power. Put most simply and usefully for our purposes, tricksters are creators and trickster stories are the stories of creation. They help us understand our environment and how it came to be. Nanaboozhoo is not just the reason that roses have thorns; he is the reason why geese fly in a line, why the porcupine has quills, why the bark of birch trees has different colors, as well as many others aspects of our lived observations and experiences.[17] Like many others of his kind, Nanaboozhoo is even responsible for the very ground upon which we walk and live in the wake of a great flood.[18]

Again, in today's modern world in which we are ostensibly much more sophisticated and knowledgeable and worldly, it is easy to cast aside tricksters and trickster stories as superstitions of the past or playthings for children. But to juxtapose trickster stories on one side of the ring against "science" or "rationality" on the other side in a winner-take-all battle for the truth is to miss the point. The literality of trickster stories is much less important than their capacity to allow us to see and test the boundaries of the society in which we live. Often by misbehaving, Nanaboozhoo shows us how we should behave lest we end up with a sore forehead and foot to go along with our empty stomach. Yet Nanaboozhoo also allows us to imagine a world beyond the lines that we have drawn for ourselves. Through his cleverness, ingenuity, and bravery he invites us to test the limits of what we believe we know and what we think we can accomplish. For example, in bringing fire to humanity (according to many of the tellings), Nanaboozhoo had to shape-shift, travel a great distance, and hide the fire on his body.[19] Obviously, this is not to suggest that Native peoples somehow believed they could, say, literally shape-shift because Nanaboozhoo and others of his ilk were able to but rather that such stories sparked contemplation and allowed the imagination to flourish. In other words, Nanaboozhoo, like any other trickster, disrupted the status quo, offering in its stead a pathway to innovation and creativity.[20]

Furthermore, while we might struggle to find the tricksters of the past in the modern world, we still admire their spirit and function. We still laud those who "change the game" or "break all the rules" in a way that alters our perspective or offers something new and beneficial to society. I first came upon the question that has led to this book about two decades before I began writing it. Back then smartphones didn't exist. Today you can hardly function in society without one. At some point between then and now, someone had to imagine the smartphone and bring it into existence. Someone had to conceptualize a vision of the world in which the smartphone was real and then made it happen. That person was operating in the space created by the trickster.[21]

With that in mind it becomes possible to recognize the story that the Supreme Court is telling about plenary power as its own trickster story. However, it is the colonizer's perverse, self-serving manipulation of the genre. Let's consider the situation from Nanaboozhoo's perspective:

> One day, Nanaboozhoo was walking along, minding his own business, when he happened to notice a group of people milling about in the distance. They were all similarly attired in long black dresses even though most of them appeared to be men. Well, you don't see that everyday, he thought to himself. But who am I to judge? I've been known to dress up like a woman from time to time.[22]
>
> Curious as to what was going on, Nanaboozhoo inched closer to the group until he could tell that there were nine of them. They were huddled together, constantly bickering in close conversation. He grew afraid at the harsh tones with which they addressed one another, but he couldn't help but wonder what was making them speak that way to each other, so he kept taking cautious steps toward the group. He figured if he could just find a place that was within earshot but out of their line of sight . . .
>
> But Nanaboozhoo was a bit too clumsy and far too curious, and before he knew it, nine heads shot up from their huddled conversation and were staring directly at him. They looked at each other for a moment before one of the nine spoke. "I'm so glad that you are here, Indian. We've got something that we need to say to you."
>
> Nanaboozhoo looked askance for a moment. What did that one just call me? he thought to himself. But he quickly gathered himself. "Well, hello folks. My name is Nanab . . ."
>
> A different one interrupted. "We are here to let you know that, now that this land is ours, we have given ourselves authority over you. Also, it is our solemn duty to protect you. In order to fulfill this obligation, we are requiring you to do everything that we say. You must live how and where we tell you to live. You must refrain from the behaviors that we don't like. You must start acting more like us. For starters, let's cut that hair."

Nanaboozhoo was immediately frightened and tried to run, but he found that he couldn't get very far. His arms and legs and body still moved like they used to, but he couldn't put any distance between himself and the nine people watching him. It was like he was trapped in a bubble. Their magic was already working on him, and he was unable to resist. They approached him and cut his hair and twisted his tongue and made him feel bad about himself.

Nanaboozhoo was flustered and sad and angry. He became compelled to challenge the group of nine. "What right do any of you have to do this to me? Why do you think you can treat me this way? Where did you get the power to act in this manner?"

The group of nine looked at each other before chuckling. Yet another spoke up. "Yes, I suppose we do have to explain it to you, don't we, Indian? How could we expect someone of your status to understand?" He shook his head at the seeming foolishness of the group.

And yet another continued. "You see, you are uncivilized. You are ignorant and unlearned. You don't use the land the right way. You talk to the natural world as if it were your relative. You don't know who to pray to or how to do it. You are brave and high-spirited, but you are also weak in the mind and in the flesh. You get too rowdy when you drink, you're not nearly ashamed enough of your body, and you are too generous with your family and community. Is any of this getting through to you? Are you starting to see what the problem is?"

Nanaboozhoo thought to himself no, he didn't see the problem, but he kept his mouth shut.

Still yet another one continued. "There are many of us who see potential in you. You could do great things . . . Well, OK, maybe not great things. I mean . . ." He paused and the words emerged a little more carefully. "What I am trying to say is that you are not irredeemable. You may not have all the natural advantages that we have, but you could be a productive member of society with a little training. You might make a fine tradesman."

And still yet another spoke. "Your primitive ways were enough for you to get along before, but now that we are here, it is only right that we who are civilized show you the proper way to live. We will protect you. But we must exercise authority over you. It is for your own good. Isn't this obvious?"

Nanaboozhoo grew increasingly frustrated, but he was still unable to escape or fight back, so he knew that his only option was to reason with the group of nine. "Great fathers, I recognize that I am ignorant of your ways, so please have patience with me. I hope that you can help me understand. I know that we have our differences, but are we so different? Are we not all human beings? Do we not all eat and sleep and breathe and love? And if we have all these things in common, then why do you have this power over me?"

Another of the nine spoke up. "We are stronger, smarter, and better than you, Indian. That is why we have this power. That is why we must use it. It is for your own good."

"But there are nine of you," Nanaboozhoo retorted. "Surely one of you is the strongest, smartest, and best. Does that person have the same power over the rest of the group?"

The nine looked at each other quizzically. "Of course not," one said. "That's no way to run a society of free men."

"Yeah," said another. "We fought a big war against this guy who lives across the ocean who thinks HE'S the great father just so we didn't have to live like that anymore. It was right next door. I can't believe you didn't notice it."

Nanaboozhoo had definitely noticed it but he was determined to stay on topic. "So what makes me so different?" Nanaboozhoo asked. "Why do you need this power over me but not each other?"

The group of nine rolled their eyes.

But Nanaboozhoo persisted. He kept asking why the group of nine needed to keep him trapped but were willing to let each other roam free. He kept demanding to know the difference between him and them. He kept inquiring over and over again what made them superior and him inferior. Nanaboozhoo could be quite insistent when he started asking questions.

For the longest time the group of nine ignored Nanaboozhoo. They pretended that he had no voice. They tried to shout him down whenever he got louder. They turned their backs to him. This went on for years and years, but Nanaboozhoo never stopped asking. And when he listened very carefully, he was pretty sure he could also hear others in the distance asking similar questions.

Much time passed in this manner. In the beginning the group of nine appeared unfalteringly confident in themselves. But as the days and months and years and decades wore on, Nanaboozhoo could see their apprehension grow. The group of nine began to look less and less sure of itself. At some point, Nanaboozhoo could tell that he was able to move about a little more freely than when the group of nine first arrived—although still not as freely as before he had stumbled across them. Eventually the group of nine looked worried. It was clear that they understood that their old magic was not as potent as it once was. They huddled together, trying to decide what to do.

Nanaboozhoo watched their intense conversation (all while still asking questions). Eventually he figured out that they were trying to make new magic. All of a sudden, each one of the nine reached toward the sky. Their arms started to grow and extended further and further toward the clouds. Their arms grew so long that they reached up too far into the sky for Nanaboozhoo to see their hands. After a long while of reaching around in the heavens Nanaboozhoo could tell that the arms were receding. As they descended, Nanaboozhoo could see that the hands were holding something. Finally he could tell what it was: a piece of parchment.

The nine looked over the piece of parchment intently for a long time before raising their heads and smiling. They sauntered over to Nanaboozhoo with contented grins. "We have your answer, Indian," one of them said.

"What is that?" Nanaboozhoo asked, looking at the parchment.

"It is the source of our magic," said one. "And it also explains why we have power over you."

The group pushed the parchment in front of Nanaboozhoo's face and pointed. They excitedly waited for Nanaboozhoo to read and understand. But he was confused. He looked up from the paper into the faces of the expectant group of nine and found no additional clarity.

Nanaboozhoo even grew a little embarrassed. He meekly said, "All it says is 'commerce.'"

"He understands!" one of the group of nine shouted.

"It makes sense!" another yelled.

"The question has finally been answered!" exclaimed another.

The group of nine celebrated by dancing, hugging, and giving each other high fives. "We have demonstrated to Nanaboozhoo why we have power over him!" one squealed. "Perhaps now he will stop bothering us with all of his questions," added another. "Thank goodness! I was wondering if we had lost our magic," another one let slip before quickly shutting up after being glared at by the others. There was a palpable relief among the group of nine after consulting the source of their magic. But as Nanaboozhoo watched, he could also tell that a sense of unease continued to linger. They were still not as sure as they had once been. He even thought he heard one particularly grumpy member of the group off in the corner by himself mumbling about "commerce."

Nanaboozhoo assessed the situation. They don't actually believe it, he said to himself. They don't believe in their magic like they once did.

I better ask more questions, he thought.

The story that the Supreme Court is telling about the constitutionalization of plenary power has many of the characteristics of a trickster story. It has powerful beings who make important choices. It has a magical conjuring that brings something new into the world. It claims to explain the natural order of things. It attempts to follow the path and demonstrate the same authority as a trickster story.

But the constitutionalization of plenary power is not an act of creation; it is an act of destruction. It truncates the humanity of Native peoples and the sovereignty of Native nations by perpetuating the process of colonization under the guise of the law. It encases Native America in a permanent state of infantilization by claiming this is the will of the colonizer's highest authority. It is not a story of growth or development, but rather it actively inhibits these things. It is a selfish story in which the self-appointed protagonists use their magical amulet to try to convince everyone, including themselves, that their oppressive acts and beliefs are legitimate and justified and even righteous. It does not open up possibilities; it curtails them.

Furthermore, trickster stories give us the ability to make sense of the world by explaining its development. But the story that the Supreme Court tells about the constitutionalization of plenary power does not describe how the natural world came to be. Rather, it forces an unnatural order on the world into existence. It is the colonizer imposing the ethos of colonization on everyone involved through the application of the colonizer's law. In order for one to believe both that "all men are created equal" with "certain unalienable rights" and also that the all-encompassing version of plenary power in which the federal government can do (and often has done) whatever it wants with Native America is justified under the U.S. Constitution, then one must also believe that Native peoples are not "men." Native peoples become—or, more in keeping with how the story is told, always were—less than human because the "magic" that is inured in this trickster story converts the racist foundations that the colonizers employed to justify their efforts into constitutional doctrine. This (ugly, manipulative, irresponsible version of a) trickster story simply does not allow for all peoples to be understood as equals.[23]

In summation, the story that the Supreme Court is telling about the constitutionalization of plenary power wants to be a trickster story. It is claiming the power, capacity, and authority of a trickster story. It uses magic to change the world. But it is a grotesque bastardization of the genre. Much like a foolish child playing with matches, it demonstrates that the Supreme Court either does not know or does not care about the capacity of trickster stories. It is not the colonizer understanding and living in harmony with the natural world but rather the colonizer pretending that the unequal world that it has created is natural and normal.

The story they have chosen to tell is wrong. They know it and we know it. ***It is the worst trickster story ever told***.

It is time to tell a better story.

So why aren't we?

It is obvious why the colonizer is invested in continuing to tell the worst trickster story ever told. To that end, I am less curious as to why the Supreme Court has manufactured a constitutional basis for the all-encompassing version of plenary power and now wants to claim that it is traditional. Rather, I am more curious about myself and the people like me. As noted in Chapter 1, many tribal advocates (as well as others operating within this body of law) continue to assert that the Indian Commerce Clause is the basis for the all-encompassing version of plenary power.[24] To be fair, this is not a universal practice, and we will sharpen this point considerably in about a page. Still, there is a whole heck of a lot of material out there produced by a lot of really smart people that asserts the constitutional nature of plenary power without much question. For example, the 2022 edition of the *American Indian Law Deskbook*, a resource developed by and primarily for lawyers in state attorney general offices, flatly states, "Congress's power over tribal affairs derives principally from the Indian Commerce Clause."[25] The most recent edition of the famous *Handbook of Federal Indian Law* (or the Cohen *Handbook*)—regarded as the most authoritative source in the field—states, "Federal power to regulate Indian affairs derives from the text and structure of the Constitution. The Constitution both defines and limits national powers, and, as interpreted by the Supreme Court, provides ample support for the national regulation of Indian affairs."[26] A leading casebook (casebooks are generally the primary resource for law students in their classes) states, "The Court has alluded variously to several federal constitutional powers, including the Treaty Clause, the War Power, the Property Clause, as supporting legislative and executive authority over Indian affairs. Today federal power over Indian affairs is accepted as tracing primarily to the Indian Commerce Clause, Article I, Section 8, Clause 3, the only express grant of federal power concerning Indians."[27] A primer for those looking to learn the field states, "By virtue of the Indian Commerce Clause, the U.S. Congress is empowered within the federal government to regulate Indian affairs. The confines of Indian affairs originally related to the acquisition of Indian land and the regulation of trade with Indians, but that definition and the accompanying power has expanded in scope over the years. Federal courts have long since recognized congressional power to enact laws well beyond trade and commerce, including laws that govern otherwise internal tribal issues."[28]

Again, to be fair, I am not the first person to notice or question the worst trickster story ever told. Tribal advocates are hardly monolithic or in total agreement in an unquestioning belief that the Indian Commerce Clause authorizes the all-encompassing version of plenary power. In fact, most folks seem to recognize the incongruity of the Supreme Court's story about plenary power.[29] And yet, as evidenced from the previous sampling of authoritative sources, there is also an undeniable thread of acquiescence to the claims of the Supreme Court.[30] Tribal advocates are also telling the worst trickster story ever told. So why are we doing it?

There are two primary reasons why tribal advocates are also telling this story, both of which help us understand why this happens, each in its own way (regardless of whether or not we find them wholly satisfactory). The first is fairly simple, easy to understand, and even somewhat reasonable. Sometimes tribal advocates echo the worst trickster story ever told because their primary concern is with something other than the worst trickster story ever told. For example, the primary purpose of the materials quoted previously—the treatises, the casebook, and the primer—are to help students and others understand the state of the law. This is a different purpose from advocating for what the law should be. Consequently, if the Supreme Court claims (as it presently does) that plenary power is justified under the Indian Commerce Clause, then any work of scholarship that seeks to aid others in understanding the state of the law will necessarily parrot the worst trickster story ever told. Along those same lines, sometimes a scholar will be concerned with something other than plenary power—say, a specific statute, case, or other aspect of the law. Often that scholar might write something like "Congress has the plenary power authority to pass Statute X under the Indian Commerce Clause" to create a pathway to consider Statute X, the true object of the scholar's attention. Thus, we might ask whether it is reasonable to critique a work of scholarship for failing to address a problem it did not set out to contemplate or solve.

The second reason tribal advocates are also telling the worst trickster story ever told is a bit more complicated. There is definitely a logic behind it, but it is circular in nature, forever leading us back to the same fundamental problem. We might call this second reason the Indian Child Welfare Act (ICWA) conundrum.

In order to understand the ICWA conundrum, it is necessary to return to the Allotment Era of federal policy. As described in Chapter 1, the Allotment Era of the late nineteenth and early twentieth centuries was defined by the attempts of federal officials (and others with their own motivations) to destroy tribes and tribalism. It was an all-out assault on Native America and Native ways of life in the name of "civilizing" Native individuals.

That being noted, how to best understand the motivations behind the Allotment Era is less clear than it may appear at first glance. Many of the folks leading these efforts regarded themselves as humanitarians (although, again, there were plenty of people who had selfish motivations as well).[31] They honestly and earnestly believed that the only way to "save" Native peoples from the obviously disastrous effects of colonialism was to make them more like the colonists who had created the ill conditions in the first place. For example, reconsider the Richard Henry Pratt quotation that we first looked at in Chapter 1. Pratt certainly wanted to "kill the Indian," yet he also wanted to "save the man." To that end, the primary target was the culture (and the acquisition of land and other resources the colonizer found valuable), not necessarily the lives of Native peoples themselves (although yet again, there were those who would have preferred genocide).

Thus, it is important to recognize that the motivations of many of the actors of the Allotment Era and thereafter were hardly evil in their intent, as it will help us understand the ICWA conundrum in the modern context. And yet, even when we take this into consideration, it is undeniable that this self-understanding was rooted in the same racism and sense of superiority that was endemic to the Supreme Court cases of the same time period.[32] The assault on Native culture was, in significant part, perpetrated by people who thought they were doing what was best. Then again, as we also know, the road to H-E-double-hockey-sticks is paved with good intentions.

Having considered some of the parties involved, let's refocus on

Native culture itself, which was very much in the crosshairs during the Allotment Era. The goal was to eradicate a way of life. And where do you attack if you want to kill a culture?

The children.[33]

One of the major pillars of the Allotment Era was education in general and boarding schools in particular.[34] Many reformers of the day considered adult Native people as a lost cause too deeply steeped in their backward ways to be saved. Children, on the other hand, still had the potential to be civilized and assimilated into the dominant American culture.[35] Schooling itself was important, but for many reformers of the day, this was not enough. Children needed to be fully removed from an environment that might hinder their development. This included not just their communities but their families as well.

To that end, the federal government developed an educational system that is best remembered for off-reservation boarding schools (although it was hardly limited to them).[36] By 1908 there were twenty-seven of these institutions, mostly in the West, as well as over one hundred more on-reservation boarding schools.[37] Many children were taken away from their families, sent to faraway institutions to discourage them from running away, and forced into patterns of colonial acculturation. In the chronically underfunded boarding schools, generally run on the model of a military academy, the conditions were often difficult.[38] Disease and death were common, as were homesickness, malnourishment, and resistance.[39] Many Native people survived, and some even thrived, but the experience as a whole took its toll on Native America.

As with many of the subjects that we have covered in this book, a fuller accounting of boarding schools and their effects on Native nations, individuals, and culture is better found elsewhere.[40] For our purposes, it suffices to note that removing Native children from Native homes became something that was not only acceptable in the Allotment Era; it was often considered a necessity. Thus began a pattern in which a Native family could expect to see at least one child, and probably more, removed from the home.[41]

The phenomenon of boarding schools and their prominence as a major tool in assimilation efforts was more or less complete by the

1930s, although they continued to exist long thereafter, and a few are still around today. Nonetheless, one of their major consequences persisted—Native children were still regularly being taken from the home. As boarding schools waned, the perpetrators of the disruption of Native family life increasingly became states. In the balance of authority between the federal government and states in the federalism model, family law issues—marriage, divorce, adoption, custody, and the like—are generally recognized as almost exclusively within the purview of the states.[42] Thus, states were well positioned to continue the efforts that the federal government and boarding schools had begun.

This troubling trend was exacerbated in the 1950s during the Termination Era of federal policy when federal bureaucrats, with help from the Child Welfare League of America, devised the Indian Adoption Project.[43] The Termination Era, introduced in Chapter 3, was akin to its older cousin, the Allotment Era, in that it sought an end to tribes and tribalism, and the Indian Adoption Project was in line with that goal. The purpose of the project was to find suitable non-Native homes for Native children who, as the thinking went, were inherently disadvantaged in a Native environment.[44] As were those who advocated for boarding schools, once again seemingly kindhearted people were perpetuating racist understandings of Native peoples and families and doing more harm than good.

The combined efforts of the federal government, the states, and adoption advocates were shockingly effective. By the 1970s the federal government had estimated that somewhere between one-quarter and one-third of Native children had been removed from their home.[45] Statistics at the state level were often even more pronounced. Native children were taken out of the home at a rate four times greater than non-Native children in Minnesota; thirteen times greater in Montana.[46] In South Dakota, Native children accounted for only 7 percent of the juvenile population yet for 40 percent of the adoptions in the state.[47] In Wisconsin a Native child was 1,600 percent more likely than a non-Native child to be removed from the home.[48]

In the Termination Era of the 1950s these numbers would likely have been celebrated by policy makers. However, in the early days of the Self-

Determination Era in the 1970s they were rightfully identified as an ongoing historical atrocity. The decades-long assault on tribal family life had significant negative consequences for tribal nations and individuals. For tribal nations, the consistent drain on the population created a perpetual threat to the continuing vitality of the nations themselves. For individuals, removal from their tribal home often meant a lack of connection anywhere. These folks often felt out of place in the non-Native homes and communities in which they were placed yet also lacked a meaningful engagement within what was or would have been their tribal nation.

In 1978 Congress responded to this crisis by passing the Indian Child Welfare Act.[49] As does any big piece of congressional legislation, ICWA does a number of things, but its main purpose was to return the authority to make choices about tribal children back to tribal nations. Without getting too deep in the weeds, ICWA grants tribal nations significant control over child custody proceedings—things like adoptions and foster care placements. Thus, tribal courts, rather than state courts, have much more say over a tribal nation's juvenile population under the law.[50]

Before we run the risk of going overboard, we ought to be clear about ICWA. The statute has not fixed everything related to Native families. Its application across the United States has been uneven in large part because many states—which tend to be reluctant to cede any of their authority, particularly in an area like family law, which has traditionally been reserved to them—have historically found ways around ICWA or ignored it altogether.[51] Thus, Native children continue to be disproportionately taken out of their homes and represented in the foster care system.[52]

That being noted, ICWA has also been a resounding success and may very well be the most important piece of legislation in the Self-Determination Era of federal policy. When and where ICWA has been implemented and adhered to properly, it has kept Native children in their immediate and extended families at a greater rate, it has shortened the amount of time Native children have spent in foster care systems, Native children have become significantly less likely to "age out" of the foster care system, and tribal nations have regularly provided more services to

Native children and families than they would have otherwise gotten.[53] Those states that have warmed to ICWA have found that the legislation has not only been to the benefit of Native children but that it has also been to their own benefit and has regularly been regarded as a model to emulate for their own state law.[54] ICWA has engendered so much goodwill that it has been lauded as the "gold standard of child welfare practice."[55] In short, ICWA has been a very good thing for Native America and for others as well.

And because ICWA has been so good to Native America, that means that someone has been determined to ruin it. To be perfectly fair, many of those who have attacked ICWA understand themselves as pure of heart and well-meaning as their forebears from the Allotment and Termination Eras. Nonetheless, the consequences are the same: to suit their own view of the world, certain non-Native peoples have sought to destroy a positive thing for Native nations that Native people overwhelmingly approve of and that protects Native children. In this instance, a coalition of forces including would-be adoptive parents and hostile states emboldened by a conservative think tank was able to bring a case to the Supreme Court with the argument that ICWA was race-based legislation that should be struck down as unconstitutional.[56] The case, *Haaland v. Brackeen*, was decided in the summer of 2023 and revolved around a question that you probably are able to anticipate by this point in the book.

Is ICWA constitutional?

And thus the ICWA conundrum begins to come into focus. The way that American law is structured does not allow for a question like "is Statute X constitutional?" to exist on its own. It is forever accompanied by its sister question: "What part of the U.S. Constitution authorizes Congress to pass Statute X?" Consequently, an American court cannot rule on the constitutionality of a statute without identifying what part of the U.S. Constitution is under question.

So it is with *Brackeen*, with Justice Amy Coney Barrett telling yet another version of the worst trickster story ever told. We will contemplate this new version of the old story shortly, but before we do, we need to briefly note a couple of important points. First, astute readers with some familiarity with ICWA might be wondering if the statute is the right example to illustrate the issue.[57] After all, doesn't ICWA mostly operate as a limitation on states, and thus isn't it better understood as an exercise of the original version of plenary power? That is a fair question and one that is answered by connecting a few ideas together. We must begin by noting that the line between those exercises of the older version of plenary power articulated by John Marshall and the newer, all-encompassing version can be blurry. Where one version of plenary power begins and the other ends is not always clear. For example, Title II of ICWA operates more directly on tribal nations, stating, "The objective of every Indian child and family service program shall be to prevent the breakup of Indian families."[58] Title II is mostly about funding and lacks the draconian overreach of more obviously intrusive legislation, yet it still seeks to shape tribal governance and services. Furthermore, as we noted in the last chapter, the Supreme Court destabilized the distinction between the two versions of plenary power in the Allotment Era, making it hard to distinguish one from the other within the law. Barrett's opinion demonstrates, once again, this lack of precision, stating that "we have explained that 'virtually all authority over Indian commerce and Indian tribes' lies with the Federal Government."[59] As a consequence, tribal advocates also tend to lack this precision as well, making larger claims than might seem necessary were American law and the Supreme Court to more fully regard distinct versions of plenary power.[60] Thus, ICWA is still eminently capable of demonstrating the conundrum that tribal advocates face, as the analysis of the issue would be no different were we to center our focus on the Major Crimes Act (contemplated in *Kagama*), the Indian Civil Rights Act (contemplated in the last chapter), the statute at the heart of *Lara* (contemplated more times in this book than I care to count), or any other American law that reaches into Native America.

The second important point to note is that the Supreme Court fully upheld the constitutionality of ICWA in *Brackeen*. The decision was understandably hailed as a significant victory for tribal nations.[61] Yet, how the Supreme Court came to its ruling is all too distressingly familiar, and the fact that it was a victory for Native America further helps illuminate the ICWA conundrum.

Getting back to Barrett's opinion, she began—as did many others before her—with the claim that the federal government has plenary power over Native America. "In a long line of cases, we have characterized Congress's power to legislate with respect to the Indian tribes as 'plenary and exclusive.' Our cases leave little doubt that Congress's power in this field is muscular, superseding both tribal and state authority."[62] Of course, a totally ripped, absolutely jacked power like this doesn't come out of nowhere. As has become the tradition in telling the worst trickster story ever told, Barrett reminded us that "a power unmoored from the Constitution would lack both justification and limits. So like the rest of its legislative powers, Congress's authority to regulate Indians must derive from the Constitution, not the atmosphere."[63]

Thus, the sister question entered the picture: Where in the U.S. Constitution does this totally buff power come from? As we noted in Chapter 3, Barrett offered four sources of authority, beginning, of course, with the Indian Commerce Clause. "The Indian Commerce Clause authorizes Congress 'to regulate Commerce . . . with the Indian Tribes.' We have interpreted the Indian Commerce Clause to reach not only trade, but certain 'Indian affairs' too."[64] Barrett also pointed to the Treaty Clause, "preconstitutional powers necessarily inherent in any federal government," and the trust responsibility.[65] According to Barrett, "In sum, Congress's power to legislate with respect to Indians is well established and broad."[66]

The incongruity and dark magic of the worst trickster story ever told are on open display for anyone willing to look. Barrett claimed that plenary power "must derive from the Constitution," yet only two of her four sources of authority engage with the text of the document. That would be like a chef stating that the only thing she can cook are vegetarian entrees such as roasted eggplant, cheese ravioli, steak tartare, and bacon-wrapped zucchini. Furthermore, the references to the text of the U.S. Constitution are decidedly perfunctory. The Indian Commerce Clause received little more than a mention, and the Treaty Clause makes no reference to any specific treaties. As we noted in Chapter 3, Barrett seemed very much aware that the foundations of this argument are not solid. "Admittedly, our precedent is unwieldy, because it rarely ties a challenged statute to a specific source of constitutional authority."[67] But, as is characteristic of the worst trickster story ever told, any concerns are rendered impotent by a self-fulfilling incantation.[68] Not only is plenary power declared "well established and broad," but we are further told that "consistent with that breadth, we have not doubted Congress's ability to legislate across a wide range of areas, including criminal law, domestic violence, employment, property, tax, and trade."[69]

That the Supreme Court would continue to tell the worst trickster story ever told—in which the all-encompassing version of plenary power is authorized under the U.S. Constitution—is not a surprise. What can be surprising, however, is how often tribal advocates repeat the story. Admittedly and characteristically of the ICWA conundrum, those in support of Native America tend to be much more careful and nuanced in their tellings, but the basic structure of the story remains the same. For example, the tribal defendants in *Brackeen* stated both that "this Court has long held that Congress has broad Indian-affairs powers—indeed, 'plenary authority to legislate for the Indian tribes in all matters' " and that "this 'plenary power' derives 'explicitly' from the Constitution."[70] In support of the tribal interests in *Brackeen*, the American Bar Association, a well-known and very influential organization of attorneys, pointed to the usual constitutional suspects, including the Indian Commerce Clause, before stating, "This Court has held repeatedly that these constitutional authorities vest Congress with unique powers over Indian affairs that it does not have with respect to other groups."[71] Senator James Abourezk of South Dakota, the main architect behind ICWA, stated, "The legislative process and ultimate enactment of ICWA fell within Congress's plenary authority in Indian affairs, a power with origins in the Indian Commerce Clause."[72]

All of which is to note that the argument in *Brackeen* over the ICWA statute sharpens the ICWA conundrum by demonstrating that plenary power has been a double-edged sword for Native America. As you will recall, we began this crazy journey way back in the 1880s in the Allotment Era with the very same question about the constitutionality of a very different statute. In 1885 Congress passed the Major Crimes Act, which purported to extend federal criminal jurisdiction into Indian

Country. The Major Crimes Act was (and remains, as it is still in force) indicative of both the types of laws that were passed during this time and the spirit of the Allotment Era in that it intruded upon the inner workings of tribal nations and sought to reshape Native lives, perspectives, and governance. Not that you could ever forget by this point, but as a reminder, our old friend Justice Stanley Miller, in a case with which we have become all too familiar—*Kagama*—upheld the constitutionality of the Major Crimes Act, further bringing the all-encompassing version of plenary power to the forefront in American law. It was the beginning of the worst trickster story ever told, and the Major Crimes Act and statutes like it are precisely the types of exercise of the all-encompassing version of plenary power upon Native life and sovereignty that tribal advocates have been questioning and challenging for years upon years.

ICWA, on the other hand, is a product of the Self-Determination Era in which the federal government (for the most part) has been actively supporting tribal governments and sovereignty. It is one of many statutes of the era that has aided Native America in its efforts to reinvest in itself. There is certainly room to critique the statutes of the Self-Determination Era: things like the Indian Self-Determination and Education Assistance Act, the American Indian Religious Freedom Act, the Indian Arts and Crafts Act, and more.[73] Yet, they are very different from their counterparts from the Allotment and other eras of federal policy in that they generally seek to foster Native governance, culture, and sovereignty rather than disrupt it. Moreover, Native advocates have not only fought for this type of legislation; their efforts have also often been directly responsible for it.

And yet, according to the worst trickster story ever told, the "good" statutes of the Self-Determination Era are just as dependent on the supposedly constitutionally grounded, all-encompassing version of plenary power for their authority as are the "bad" statutes of the Allotment and other eras for their authority. To point to a particularly on-the-nose example, pretty much the first thing that the ICWA statute itself declares is that "clause 3, section 8, article I of the United States Constitution provides that 'The Congress shall have Power . . . To regulate Commerce . . . with Indian tribes' and, through this and other constitutional authority,

Congress has plenary power over Indian affairs."[74] Plenary power is at the heart of every engagement between Native America and the United States under American law.

Therein lies the ICWA conundrum. Tribal advocates would rather be without the "bad" stuff from the Allotment and other eras but very much want to keep the "good" stuff like ICWA. In fact, keeping the good stuff becomes vital and necessary to defend against the bad stuff. However, in American law the same rationale that allows for the good stuff also allows for the bad stuff. Thus, tribal advocates are compelled to repeat the worst trickster story ever told in their efforts to defend, perpetuate, and expand ICWA and the rest of the good stuff. But, as we noted a handful of pages ago, the logic is circular, which makes it a conundrum. In order to defend against the colonizer, tribal advocates end up reinforcing the work done by the colonizer in the name of colonization. The worst trickster story ever told works its magic on all of us by making us tell it over and over again.[75]

So is there any solution to the ICWA conundrum? How do tribal advocates escape the self-realizing circle in which they can deconstruct the effects of colonialism only by reinforcing them? Are there no alternatives?

At the risk of boring you with repetition, I have to again note that I am hardly the first person to notice or question the worst trickster story ever told. In fact, lots of very smart people for whom I have the utmost respect have confronted the ICWA conundrum.[76] We will consider some of what they have had to say and propose in more depth in the next chapter. But for now, it suffices to note that there seems to be one more really important reason that tribal advocates are not always as forceful as they could be in offering and advocating for alternatives to the worst trickster story ever told. Obviously, some of it is simple pragmatism. Lawyering is, first and foremost, a results-based business. Lawyers have clients and clients want to win their cases. To that end, clients tend to be less interested in testing novel legal theories that do not have any track record of success and more interested in going with what has worked in the past. As noted previously, winning cases often involves retelling the worst trickster story ever told, so that is what tribal advocates do for their clients. But there is another motivation that is lurking behind this and is often obscured by an easily assertible pragmatism. It is an especially powerful force that we tend not to want to acknowledge but that seems to be exerting a significant amount of influence in this matter.

Fear.

Many tribal advocates—not altogether unreasonably, it is important to note—are of the belief that any alternative that the Supreme Court would come up with to the worst trickster story ever told would inevitably be worse than the worst trickster story ever told. Again, this line of reasoning is hardly unfounded, particularly since, as we noted in Chapter 3, the main proponent for rethinking the basis of federal engagement with Native America has been Justice Clarence Thomas. As we also noted in Chapter 3, Thomas is a polarizing figure, and reactions to him can sometimes seem visceral, especially since he has often (although hardly exclusively) voted against tribal interests. Thus, tribal advocates who agree with Thomas's basic premise that the Supreme Court ought to rethink the relationship between the United States and Native America are nonetheless leery of what the end result of such a process would be under Thomas's stewardship.

Thomas's own words very much create the space for ambiguity if not outright skepticism. For example, in *Lara,* the case where he began his campaign for reform (and which been central to our examination of the worst trickster story ever told), he very explicitly laid out the problem as he saw it. "In my view, the tribes either are or are not separate sovereigns, and our federal Indian law cases untenably hold both positions simultaneously."[77] Thomas focused on what he saw as the weaknesses of both sides of this are-they-or-aren't-they-sovereigns question without offering a conclusion. But his critique of tribal sovereignty in the case hardly inspired confidence among tribal advocates. "It is quite arguably the essence of sovereignty not to exist merely at the whim of an external government."[78] In the last ICWA case to reach the Supreme Court before *Brackeen,* Thomas fervently argued against the Indian Commerce Clause or any other portion of the U.S. Constitution supporting federal plenary power over Native America.[79] Yet, in the type of twist that tribal advocates feared after *Lara,* his rejection of the worst trickster story ever told led him to vote against tribal interests in the case.[80] However, in another case in which he once again challenged federal claims to plenary power—one in which tribal court criminal convictions were held in the same regard as state and federal criminal convictions—Thomas voted in favor of tribal interests. As has become his custom, he expressed discontent with both sides of the are-they-or-aren't-they-sovereigns coin.[81] But he also took a significant swipe at the concept of plenary power and its birthplace in American law, *Kagama*. "Until the Court rejects the fiction that Congress possesses plenary power over Indian affairs, our precedents will continue to be based on the paternalistic theory that Congress must assume all-encompassing control over the 'remnants of a race' for its own good."[82] Then again, he voted against tribal interests in *Brackeen*.

This is, more or less, where we stand today (although we will consider if we haven't taken a few extra steps in the next chapter). With a very unlikely leader in Thomas trying to move the Supreme Court in who-even-knows what direction, it is not an altogether unreasonable fear among some tribal advocates that anything that replaces the worst trickster story ever told would only be worse (than the worst).[83] After all, can Thomas be trusted to invoke something that is more understanding and respectful for Native America? How could anything of value that is new or different be built on ground this shaky? Isn't it better to just keep telling the story that we do know, warts and all, rather than risk losing the space that we have managed to maintain? Isn't it better to deal with the devil we've gotten to know and all that?

As you may have noticed, I have tried to be as deferential as possible to anyone who holds this viewpoint.[84] I have been doing this because, as I have noted more than once now, there is a strong thread of logic behind this thought process, and I have nothing but respect for others who have deeply considered and been forced to act under what we have been calling the ICWA conundrum. Nor do I want to cast aspersions on tribal advocates who have invoked the worst trickster story ever told in an effort to better Native America. This is not an easy space to live in, and tough choices have had to be made.

That being noted, one of the biggest problems with fear is that it tends to blind us to our situation rather than illuminate it. The dominant metaphor that people like me who teach this stuff tend to use to describe federal Indian policy is that of a pendulum. As history has shown, the general tenor of the times swings back and forth between eras when the federal government is more intent on limiting or even eliminating tribal sovereignty and times when the federal government is more tolerant and even supportive of it. The Self-Determination Era has, of course, been one of the stretches of time when the federal government has been supportive of tribal nations. To that end, we have seen a number of "good" uses of the all-encompassing version of plenary power. But if this pattern holds, eventually the Self-Determination Era will end and a new era will be marked by "bad" uses of plenary power. It has happened before; the threat remains ever present; who among us would ever bet on it never happening again? We should not let our fear prevent us from seeing what the future is likely to hold in our efforts to preserve the status quo.

Consequently, when that likely time comes, what will those of us who consider ourselves tribal advocates do?[85] What happens when we want to stem the tide of plenary power rather than enhance it? What do we do when the shaky ground we are currently on falls out from underneath our feet? Do we have a strategy for when the ICWA conundrum turns back into something like the Allotment conundrum or the Termination conundrum? What alternatives are available to us when we can no longer tell the worst trickster story ever told to protect ourselves?

Nanaboozhoo sat on the ground with his head in his hands for a very long time. He tried to think of a way out of his predicament, but he wasn't coming up with anything. This was unlike any other problem he had encountered before. He could not make magic like he had in the past. Answers were not easily within reach. He felt like he had lost his power. Sometimes all he could do was keep himself from crying. Sometimes he couldn't even do that.

Nanaboozhoo was about to give up all hope when all of a sudden he felt something he hadn't felt since he couldn't remember when. As he sat on the ground, a ray of sunshine spread across his back. It was just a small sliver, but it was warm and familiar and comforting. Nanaboozhoo raised his head for the first time in a long time. Then he smiled for the first time in a long time.

As is his way, curiosity eventually got the best of Nanaboozhoo. He stood up and turned around to look for the source of the light. At first the brightness overcame him, as it had been so long since the pale man's hands descended and left Nanaboozhoo and the other partygoers in darkness. But the light was not so great as to blind him, and eventually his eyes adjusted.

Nanaboozhoo could see that there was a very small opening between the pale man's hands that let in the shaft of light. The open space was not nearly big enough for a person to escape from the dome, but it did offer some illumination and some cheer. Nanaboozhoo watched as the other partygoers started to notice and gather around the light. Many remained grumpy about their situation and claimed that they preferred to sit in the dark, but others were joyful about the change. They planted a few things on the patch of ground where the light settled and watched them grow. They started to talk and laugh and share among each other again. The air seemed a little less thick and easier to breathe. Things were not the same as they had been when the party had started. There was still often too little to eat or too much burden to carry. But the situation was not quite as bad as it had once been. They were not completely in the dark. Nanaboozhoo tried to be thankful for this small blessing and was generally successful in his effort.

All of a sudden, the pale man's hands began to rumble. The tremendous sound and commotion frightened the partygoers. There was much yelling and cowering and scurrying to find a safe spot among the group. Nanaboozhoo had to admit that he also had ducked under something and hid his head in his arms again. However, before long the noise and motion subsided. The partygoers looked around, trying to assess the damage. What they found surprised them. Not only was there no additional damage; they could see more than they ever had been able to since the pale man's hands first descended upon them. There were now a number of small openings between the pale man's fingers, letting in even more light.

As with the first, none of these new openings were large enough for any of the partygoers to escape from under the pale man's hands. But they did allow the partygoers to see more and to do more. Many remembered their old ways and began to rekindle them. Many remembered the gifts that the pale man had given them when he first arrived and figured out how to use them. Many blended the old and the new into something that made sense in the present. The situation was still not ideal. The sky was still mostly clouded by the pale man's hands. But the partygoers, including Nanaboozhoo, made the best out of their circumstances.

And so it was for a period of time. But after a while the pale man's hands again rumbled and shook. This time they constricted. Many of the sources of light closed. The things that had been growing started to wither. The tools that the partygoers had used became less potent. Space became more cramped again, thickening the air and making it harder to breathe. Old grievances rose to the surface again, causing more fighting and arguing and harm. Not every source of light had closed, but not enough remained open to perpetuate the meager existence of the partygoers. Some lost their way. Some died. Others were stolen. Nanaboozhoo watched as the partygoers endured increased suffering.

And thus a pattern developed. At unpredictable intervals the pale man's hands would move. Sometimes they would expand, allowing more freedom and room to flourish. Sometimes they would constrict, imposing more suffering and oppression. None of the partygoers knew when it would happen nor what would happen. All of a sudden, without warning, they would hear the rumbling. Sometimes it made things better; sometimes it made things worse. Eventually it began to feel normal.

So it was one day when Nanaboozhoo heard the rumbling once again. He prepared for something bad to happen but was pleasantly surprised; after it was said and done, there seemed to be more light and space and opportunity than there had ever been under the pale man's hands. Sure, there were still problems. After all, aren't we all human? But as he looked upon all that he had grown and built and developed, he was as content as he had been in a long while. Many of the other partygoers also seemed to be doing as well as if not better than him. He may not have had all of his old magic back, but it was the strongest he had felt in a long time. As he paused for a moment to take it all in, a thought popped into his head.

"I can live like this."

All of a sudden, Nanaboozhoo could have sworn that he thought he heard the rumbling again. At the very least, he was sure that he had heard the first low groans that precipitated when the hands moved. He looked around and could see in the other partygoers' eyes that they had heard it as well. Everybody under the dome seemed to stop and listen and wait for what was coming next. After a number of tense, eerily quiet moments with breath held and tensions high, one of the partygoers let out a deep sigh of relief. Soon others did the same. Perhaps it had been a false alarm. Or maybe someone had figured out how to prevent this one from happening. Whatever the reason enough time had elapsed that the partygoers became convinced that the moment had passed. Nanaboozhoo had to admit that he felt the same way. But as the other partygoers joked about the non-incident and returned to their daily lives, Nanaboozhoo could not so quickly recover. He remained wary of what had almost happened and what might happen in the future. Another thought popped into his head.

"Can I live like this?"

FIVE *The Resolution?*

Nanaboozhoo decided to call a council and invited all of the other partygoers. Most of the partygoers were surprised by the invitation. Some didn't see the point. Others were skeptical, especially after what had happened the last time Nanaboozhoo had asked them to a gathering. Some openly grumbled about Nanaboozhoo wanting to stir up trouble again. But all were curious and decided to attend.

Nanaboozhoo knew that the council was going to be important, maybe the most important thing that he had ever done. So he got himself ready. He put on his fanciest, most oratorically inspiring clothes. He warmed up his voice and gathered his courage by practicing what he was going to say. He even ran some laps and did some push-ups to work off his nervous energy. He asked the giver of life to help him put his best foot forward.

As the council was about to start, Nanaboozhoo steeled himself. He was nervous, but he knew that he needed to be strong and humble enough to seek the wisdom of his compatriots. As he stood to start the proceedings, he could hear the murmur among the crowd dissipate. Eventually there was silence, and Nanaboozhoo knew it was now or never.

"My friends," he started. "I have asked you here today because I have had a question that has been troubling me for a long while now. I need to ask it and benefit from our collective wisdom. We must answer it because it is critical to our future. It may well be the most important question I have ever asked . . ."

Nanaboozhoo waited for a beat to let the gravity of the moment sink in. Then he raised an open hand with his arm bent at a slight angle toward the sky. "Can we live like this?" he asked with all of the drama in his voice that he could muster.

Would it be too cliché to claim that the only sound was crickets as a lonely tumbleweed drifted by? Anyway, there was a big, long pause when nobody moved or spoke. Nanaboozhoo felt himself frozen in place, not sure of what to do next since the obviousness of the situation was not as apparent to everyone else as it was to him. Finally, a voice from the back rang out and broke the impasse.

"What the &$#@ are you talking about, Nanaboozhoo?"

Thawed by the very direct question, Nanaboozhoo gathered himself. He cleared his throat and tried again. "I'm trying to ask if we can live like this," he said gesturing again with his own open hand toward the giant hands of the pale man that still enveloped them. "Aren't you tired of being afraid every time the big hands move?"

Another voice from the crowd rang out. "You got a big plan to get rid of the hands, Nanaboozhoo?" This made many of the partygoers chuckle.

"Well, no . . . Not exactly, I guess . . . But this isn't right, is it? We have to do something, don't we?"

Yet another voice from the crowd. "So what IS your plan, then?"

Nanaboozhoo stammered. "Well, uhhhhh, ummmm . . . I guess I'm not sure really. It just seems like someone should do something!"

Another partygoer challenged him. "Are you trying to cause trouble, Nanaboozhoo? Why do you want to start something? Don't you remember what happened the last time you called us all together?" This time the partygoer raised his own open hand to the sky. "Now we are all stuck here because of you, and you want us to listen to you again?"

With the crowd clearly turning against him, Nanaboozhoo became defensive. "That was not my fault! I didn't invite that guy to the party. I didn't make him fall out of a tree into our gathering. Sure, I did invite him to sit with us, but how was I supposed to know that he would grow the way that he did? How am I to blame?"

"What are you trying to do to us, Nanaboozhoo?" another partygoer wailed. "Do you have any idea what could happen if you disrupt the big hands? It could all come crashing down on us! We could all be squished! What would happen then? Do you want the big hands to wipe us out completely?"

"But this is what I am talking about!" Nanaboozhoo retorted. "The hands move whether we want them to or not. They could fall down upon us at any moment even if we are on our best behavior." And this crowd is never on its best behavior, Nanaboozhoo thought to himself. "Right now we are powerless to stop it. So shouldn't we do something to protect ourselves? I know that we've become reasonably comfortable with the status quo. Yes, sometimes the hands give us more space, but sometimes they give us less space, and I am tired of being afraid every time there is even the slightest indication that the hands might move again." Nanaboozhoo took a deep breath. He looked over the crowd. He couldn't tell if he was reaching them or if they were growing more angry with him. Mostly they seemed unmoved. He decided to make his final pitch. "Do you want to live like this? Are you willing to accept the constant fear of the hands moving just because it's not too bad right now? Or are you willing to try something different and new? Sure, I guess there is the possibility that it might make things worse, but it might make things much, much better. Maybe we don't have to live in constant fear of the hands moving. Maybe we can do something about it."

Another long pause ensued. Nanaboozhoo held his breath as he looked over the crowd. He wanted to talk more, to force the others to listen to his words until they agreed with him. But he knew he had had his say. It was up for the others to decide for themselves.

Finally another voice from the crowd emerged. "Well, you do whatever you want, Nanaboozhoo, but I'm going home."

Another partygoer stood up. "Yeah, I'm going home too. But whatever you do, Nanaboozhoo, don't mess everything up." Others snickered at this.

The floodgates were open. Soon nearly everyone was standing. Some drifted away by themselves. Others ambled off in groups, talking and laughing (probably about him, Nanaboozhoo thought). Despondent, Nanaboozhoo sat down and stared at the ground. He listened but could not make himself watch as nearly everybody left the council. Not long thereafter nearly everyone was gone. Nanaboozhoo tried to keep himself from crying. I have failed, he thought to himself. I couldn't get them to understand. Nanaboozhoo could not hold back the tears anymore. I'm not sure I want to live like this . . .

One partygoer remained with Nanaboozhoo, however. It was Coyote. Once everyone else was completely gone and once Nanaboozhoo looked like he might be ready to listen, Coyote approached.

"Nanaboozhoo, my friend," Coyote said as he pretended not to notice Nanaboozhoo trying to discreetly wipe away what remained of his tears. "It has been so interesting reading this book. You know, whenever someone needs a spokesperson for our kind, they usually come to me. But I am glad that Keith came to you this time. You are the right person for the job."

Nanaboozhoo lifted his head and saw Coyote's smile. "The thing you have to remember, my friend," Coyote said adding underlining for extra emphasis, "is that we are troublemakers."

Coyote's smile grew a little more wry. "We are never satisfied with the status quo. We change things. We shake things up. We make things new. We are meant to disrupt this world and make it see itself in ways it had never imagined before. We have a role to play and we play it well."

Coyote chuckled as he watched the cloud over Nanaboozhoo's head start to lift. "We anger the gods and we amuse the humans. We bumble and stumble, but we also make magic and goodness and life. We can't be anything other than what we are."

Then Coyote got surprisingly serious and looked directly into Nanaboozhoo's eyes as his own grew more intense.

"So be who you are, my friend."

A moment later Coyote's eyes softened and he smiled again. "Say, has anyone ever told you that you are the spitting image of Keith's son, Steven? Have you ever met Steven? Now THAT GUY is a trickster . . ." And with that Coyote darted off. Nanaboozhoo could hear Coyote mutter to himself as he sprinted away, "I could really use a good meal and a lonely woman to share it with . . ."

Nanaboozhoo was flabbergasted and had to take a moment to gather himself. But as he slowly stood, he realized what he needed to do. Without wasting any time, he set off to the giant hands.

When he got to a place where the hands met the ground, Nanaboozhoo looked up. The hands were larger and more vast than he had realized. But with his newfound resoluteness Nanaboozhoo remembered that he had encountered many formidable tasks, so he set out on his plan. He started climbing. Up and up and up he went, occasionally looking forward but never seeing an end in sight.

Finally, after days and days of climbing, Nanaboozhoo reached as high as he could go. He began to look around, and he noticed all of the gaps between the fingers that let in the light and the air for the folks below. He searched for the largest one and eventually found it. It was, of course, not big enough for him to escape his predicament, but it did allow him to squeeze his head through and see the pale man's face in the distance. The pale man's face was so far away that Nanaboozhoo was unsure that he would ever be able to hear him, but Nanaboozhoo hadn't come all this way to give up now. Nanaboozhoo shouted at the top of his lungs.

"Hello there . . . KingGeorgeWashingtonRedskinsThomasJefferson LouisanaPurchaseJohnMarshallTrilogyJohnsonMcIntoshGeorgia WorcesterRemovalTrailofTearsBrokenTreatyGrantPeacePolicyAllotment AssimilationCivilizationSandCreekCusterWoundedKneeOklahoma SoonerCarlisleRichardHenryPrattLactoseIntoleranceRacialIntolerance CulturalIntoleranceReligiousIntoleranceKagamaLoneWolfSandovalJohn CollierTerminationRelocationSubjugationReservationChiefWahooIron EyesCodyTomahawkChopMarkDavidOliphantRehnquist the Third. Do you remember me? Of course you do! I'm always going to be somewhere in the back of your mind, aren't I?

"We need to talk. Or at least I need to say something, and I hope that you are listening. Are you listening?" There wasn't any response, but Nanaboozhoo decided to push forward regardless. "Good. Anyway, I think that at some point we got off of the same wavelength as each other, and I was hoping that we could figure out how to find a little more coordination between us.

"Us folks down here know that you are not going away anytime soon. And we know that there are some real benefits to the shelter that your hands provide. Those are two things that we have come to accept, and even in some cases appreciate." Nanaboozhoo nodded reassuringly.

"But there are some real drawbacks as well. Whenever you move your hands without any warning, it scares the bejeebus out of us. We scramble and act out of fear. Even worse, sometimes it can really hurt us. And I mean really hurt us. I don't even know how to describe some of the pain and anguish and devastation your hands have caused." Nanaboozhoo shook his head as he remembered.

"For the most part, a lot of us are doing OK down there for the time being. Or, at least better than before. There are a lot of us, so it's hard to say it's one way for everybody. Some of us are a little worse off and could use more of your shelter and aid, even if it makes things more cramped. Others of us are a little better off and could use more space."

Nanaboozhoo gathered himself for a moment so that he could really shout. He wanted the pale man to hear what he had to say next most of all. "This is what I propose. Why don't you just ask us before you move your hands? Some of us will want to be sheltered and will be happy to reside in those spaces, and others of us will want more room to maneuver and will reside where it is less constricted.

"But if you ask us first, then we can prepare. We can make the decision for ourselves. We won't have to live in fear and be frightened or even hurt every time you move your hands. All you have to do is just ask us first and respect our answers.

"So will you please just ask first?"

Nanaboozhoo could not tell if the pale man had heard him. He hoped that he had. He hoped that the pale man was listening . . .

The answer is consent.

Before we go any further, let's catch our breath. Admittedly, we have worked through a lot of stuff to get to this point in the book. We have considered, in one way or another, over one hundred Supreme Court cases, an even longer list of books and articles, and all kinds of other stuff like laws and treaties and government publications.[1] It has been a lot of ground to cover, and I wouldn't blame you for not remembering every detail or needing a reminder of why we've done all of this.

Fortunately, our task has been pretty simple and straightforward. We wanted to figure out when plenary power became constitutional. More specifically, we wanted to know when the Indian Commerce Clause became the basis for the all-encompassing version of plenary power. In 1886 in *Kagama* the Supreme Court rejected the Indian Commerce Clause, opting for blatantly racist rationales for federal authority. This was part of a larger trend in the late nineteenth and twentieth centuries in which the Supreme Court was complicit in the further subjugation of non-White peoples under American law. By 2004 in *Lara* the Supreme Court was claiming that it had "traditionally identified" the Indian Commerce Clause as the source of the all-encompassing version of plenary power. Something drastically changed between *Kagama* and *Lara*, and we wanted to identify when it had changed in order to figure out why it had changed. Had the Supreme Court reasoned out a logical and justifiable connection between plenary power and the U.S. Constitution that was in keeping with other justifications for American governance, or were the old, racist rationales merely hiding behind the U.S. Constitution?

We came to find that we didn't have a seminal moment when we could definitively mark the change from *Kagama* to *Lara*. Nonetheless, during the mid- to late twentieth century there were two major trends that perpetuated the shift. First, the Commerce Clause as a whole became a major tool in American governance. Consequently, as the much more reasonable and legitimate original version of plenary power—as against the states—had already been mostly subsumed by the later all-encompassing version—as evidenced most clearly in various liquor cases—it became all too easy for an imprecise Supreme Court to turn to the Commerce Clause in the era of its ascendency to justify essentially unlimited federal authority over Native America. Second, at a time when civil rights were a prominent part of the legal and political landscape, the Supreme Court appeared to grow increasingly embarrassed by the racist language and rationales it had previously openly employed to describe Native peoples and the reasonings for plenary power. To that end, the justices of the Court began using softer language and lines of argument that fit the pattern of more traditional and established exercises of American law and governmental authority. With the Indian Commerce Clause within easy reach, the Supreme Court could claim that the all-encompassing version of plenary power was constitutional while leaving behind the increasingly unpleasant rhetoric of wardship, savagery, and protection.

Tracing this history has left us with two troubling conclusions. First, nothing has changed but the words. The Supreme Court has not found a legitimate basis for the exercise of the all-encompassing version of plenary power in the U.S. Constitution. Rather, it has changed how it writes about plenary power to obscure its racist origins and sloppy reasoning and to shield a doctrine that is discordant with the basic theory of American governance behind the U.S. Constitution. The reason the Supreme Court maintains this clearly troublesome doctrine is that it is convenient, especially since it is now often used to benefit tribal nations rather than openly oppress them.[2] Second, the Supreme Court does not actually believe what it claims to be the law. Rather, it is reciting a story that it recognizes is false because it has the rhetorical authority to make the untrue function as if it were true. Doing so absolves the Court of having to confront the difficult origins of the all-encompassing version of plenary power specifically and colonialism generally while preserving a status quo that appears to be less threatening than it actually still is once the more overt and disconcerting (and honest) language is scrubbed away. Both of these troubling conclusions can be summed up in a single statement: the Supreme Court is telling the worst trickster story ever told.

Again, this is relatively simple and straightforward to understand. Where it becomes more difficult is trying to think beyond the worst trickster story ever told. Colonialism has a real funny way of provoking all of us—the colonizer and colonized alike—to repeat and reinforce that which it has established. Thus, tribal advocates also participate in telling the worst trickster story ever told because it is often as useful for them to tell it as it is for the colonizer to tell it and/or because we are afraid of the unknown alternatives.

The result is that we all keep telling the worst trickster story ever told and the all-encompassing version of plenary power lives on. As I write these words, such a set of circumstances may not seem like an impossible thing to live with. After all, plenary power has done more good than harm in the Self-Determination Era. But it will not always be this way. History has demonstrated that eventually the tide will turn against tribal nations, peoples, and sovereignty again. What will we do when this inevitably happens? Even today, when things are generally positive for Native America, there is no shortage of issues that arise or conflicts that ensue or cases that are filed that might be the next big turning point in this area of law. Being a tribal advocate, even in the midst of the most robust moment for tribal nations since contact, means having to be unyieldingly vigilant and living with a perpetual sense of dread of what will come next. It is a hard way to live, to always be on edge even during the best of times. But this is the way that it is going to be as long as we keep pretending that the all-encompassing version of plenary power is constitutionally sanctioned.

All of which leads us to one last question to consider: Is there anything to be done about it?

As I have noted elsewhere in this book, I am hardly the first person to notice or question the worst trickster story ever told. A lot of very smart people for whom I have the utmost respect have been deeply troubled by the all-encompassing version of plenary power's origins and continuing place in American law and have offered alternatives to this unlimited, unhinged doctrine.[3] Some of the more prominent suggestions have been relying more on increasingly progressive international law principles,[4] seeking to domesticate those international law principles within American law,[5] reinvigorating the treaty-making process,[6] and adopting a constitutional amendment that recognizes tribal nationhood and sovereignty.[7] Any one of these alternatives has the potential to offer an effective alternative to plenary power, and I encourage tribal advocates to continue to pursue any and all of them.

That being noted, we should also acknowledge that there are significant barriers to each of these proposed solutions that pose obvious difficulties to their acceptance and implementation: American courts tend not to be persuaded by international law or consider themselves bound by it; Congress decided to "end" treaty making with tribal nations in 1871, and reinstituting the process with over 570 federally recognized tribal nations would require a major bureaucratic effort in an area of governance that the federal government has traditionally left underfunded and underdeveloped; passing a constitutional amendment is a significant undertaking that requires an enormous amount of political will, cohesion, and action, and it seems unlikely that Native peoples, who make up only around 3 percent of the U.S. population, could muster the necessary enthusiasm to do so, particularly in the current political climate in which I am writing this book.[8]

Again, each of these proposed solutions has potential, and I do not mean to discourage anyone who cares to pursue them. Yet, the path forward for any of them is challenging at best. Furthermore, none can match the convenience, ease, and relief that the worst trickster story ever told offers the Supreme Court. Of course, one could very reasonably argue this might well be the whole point of these alternatives. Perhaps we ought to seek to make the Supreme Court less comfortable in sanctifying an unbounded authority of racist origins that presents a ceaseless threat to Native America.

But part of the effectiveness and resiliency of the worst trickster story ever told is that it fits comfortably into the types of stories that the Supreme Court likes to tell about American law and it absolves the Court from having to think too much about the origins of plenary power. It is easy in the same way that not leaving your couch to go to the gym is easy. Consequently, is it realistic to imagine that enough members of the Court are going to reject a familiar way of thinking and reasoning that fits seamlessly into how they understand the law to operate for something significantly or even radically different? Do we trust the Supreme Court to ever become uncomfortable enough with plenary power and the worst trickster story ever told to reject it in favor of something it has not previously embraced? What evidence do we have to suggest that the Supreme Court would be willing to go to the gym, so to speak? Compounding the conundrum, we might also ask what tribal advocates want. What is the end goal of disrupting the all-encompassing version of plenary power? Is it reasonable or even desirable for tribal nations to, say, want to be recognized as full-fledged nations? How do we account for the tremendous diversity of capacities of tribal nations under any alternative to plenary power? How can we ask the Supreme Court to change course unless we are able to guide them along the way? How do we replace plenary power with something beneficial, as opposed to making things worse? How do we keep the good while getting rid of the bad?

In short, is there a principled way to rearticulate the relationship between the federal government and tribal nations that will actually move the Supreme Court to action, will maintain and strengthen tribal sovereignty, and can speak to the many needs and desires of a diverse Native America?

Obviously the answer is no.

I'm just kidding. I wouldn't have written almost a whole book to this point if I truly believed that all hope was lost. But I do think that any rearticulation of the relationship between the United States and Native America will need to contain three essential elements. Each one is critical if the Supreme Court is to be convinced to abandon the worst trickster story ever told and a more proper balance is to be established.

This is where consent comes back into the picture, as it is the first essential element in disrupting the continuing telling of the worst trickster story ever told. As we noted in Chapter 2, the easiest way to understand American claims to the legitimate exercise of authority over its citizenry is through the metaphor of the social contract. And the defining characteristic of any contract is a meeting of the minds, or a willingness by both parties to be bound by the terms of the contract. A contract requires that the parties involved freely consent to accept the obligations and the benefits of their agreement.

Consequently, any legal theory that seeks to upend or replace plenary power must, first and foremost, be premised on the concept of consent. This is not to suggest that the other theories that we briefly described a few pages ago necessarily lack this crucial element. Rather, it is to note that any potential replacement for plenary power must clearly and obviously foreground consent as its foundational basis if it is going to have any resonance both in American courts and within Native America. The concept of consent becomes internalized by judges, lawyers, and other folks who are trained in or participate in American law. Thus, it speaks to this cohort on an intuitive level and can lubricate changes in thinking. Judges who might be reluctant to abandon the worst trickster story ever told may be persuaded by a theory that follows in the footsteps of their basic conception of the legitimate exercise of political authority, and judges who are actively seeking a change may be enthusiastic to follow a pathway that will feel familiar to them and those of their ilk. Furthermore, tribal nations have, from the very beginning, been advocating for reciprocal relationships with their colonial counterparts, through treaties and other means. Foregrounding consent, in which all parties involved have a say in the nature and direction of the relationship, will speak to a long-standing concern for Native America.

The second essential element is the U.S. Constitution. The "magic" of the worst trickster story ever told, such that it is, is that it pulls something out of the U.S. Constitution that wasn't there in the first place. There is no natural or reasonable reading of the text that authorizes an unfettered American authority over the original inhabitants of the lands now claimed by the United States. To pretend otherwise is to argue that the rabbit really does reside inside the magician's hat. Like a magic show, plenary power is a falsehood that we know simply cannot be true, yet many folks engaged in American law, including Supreme Court justices, suspend disbelief to accept it as real.

Nonetheless, this particular magic show reveals something else that is important to rebalancing the relationship between the federal government and tribal nations. The whole purpose of the "trick" in the worst trickster story ever told is to convert a colonial articulation of law and race into something that is constitutionally sanctioned. The ostensible legitimacy of plenary power is not as a legal principle that stands on its own—such as the elements of a contract or what constitutes negligence—but rather its connection to the U.S. Constitution. It is the U.S. Constitution that makes plenary power what it is today in the worst trickster story ever told. It is the source of the magic.

Consequently, any rebalancing of the relationship between the federal government and tribal nations must have some significant grounding in the U.S. Constitution. This is not to suggest that the worst trickster story ever told somehow gets it right or offers a model. Rather, it is an acknowledgment that American law does treat the U.S. Constitution as if it can make magic. As we noted in Chapter 1, it separates the "haves" and the "have-nots" when it comes to rights and authority, and there is a reason why the worst trickster story ever told seeks to drag plenary power into the realm of that which is constitutional. Any theory that seeks to displace the current state of affairs must acknowledge that the power of the worst trickster story ever told is that it ostensibly connects plenary power to the greatest source of authority in American law and that it is unlikely that American courts are going to embrace anything that they perceive as having a more tenuous connection to the U.S. Constitution. Thus, any alternative theory must also look to the U.S. Constitution if it hopes to maximize its chances of gaining traction in American courts. This magic cannot be denied.

We must be careful in how we understand and describe the third essential element because we have already seen how other, less well-formed articulations of the same basic idea have been used to support rather than diminish plenary power. Put directly, the third essential element to a rearticulation of the relationship between the United States and Native America is an acknowledgment that the United States has an obligation to Native America. Admittedly, this element is reminiscent of the concepts of wardship, trust, and protection that we explored in Chapter 2, but it is far from the same as them. The concepts from Chapter 2 are hierarchical in nature and result in one party exerting power over a second party, sometimes against the second party's will. An obligation, on the other hand, is not about one stakeholder exerting power over another but rather about that stakeholder needing to perform or behave in a certain way for the other. Thinking in terms of an obligation drastically shifts the dynamic from, say, wardship, in that it does not authorize the United States to dictate over Native peoples but instead places the United States in service to them.

The easiest way to understand the third essential element is through a metaphor that Native peoples have been using for years and that we also considered in Chapter 2: familial relationships. Rather than, again say, a guardian and a ward, the relationship between the United States and Native America is best understood as something like an older sibling to a younger sibling. The older sibling cannot dictate the choices and actions of the younger sibling (no matter how bossy she or he is) but is expected to offer an example and guidance and aid when necessary. The United States has accepted this role, and Native nations have also accepted their role, time and time again through treaties. The United States has also done so through its own law. For example, the Northwest Ordinance, one of the earliest American laws to consider Native peoples, stated, "The utmost good faith shall always be observed towards the Indians."[9] Describing the connection between the United States and Native America through the cold, technical language of trust law does not do it justice. Along those same lines, any hierarchical articulation of this connection is incompatible with the first two essential elements. Understanding the third essential element to rebalancing this relationship as something akin to a familial obligation much better encapsulates a truly healthy and reciprocal engagement among each of the parties and the bonds between them and offers a much more plausible pathway to something other than plenary power.[10]

So there we have it, the three essential elements to dislodging the worst trickster story ever told: consent, the U.S. Constitution, and the recognition of an obligation on the part of the United States to Native America. But what do we do with them? How might they fit together in a manner that will disrupt the ceaseless telling of the worst trickster story ever told? What can we build with these tools?

The answer to this particular riddle is, of course, to give up because it is too hard. No, I'm just kidding again. The real key to imagining a workable alternative to plenary power is to center one of the elements—consent—and build a logical progression from there. Obviously the first step is to reject the all-encompassing version of plenary power that has plagued this area of law (and others) for far too long. From there, we can assert the basic premise that should replace plenary power:

> Congress still has significant latitude to legislate concerning Native America ***as long as that legislation requires the consent of tribal nations and peoples to come into force***.

Put slightly differently, under this rearticulation of the relationship between the federal government and Native America a congressional law that affects or alters or engages with Native America is valid only if it allows for a tribal nation to decide for itself whether it will come under its auspices. A tribal nation must consent to the law before it comes into effect. This places a crucial limitation on federal authority that is currently lacking under the plenary power regime. It also recrafts the relationship between the federal government and tribal nations as something closer to the familial arrangement that Native nations have been advocating for from the beginning rather than the hierarchical structure presently in place.

And where in the U.S. Constitution does the congressional authority to legislate concerning Native America under this new understanding come from? The source of this power is the Treaty Clause as long as the scope of the power is truncated by tribal consent. We will explore this idea in greater depth shortly, but in essence this proposed regime will be a version of treaty making for today's circumstances. In summation, consent is the key to legitimizing federal authority, for allowing the federal government to fulfill the obligations it has previously undertaken on behalf of Native America, and for moving forward with those obligations in the present day.

Allowing for continuing significant congressional leeway in legislating regarding Native America while also requiring tribal consent checks a lot of important boxes. First and foremost, as noted previously, it places a limit on what has otherwise been a limitless authority. At present, Native America is stuck between the proverbial rock and a hard place. On the one hand, to the extent that the Supreme Court ever bothers to assert that there is a standard by which it assesses federal action through the plenary power doctrine, it is under the decidedly ephemeral nonstandard of asking whether congressional legislation can be rationally tied to the federal government's "unique obligation" to Native America.[11] No piece of congressional legislation has ever been struck down by the Supreme Court under this bundle of fluff. On the other hand, as we noted in Chapter 1, the Supreme Court, starting in *Oliphant*, gifted itself the capacity to decide the boundaries of tribal sovereignty by considering whether an exercise of tribal authority is "inconsistent with their status." The type of fancypants folks who write the kinds of books and articles that I tend to read call this the doctrine of implicit divestiture, and it is equally as unlimited and unanchored in the U.S. Constitution as plenary power.[12] Thus, at present, when a tribal nation finds itself in front of the Supreme Court, it is facing an institution that has proven unwilling to limit either Congress or itself.[13]

Requiring tribal consent curbs these excesses. It does not prohibit the federal government from acting on behalf of Native America, yet it prevents tribal nations from having to endure federal legislation that it finds onerous, incompatible with its own goals, or threatening. Extensive federal power still exists, but it is mediated by tribal choice. By accepting consent as the foundational principle for understanding the relationship between the federal government and tribal nations—by adopting the foundational principle for the legitimacy of American governmental authority more generally in the field of Indian law—federal authority becomes much more fully aligned with the principle of a government of limited and enumerated powers.

Speaking of enumeration, placing consent at the center of this relationship and analysis allows for a much more reasonable and natural reading of federal authority under the U.S. Constitution than the current empty gestures toward the Indian Commerce Clause. I will admit that the reasoning may seem a little novel at first, but I promise that the more you think about it, the more it will make sense, so please hear me out. The real basis for a continuing and extensive federal authority to legislate as it concerns Native America—if we place consent at the center of the analysis—is the Treaty Clause.

Let's be open and honest with each other: I can feel some skepticism on your part. For one thing, haven't we seen more than a few times during the course of this book the Supreme Court already trying to use the Treaty Clause as one of the sources of plenary power, often in conjunction with or as backup to the Indian Commerce Clause? Well, yes we have. But the critical difference between what the Supreme Court has been doing with the Treaty Clause and the consent-based theory we are developing is the actual participation of Native America. Whereas the Supreme Court has often acted as if the very existence of the Treaty Clause has conferred plenary power to the federal government regardless of any action or knowledge on the part of Native America, the understanding that we are developing demands Native participation in a manner that is much more akin to how treaties are made and function.

Allow me to explain further. The primary characteristic of tribal nations is, quite obviously, their nationhood. How to define tribal nationhood is a matter of great debate, and one could make a very cogent argument that the totality of federal Indian law is nothing more than wrestling with this question. Nonetheless, from the beginning and to the present day, the federal government has recognized this political status of Native nations.[14] And the way that nations come to agreement with each other is through treaties. There is obviously plenty of precedent for understanding the tribal/federal relationship in these terms.[15]

As noted elsewhere in this book, Congress "ended" treaty making with tribal nations in 1871. Whether Congress actually has the authority to do this is perhaps an open question, but this action eventually inaugurated a long and continuing period in which tribal nations and the federal government have not engaged with each other in this manner directly.[16] Nonetheless, treaties are bi- or multilateral agreements between national entities. Placing consent at the center of the analysis allows us to reimagine the relationship between tribal nations and the federal government in these bi- or multilateral terms in ways that make sense for the present and offer a better, more structured, more reasonable reading of American authority under the U.S. Constitution.

Let's put it as simply as possible. Allowing the federal government to maintain extensive authority to legislate concerning Native America, yet also recognizing that tribal nations must consent to that legislation before it becomes operative, mimics treaty making—and thus an enumerated federal power in the U.S. Constitution—in a manner that works best for the present day.[17] The process that we are considering—with consent at the center—is like a treaty in that it requires the assent of all of the political parties involved. It also allows for the federal government to legislate more extensively than it otherwise could, as American law already recognizes that treaties allow the federal government to exert authority in areas in which it is otherwise more limited in the purely American context.[18] It also honors the relationship that has already been established through the treaty-making process by engaging in something closer to a familial connection than a hierarchical one. In short, it is much easier to craft a justifiable theory of federal authority under the Treaty Clause than it is under the Commerce Clause—as long as consent is at the center of the theory.

Well, OK, fine, you might be saying to yourself, if treaty making and the Treaty Clause are so great, why don't I just advocate for reinstating that process as some other (much more) well-respected minds have? What makes this method any different or better? This is a very reasonable question, and I am not at all hurt that you would express such doubt (and snark) after all we have been through together.[19]

My answer to this very understandable and, again, not at all hurtful question boils down to a straightforward assertion: Reinstating treaty making in the manner akin to how it was practiced before 1871 is not a viable request, particularly when there is a simpler, more elegant solution. At the time that I write this, there are over 570 federally recognized tribal nations in the United States. Engaging in the version of treaty making that occurred prior to 1871 would be a massive bureaucratic undertaking on the part of the federal government. And since the federal government doesn't exactly have the most pristine reputation when it comes to fully funding or otherwise supporting its efforts in Native America, it is difficult to see how treaty making in the modern day would be effective even if it were to appeal to the parties involved. Not to mention the awkwardness of negotiating treaties with Native peoples, who are now regarded as American citizens under American law. It is difficult to see how such a process would function well even if it could get off the ground.

A process with consent firmly at its center, on the other hand, can effectively capture the spirit and purpose of the Treaty Clause—and thus a much more tangible and legitimate claim to constitutionality than the Commerce Clause—with much less effort and in a manner that is better suited to the present-day context. The federal government retains significant authority to pass legislation that touches upon Native America without having to negotiate directly with each and every tribal nation. Tribal nations have the capacity to accept or reject the effects of that legislation without having to wait their turn or otherwise manage an impenetrable bureaucracy to engage with the federal government directly. And yet, both parties have a say in the outcome, just as they would if they had negotiated a treaty. A process with consent at the center allows for a modern-day version of treaty making that establishes the type of real and substantial connection to the U.S. Constitution that will be necessary to eradicate the worst trickster story ever told.[20] It also allows the Indian Commerce Clause to move back into its original, more natural setting—as a tool that both limits state intervention into Indian Country and allows for the regulation of those who would engage with Native America.

And after all of that there are still more boxes left that we can check! One of the most pernicious and least recognized effects of colonialism in what is now the United States is that it has flattened the totality of Native America into a homogeneous singularity in the minds of most. Or, to use fewer top-shelf words, most folks still tend to think of "Indians" as one category of people.[21] However, as we have noted a few times in this chapter now, there are over 570 federally recognized tribal nations in the United States. There are undeniably commonalities among various pockets of peoples and the group as a whole, and sometimes we need to speak about Native America as a whole to understand big ideas, such as plenary power. But this is also over 570 distinct social, political, cultural, historical, and legal contexts, each deserving its own acknowledgment, respect, and understanding. The best way to conceptualize it is to recognize that using the word "Indian" (or whatever word or term you prefer) is a lot like using the word "European." There is certainly something that connects all Europeans together, but it is at a highly abstract level, and if you behave like you were in France when you are in Greece or treat people like they were Spanish when they are Hungarian, then obvious issues will arise.

American law has not always known what to do about this diversity (nor has it always cared), which has occasionally been a cause for concern for Supreme Court justices. Unfortunately, this concern has often been raised in terms of questioning the continuing validity of tribal sovereignty. Put slightly differently, sometimes a Supreme Court justice will question whether a tribal nation is too small to retain its national character. For example, writing in concurrence in one of the Marshall Trilogy cases, Justice William Johnson asked about the recognition of tribal sovereignty. "Where is the rule to stop? Must every petty kraal of Indians, designating themselves a tribe or nation, and having a few hundred acres of land to hunt on exclusively, be recognized as a state?"[22] Much more recently, Justice Clarence Thomas has stated that "by treating all tribes as possessing an identical quantum of sovereignty, the Court's precedents have made it all but impossible to understand the ultimate source of each tribe's sovereignty and whether it endures."[23]

A consent-based approach addresses the diversity of tribal nations by disrupting what has often been a one-size-fits-all approach to federal Indian law and legislation. Moreover, it does so in a way that eases the administrative burden on the federal government and speaks to the reasonable-if-we-read-them-in-the-very-best-light concerns articulated by Johnson and Thomas. Under the consent-based approach, Congress is still authorized to pass legislation that it believes is generally for the betterment of Native America without having to constantly account for every unique set of circumstances or concerns that arise for any particular tribal nation or group of tribal nations. Tribal nations, on the other hand, will not have to constantly lobby to make sure that their interests are heard or that a large bill does not inadvertently negatively affect them. Instead, they can simply opt out of legislation that is not right for them. Whether big or small, tribal nations can find the appropriate level of authority and sovereignty for themselves. It also greatly mitigates the chance that any one single tribal nation will significantly disrupt tribal sovereignty for Native America as a whole under the auspices of a piece of federal legislation for which it is mismatched.

Along these same lines a consent-based approach rebalances the relationship between the federal government and Native America into something more familial by respecting the choices that tribal nations make for themselves. Some tribal nations are larger in population and land base with a well-developed, long-standing infrastructure to serve their citizenries, including schools, court systems, social services, and more. Others are smaller in population with little to no land base and are not as well equipped to provide the same level of support to their citizenries. All are somewhere along this spectrum with needs and desires that can vary greatly depending on the circumstances. No entity is better equipped to assess where any given tribal nation is on this spectrum and what it needs and wants from the federal government than the given tribal nation itself. By moving out of the hierarchical plenary power regime and into a consent-based approach, the federal government will more fully adopt the role of the older sibling who offers aid, guidance, and advice when necessary and steps back when the younger sibling needs to act and take responsibility on her or his own. It will also reduce the opportunities for the federal government to come across as overbearing or overreaching. As the younger sibling, tribal nations will make choices that make the most sense for them. Tribal nations with a stronger, more robust infrastructure may not want or need significant federal involvement, whereas tribal nations that have a lesser developed infrastructure might depend on federal involvement. Each can shape the contours of its own individual connection with the federal government, which, in turn, will make it more responsible to its own citizenry. Successes and failures will become that much more attributable to tribal stakeholders than federal bureaucrats and will leave the future of any particular tribal nation much more fully in its own hands. All parties enjoy greater benefits and a stronger bond—underscored by consent—under a familial approach.

Now, before we go any further, we should take one moment to address a looming question that you very well might have but are perhaps afraid to ask—or at least one that someone is inevitably going to have and will definitely ask. Let's put it gently, shall we? Doesn't our consent-based approach put too much power in the hands of tribal nations? If a tribal nation can reject any piece of federal legislation that might apply to it, doesn't that mean that there is no check on tribal authority? Wouldn't a tribal nation just take all of the privileges and none of the responsibilities in its relationship with the federal government? Can we really trust tribal nations to behave properly under a consent-based regime?

First and foremost, I want to acknowledge that I understand why you might ask such a question, and I appreciate the opportunity to address it. Perhaps you know of some act of malfeasance on the part of a tribal politician or official, or have heard of something unfortunate happening somewhere on a reservation, or just have a vague, uneasy sense about tribal governments. And even if you don't have that sense or experience, we should just confront the fact that there is a negative stereotype about tribal governments and politicians. Some of that stereotype is earned, as there certainly have been plenty of bad actors in tribal governments. Native peoples are human after all. But non-Native folks are also human, and it seems like you can't go even a week without hearing about some act of malfeasance on the part of a federal, state, or local official. Bad actors are hardly the sole purview of tribal governments. In fact, as I write this, news that a former U.S. president has been indicted for a fourth time has come to light. All of which is to note that there really doesn't seem to be any evidence that tribal governments are any more corrupt or untrustworthy than any other government in the United States.

With that in mind we can reconsider the question that led us to this point and once again do the professorial thing and answer the question with a bunch of other questions: Why would we assume that a tribal nation would behave poorly if afforded the leeway to choose its own path under a consent-based approach? Why do we make this assumption? Why wouldn't we assume, as we do in so many other contexts, that tribal nations are rational actors capable of assessing their own needs and desires and acting appropriately on them? Why would we assume that tribal self-interest would lead to greedy choices instead of smart ones? What does that starting point tell us about our own thinking about tribal nations and peoples?

Some tribal nations are smaller and are in greater need of help to provide for their citizenries and, it seems reasonable to presume, are more willing to accept federal aid and the conditions that come with it. Other tribal nations are bigger and more self-sufficient and, it also seems reasonable to presume, are willing and capable of forgoing more of what the federal government has to offer. It seems highly plausible that any tribal nation would best understand its own context and make the appropriate decisions for itself and its citizenry rather than act irrationally just because it was entrusted with a greater level of choice.

Furthermore, even if a tribal government did behave badly (however we might measure such a thing), why would that be a big enough problem to disrupt or forgo a consent-based approach? Thanks to a famous quotation from a Supreme Court case, we regularly conceptualize states as "laboratories of democracy" in which different governments can try different things for their citizenries.[24] One need only remember that Nevada and Utah share a border to recognize how this works in practice. So why shouldn't tribal nations be afforded the same opportunity as states to try new things and make mistakes and follow their own path? If things go wrong, aren't tribal nations just as answerable to their citizenries as states? In fact, considering they are much smaller, isn't it easier to imagine that tribal nations have a greater flexibility than states to correct "mistakes"? So what is there to be worried about?

All right then, that covers a lot of ground, doesn't it? And after all of that there couldn't be any more boxes that we could possibly check, could there? We must have totally and completely exhausted all of the ways we could think of that our consent-based approach is superior to the worst trickster story ever told. We noted that it places a tangible and substantial cap—for a government that claims to consist of limited and enumerated powers—on the presently unlimited scope of plenary power; it offers a more logical and reasonable constitutional basis for the exercise of federal authority than the Indian Commerce Clause; it actually takes the wide diversity within Indian Country into account; and it sets the foundation for a relationship that is more familial and less hierarchical in nature, which is to the benefit of everyone involved. What more could anybody possibly want? This already makes a compelling case for rethinking the engagement between the United States and Native America, and I don't know how anyone could need any other convincing . . .

Hey, wait a minute. What's that thing just right over there? That thing that is just within arm's reach . . .

There, got it. Well, wouldn't you know it. It turns out that there is one more box to check. Our consent-based approach also falls much more fully in line with emerging standards in international law concerning Indigenous peoples. This is most evident when we look at the United Nations Declaration on the Rights of Indigenous Peoples, which was adopted in 2007.[25] That title is a little cumbersome, so we are just going to call it UNDRIP for the time being.

There are a few things that we should note before we check this last box with ink. The first is that international law can be a little quirky, primarily because it is much harder to enforce than domestic law. Thus, American courts, particularly the Supreme Court, tend to not always hold it in the highest regard. And UNDRIP, at the title makes clear, is only a "Declaration" and not a treaty or other instrument that would have greater binding legal authority. When the United Nations originally adopted UNDRIP, the United States voted against it. Eventually the United States did vote in favor of UNDRIP, but only as a statement of purpose, noting, "The United States supports the Declaration, which—while not legally binding or a statement of current international law—has both moral and political force."[26] Tribal nations have had little success in gaining enforcement of UNDRIP in American courts.[27]

That all being noted, UNDRIP is perhaps the strongest, and at this moment certainly the most prominent, statement in support of Indigenous rights the world has ever seen. It was the culmination of years of work by Indigenous peoples in conjunction with the United Nations and offers the clearest articulation of the Indigenous perspective in international law.[28] To that end, it offers a particularly useful measure of any construction of the legal and political relationship between a colonial nation and its original inhabitants.

The most on-point part of UNDRIP for our purposes is Article 19, which explicitly calls for nations to "consult and cooperate in good faith with the Indigenous peoples concerned . . . in order to obtain their free, prior and informed ***consent*** before adopting and implementing legislative or administrative measures that may affect them." (The extra emphasis I put in there might be a little overkill, but I can imagine you can see why it's there.) Thus, the approach we are developing in this chapter falls directly in line with the current international standard, one that was developed with and takes into account the perspective of the Indigenous world. Furthermore, that one single article is hardly the only part of

UNDRIP that supports our consent-based model. For example, Article 5 states, "Indigenous peoples have the right to maintain and strengthen their distinct political, legal, economic, social and cultural institutions, while retaining their right to participate fully, if they so choose, in the political, economic, social and cultural life of the State." Article 5 is perhaps best understood as enshrining two related principles: the right of Indigenous peoples to "maintain and strengthen" themselves and their right to "participate fully" in their larger political environment. Our consent-based model clearly falls in line with both parts of this standard. It both protects tribal sovereignty by limiting the scope of plenary power and allows for tribal nations to choose their level of engagement with the colonial nation. The worst trickster story ever told, on the other hand, clearly violates this standard by enshrining the federal government's capacity to dictate the terms of its relationship to Native peoples—including disavowing it completely—in its foremost governing document.

So there you have it. Our consent-based model is superior to the worst trickster story ever told by any measure. And do you want to know what the best part is? It's not going to take any sort of radical change in our practice if we change the law because in many ways we are already more or less operating under a consent-based model. Deciding to replace the worst trickster story ever told with something better would be remarkably easy in most circumstances because we mostly wouldn't have to do anything at all.

As in Chapter 4, once again the Indian Child Welfare Act is instructive. ICWA returned the authority to make choices about tribal children in placement proceedings back to tribal nations. However, recognizing their various capacities, the legislation did not force this obligation on tribal nations who were not capable of accepting this responsibility. This is most evident in two sections of the statute. The first is §1911(b), which requires state courts to transfer child placement proceedings over Native children to tribal court under most circumstances. However, the statute also states "that such transfer shall be subject to declination by the tribal court of such tribe."[29] Thus, if a tribal nation was not ready to engage in child placement proceedings, it was not required to do so. The second is

§1919(a), which authorizes tribal nations and states to "enter into agreements with each other respecting care and custody of Indian children and jurisdiction over child custody proceedings, including agreements which may provide for orderly transfer of jurisdiction on a case-by-case basis and agreements which provide for concurrent jurisdiction between States and Indian tribes."[30] This clearly allows for tribal nations without a robust tribal court system (particularly in 1978 when it was passed) to nonetheless still have some control and say about its juvenile population without having to take on the full responsibilities of the statute. The next part of this section allows for the revocation of such agreements, presumably so that tribal nations that developed a functional court system in the wake of ICWA could regain their fullest authority under the statute.[31]

In short, tribal nations in essence must consent to ICWA before it becomes applicable to them. This is hardly the only federal statute that operates in this sort of manner, particularly in the Self-Determination Era.[32] Perhaps the most prominent examples concern environmental legislation. For example, the Clean Water Act authorizes states to set their own water quality standards. Yet it also authorizes tribal nations to be regarded as states under the statute as long as the tribal nation meets certain criteria.[33] We will concern ourselves with how to regard the criteria the United States imposes shortly, but for our immediate purposes it suffices to note that tribal nations can choose for themselves whether they have the capacity and the will to regulate their own water standards under the act. Although we do not always talk or write or think about it in these terms, consent is a hallmark of the legislation of the Self-Determination Era, and thus Congress would not have to radically alter how it currently operates as it concerns Native America if we replace the worst trickster story ever told with a consent-based regime.[34]

Furthermore, the various governments in the United States—tribal, state, and federal—have increasingly come to appreciate that lengthy, contentious litigation in an effort to test the metes and bounds of their sovereignty can often be costly and counterproductive. To that end, these various governments have increasingly turned to what we call cooperative agreements to share responsibility for the governance or management of a territory or subject matter.[35] In essence, the governments engage in a treaty-like process to come to a mutually beneficial arrangement on how to manage a common problem or issue, such as law enforcement, education, taxation, and more.[36] As with congressional legislation in the Self-Determination Era, consent is the hallmark of the increasingly popular cooperative agreements. It is fair to say that we are moving closer and closer toward where we need to be in this field of law.

All of which then raises another question you might have at this point: If we are already moving closer and closer to where we want to go, then what is the point of this book? Not to mention the fact that others have already called for a greater focus on consent in various ways in this area of law.[37] It kind of seems like a big waste of time if we really don't have much work to do from here, doesn't it? Why did you write this thing and why am I reading it, you might be saying to yourself?

Again, you ask a very fair (if kind of meanly worded) question. Fortunately, the answer is straightforward:

Because the Supreme Court keeps telling the worst trickster story ever told.

The federal government is similar to Native America (and Europe for that matter) in the respect that we often think and talk about it as if it is a singular entity, but it is actually very diverse with many branches, departments, and people engaged in a wide range of goals. For example, the Post Office is not the same as the military, which is not the same as the Food and Drug Administration, and so on. Consequently, regarding the federal government as a singular entity can obscure the fact that its many tentacles are not always pulling in the same direction.

All of which is to say that congressional and executive efforts toward a consent-based process will forever be limited as long as American courts keep telling the worst trickster story ever told.[38] The perpetuation of the all-encompassing version of plenary power (along with its equally pernicious sibling implicit divestiture, which we noted earlier in this chapter[39]) prevents the Self-Determination Era and its general tendency toward a more familial, less hierarchical relationship from fulfilling its fullest potential. The basic doctrine within federal Indian law must change, and it must change in and through American courts if we are ever going to escape the unyielding legacy of the worst trickster story ever told.

Put differently, if we are ever going to root out the worst trickster story ever told, we must dig it up from where it is most deeply entrenched—within American courts. To do this, two things must happen. First, tribal advocates must start asserting a consent-based model grounded in the Treaty Clause as the true source of the relationship between Native America and the United States. They must argue that any legislation that touches upon Indian Country must allow for tribal nations to choose whether or not to come under its auspices for it to be a valid exercise of constitutionally sanctioned authority.

As we noted in Chapter 4, clients want to win cases, and offering a new legal theory might seem, at first blush, like too risky a strategy to pursue when the stakes in litigation concerning Native America can be so high. However, we can mitigate the risk, particularly as this new approach gets off the ground. Lawyers in American courts are allowed to "argue in the alternative," or assert different claims that need not necessarily be logically consistent. The way that it was explained to me in law school is that it is perfectly valid for a lawyer to argue all of the following in a single case: (1) My client's dog did not bite the plaintiff; (2) My client doesn't even own a dog; (3) The plaintiff bit my client's dog first. Since American courts do not require logical consistency among the claims a party asserts in a case, tribal advocates who feel, for whatever reason, that it is necessary to continue to argue under the worst trickster story ever told can do so while simultaneously arguing for a consent-based approach rooted in the Treaty Clause as an alternative or secondary theory. Tribal advocates do not necessarily have to put all of their eggs in the consent-based basket, but they do need to offer American courts a new and better pathway if we ever want to get off the treadmill that always leads us back to plenary power.

Second, American courts must change the questions that they ask about the relationship between Native America and the United States. As we noted earlier in this chapter, under the plenary power regime, American courts, when they bother with it at all, assert that they measure congressional actions under plenary power by the standard of whether the action is rationally tied to the federal government's "unique obligation" to Native America. Furthermore, as we also noted, the Supreme Court has given itself a wide latitude to ascertain what is "inconsistent with [the] status" of tribal nations. Asking vague questions about rationality and consistency offers no resistance whatsoever to the brute force of plenary power. It is like trying to stop a bullet with a single marshmallow.

A consent-based regime offers the kind of more tangible and reasonable question that American courts are actually equipped to ask and answer: Does an act of federal authority allow for the opportunity for tribal nations to consent to it? If it does, then the act of federal authority is constitutionally sanctioned under the Treaty Clause and should stand. If it does not, then it is not constitutionally sanctioned and should be struck down. Such a question is simple, clean, and within the competency of American courts.

This is not to suggest that a consent-based approach is completely foolproof. There is still much that would need to be figured out, and there remains room for potential abuses within such a regime. For example, I suspect that most would agree that it is not outrageous for the federal government to require at least some conditions in its various arrangements with tribal nations, such as with the Clean Water Act, which requires a basic capacity and competency from tribal nations before regarding them as states under the statute. However, there is also a point at which conditions or requirements can become so onerous that they would amount to an act of plenary power. In other words, at some point we must acknowledge that a set of conditions may be so overbearing that it amounts to coercion disguising itself in consent's clothing. This is a valid thing to be concerned about. That being noted, American courts are much better equipped at assessing whether consent exists between two parties than they are at measuring more amorphous concepts that are far less well developed in American law like rationality or inconsistency. A consent-based regime gives American courts a task they can actually accomplish and is much more in keeping with how they reason, as opposed to the ineffectual gesticulating toward a void of nothingness that the plenary power regime has them do.

There is a better way to assess the relationship between the United

States and Native America if tribal advocates are courageous enough to blaze the path and American courts are humble and wise enough to follow it. But how might it work in practice? What would a consent-based regime look like if it were instituted?

Well, I am glad you asked because this is one of those beautiful moments in life when serendipity rises from her slumber and blows a kiss in our direction.[40] We have a contemporary (at least as of the time that I am writing this) real-world example to help us think this through. During the fall of 2022 into the spring and summer of 2023, when I did a good portion of the drafting of this book, the folks who inhabit my corner of the legal world were sitting on pins and needles awaiting the decision in *Haaland v. Brackeen*. This group of folks were surprised—perhaps even shocked—and delighted when in the summer of 2023 the Supreme Court handed down a decision fully and completely in favor of ICWA and tribal interests.

The result in *Brackeen* is to be celebrated if you are an advocate for Native America. And yet, as we noted in Chapter 4, the decision itself is yet another recitation and reaffirmation of the worst trickster story ever told. ICWA, according to Justice Amy Coney Barrett, is constitutional because the federal government has plenary power primarily under the Indian Commerce Clause. Others, as we have seen over and over, have told this same tale. However, as should be clear by now, this rationale is nothing more than the racism of the Allotment Era hiding behind the most powerful document in the country.[41] Despite it being a win for tribal interests, the decision in *Brackeen* further ensnares Native nations and peoples in the same precarious and vulnerable state that simply cannot be escaped under a plenary power regime. It is one of the many victories that is much hollower than it ought to be that litter this area of law.

Now let's imagine how *Brackeen* might look under a consent-based regime. Under a consent-based regime the question of the case would not be whether ICWA was constitutional because the federal government had such a broad expanse of authority over Native peoples and nations as to overcome any other objections to the legislation. Rather, the question would be whether ICWA was constitutional because it allowed tribal nations to decide whether or not to come under its auspices. The

Supreme Court would not be measuring the scope of the constitutionally unhinged, unwieldy, all-encompassing version of plenary power (or its own authority to dictate the terms of tribal sovereignty through implicit divestiture for that matter). Rather, the Supreme Court would engage with the much more manageable question of whether the federal government was fulfilling its obligation to Native America by offering a real and legitimate opportunity to consent to an exercise of federal authority. There would be no need for an unnatural (and unhealthy) reading of the Indian Commerce Clause. Rather, there would be wise and considered reading of the Treaty Clause that best fits the contemporary moment. ICWA would not survive because of a hierarchical power dynamic that affords the federal government more authority over Native peoples than any other peoples within its jurisdiction. It would survive because it establishes something much closer to a reciprocal, familial relationship that just so happens to also coincide with justifications of federal authority more generally and emerging international law standards concerning Indigenous peoples.

That seems a lot better, doesn't it?

But it can happen only if we find a way to disrupt the worst trickster story ever told. And the most straightforward way to disrupt the worst trickster story ever told is to, first and foremost, grab hold of the concept of consent and never let go. Everything flows from that basic understanding. It will also be necessary to ground federal authority in the U.S. Constitution, as it is the source of the magic. I have made my case that the Treaty Clause makes the most sense, but if you have a better idea, I would be happy to learn about it because we definitely need something. And it is also imperative to rearticulate the relationship between the federal government and Native America away from hierarchical terms and into more familial and respectful terms. But those can happen only if we place consent at the center of the analysis. Fortunately, it's not a radical ask, as consent is the basis for American governmental authority more generally, and we are in so many ways already operating under this model.[42]

And now that we have nearly reached the end of our time together, let's pause, take a deep breath, and reflect on what we have accomplished on this journey and where we can and should go from here. My hope is that you are excited and energized by what you have read, but we should also be mindful that what I have proposed should be understood as a point of departure, not the solution unto itself. Merely yelling "CONSENT" at the top of our lungs in a courtroom is not going to win a lot of cases, nor will it adequately address the many and varied challenges that face Native America and this field of law. Instead, advocates and courts should confront exercises of federal authority (and state authority for that matter) with consent as the central tool of their analysis. It should be the guiding principle in reimagining a more just and humane relationship between Native America and the United States. That being noted, I will be honest with you and admit that it is going to take much more thought and effort than I can devote in this (already lengthy enough) book to imagine and articulate how consent is effectuated in any particular set of circumstances. Native America is full of all sorts of unique situations and derivations and aspects to consider. This book cannot solve any particular problem unto itself, but rather it offers a way to think about those problems anew. And that means there is more work to be done.

But it is work that needs to be done. And it needs to be done because it might save us from continuing to do the colonizer's work for the colonizer. Tribal advocates (myself very much included) need to stop regurgitating the worst trickster story ever told. We need to stop being afraid of what might happen in a world without plenary power. We need the courage to fight for something better. We can do this. We need to do this.

The story they have chosen to tell is wrong. They know it and we know it.

It is time to tell a better story.

Acknowledgments

I began to get serious about writing this book around the same time that my wife, the historian Jenny Tone-Pah-Hote, was diagnosed with leukemia. In the all-too-brief yet still painfully long period when she was fighting for her life against a terrible disease—which happened to coincide with the onset of the COVID pandemic—during those moments when I couldn't think of anything else to talk about, I would tell her my latest thoughts on this project and ask her opinion. In the early months of her ordeal she would indulge me and help me think it through; in the later months when everything was harder, she would mostly just listen. She passed away long before I could take the project seriously enough to begin writing, which is a shame for you because this would be a much better book with her input. All of which is to note that the first thing I want to acknowledge is that cancer is just the worst.

More important, I want to acknowledge that there wouldn't even be a book for you to read were it not for Jenny. She was exactly what a spouse should be—a true partner in this life. During her illness I finally worked up the courage to tell her that I didn't (and still don't) think I would have finished graduate school if not for her caring and generosity and love. She guided me through my first research trip to the archive, which allowed me to complete my dissertation, and discovered the key issue that became the foundation for my first book. I truly do not know where I would be without her patience and direction in that seminal moment. She supported me in a million other ways as well, all of which I would like to tell you about but which I will refrain from doing because otherwise I would blow past the word count that I am contractually obligated to keep this book under. Just know that what I really want to acknowledge is that I loved her and I miss her.

Anyway, it turns out that there are a bunch of other people and entities that deserve acknowledgment, and that, to the best of my knowledge, I have never been married to and/or that haven't died at a tragically early age. And since I am not clever enough to come up with a smooth transition, I will just start listing them.

First and foremost, there is my son, Steven, who somehow managed to find his way into this book a few times. As of this writing he is eight years old, and "precocious" is not nearly a strong enough word to describe him. A parent of his best friend at school once told me that she needed to talk to the principal at their school about something. During the course of the conversation the parent mentioned that her son was friends with a kid named Steven, without providing a last name or any further detail. The principal, knowing immediately whom she was referencing, stated, "Oh, you mean the man in the little boy's body?" That is Steven—a trickster who can already shape-shift. He is beautiful and athletic and funny and intelligent and kind, and, thankfully, he loves hockey as much as his dad. Moreover, the absolutely most true and best thing that I can say about the boy is that Jenny would be so very proud of her son. I was exceptionally fortunate that, the day after Jenny died, I still needed to get up and make breakfast for him.

There is also the rest of my family as well, to whom I remain grateful. I won't get too specific because I don't want to leave anybody out and I have already acknowledged many folks in other places. However, I do want to note my maternal grandmother, who passed away while I was writing this book. Reine Freeman was very patient and loving and generous with her oldest grandchild, taking the time to teach me cribbage as well as other card and board games and many other things. During the course of overlapping lifetimes we went from her making sure that I counted my cards correctly and that I took all my points to me making sure that she did. I wish that I could have one more game of cribbage with her. I wouldn't even gloat if I skunked her.

And then there are Uncle Ian and Aunt Michelle. Although not related by blood, they are a significant part of our family. Aunt Michelle was Jenny's closest friend at the University of North Carolina, and probably overall. Uncle Ian is just a really good dude. They were kind enough to set up and endure regular Sunday-night dinners with Steven and me at a time when I wanted to hide from the world. It is a tradition that I am glad we started, am thankful that we continued, and am going to miss as I transition to the next stage of my career. I will also never forget how much they loved donkey meat.[1]

Without the generous support of the National Humanities Center this book would have only happened many years later, or maybe not at all. My year at the NHC was foundational and came along at just the right time. I was growing increasingly frustrated and restless with students, colleagues, and the rest of the trappings of an academic life. For the first time that I can remember, I didn't want to be on campus. Receiving the call that let me know I was being awarded an NHC fellowship was one of those rare moments of satisfaction in a profession that is definitely not for those who need instant gratification. Moreover, the experience at the NHC was second to none. It was a joy to go to my office every day and to have the time and space to read and think and write (and nap). I am also so thankful to note that each and every one of the other fellows during that year was an absolute delight (with the exception of one jerk who shall go unnamed[2]). In addition, the staff at the NHC is world class and honored every silly request promptly and with the utmost professionalism. I won't single out individuals at the NHC for fear of not mentioning someone who truly deserves it, but I will note that, without question, the most important people in the building were Jim and Tom, who made an amazing lunch for us every day. Life is always better when someone makes you a good meal and there is a plate of cookies waiting afterward. Also, churro day was the best.

My year on fellowship was incredibly productive for many reasons, not the least of which was that I more or less began it at the Native Peoples, American Colonialism, and the U.S. Constitution Interdisciplinary Summer Workshop at Yale University in the summer of 2022. The workshop, cosponsored by the Institute for Constitutional Studies and the NYU–Yale American Indian Sovereignty Project, brought together an absolutely wonderful collection of scholars at various stages of their career to think and converse deeply about the relationship between Native America and the U.S. Constitution. Those four days with folks who were interested in many of the same questions I was interested in was precisely the spark of inspiration that I needed to finally tackle the question at the heart of this book, a question that had plagued me for over two decades by that point. I am truly grateful to the convenors and hosts of the workshop, Ned Blackhawk, Maggie Blackhawk, and Greg Ablavsky, for allowing me to take part and to the other participants who were just delightful. My only regret is that we didn't follow through on our plan to all stay in Ned's basement and continue the workshop into perpetuity.

As I write this, I have not yet begun in my new position as director of the Indigenous Peoples Law and Policy Program and professor at the Rogers College of Law at the University of Arizona. Nonetheless, I want to acknowledge my soon-to-be colleagues and thank them for taking a chance on me. I got my LL.M. at Arizona, and that year in the IPLP Program was far more critical in my development as a scholar and person than I realized then and perhaps even now. I hope to bestow at least some measure of that same positive experience on the students I will soon be working with. I must also thank the current IPLP director, Robert A. Williams Jr. More than just a titan in my chosen field whose work has deeply influenced my own, Rob has been an exceptional mentor and guiding light during my career. He is a kind man who cares deeply about Native America, and I can't believe I get to be his colleague.

My (as of this writing) impending departure from the University of North Carolina–Chapel Hill has been a little weird.[3] Nonetheless, I am more than happy to acknowledge that my time at UNC was positive and helped me further develop as a scholar and person. There are lots of good folks at UNC fighting the good fight, and, again without naming them all, I will take note of Kathleen DuVal. She is a tremendous historian and kind person who recognizes that I am hilarious and who was generous enough to read drafts of every chapter of this book. I assure you, it is much better for her insight. Also, Duke sucks.

Before I got to UNC, I was an assistant professor at the University of North Dakota School of Law. And before that I was a graduate and law (and undergraduate!) student at the University of Minnesota. I have acknowledged these places and the people within them before, so I won't spend a lot of time on them here. But I would be remiss if I didn't continue to take at least some small note of the significant influence these places had on me. I am grateful to have been a part of both.

I also want to thank my good friend Emma Hughes for her encouragement and support as I finished writing the manuscript and began marching down the long road to publication. Emma is an incredibly hardworking, dedicated, compassionate barrister in London, and she was kind enough to show me around the city. It was fun.

I also want to thank and acknowledge Skylar and (a different) Emma. Once I became a single father, I also quickly became disabused of the notion that I could do it all alone. Both Skylar and Emma were trusted, reliable babysitters who offered much-needed relief many times and allowed Dad to keep playing in his old-man hockey league on Sunday nights. Those games, as well as the many other times that Skylar and Emma (and plenty of others who are represented by these two) came to my rescue, kept me sane. Skylar and Emma's help made way more than just this book possible. Steven really loves the both of you.

I also want to thank my old-man hockey league at the Orange County Sportsplex in Hillsborough, North Carolina. Those were some good games, boys.

And then there are the gentlemen-scholars of the Great Baseball Road Trip. Around thirty years ago my best friend since the seventh grade, Michael Rand, and I decided to take a multiday road trip to various baseball parks. It was a really good time. Since then, a core group of friends turned it into an annual tradition. Participation waxed and waned as lives and families and careers changed, but for a very long while the GBRT always occurred. Then COVID happened and there hasn't been a proper GBRT since. Despite this, we have managed to stay connected, usually with weekly Mario Kart sessions. I'm sure those evenings playing a goofy video game was good for all of us as the world was stuck at home, but it was especially critical for me as I was also coping with my wife's passing. Thank you, boys; it meant a lot. And I look forward to the teasing that this earnest and genuine expression of emotion will undoubtedly provoke.

Last but certainly not least, I want to acknowledge and thank all of the haters.

Notes

Preface

1. For a brief detailing of some of the trickster figures found in Native America, see Richard Erdoes and Alfonso Ortiz, "Introduction," in *American Indian Trickster Tales*, by Richard Erdoes and Alfonso Ortiz (New York: Penguin Books, 1999), xiii–xxi.

2. For a story about how Rabbit can talk too much, see Tim Tingle and Pat Lewis, "Rabbit's Choctaw Tail Tale," in *Trickster: Native American Tales, a Graphic Collection*, ed. Matt Dembicki (Golden, CO: Fulcrum Publishing, 2010), 79–88.

3. This story is adapted from Michael Thompson and Jacob Warrenfeltz, "Rabbit and the Tug-of-War," in Dembicki, ed., *Trickster*, 63–70.

4. My wife, Kiowa historian Jenny Tone-Pah-Hote, used to tell me that there was a Saynday story like this one. However, she would only tell me that such a story existed, not what the story was. Jenny was a modest woman, and, as you will see, this is the type of story that would easily redden her cheeks were she to tell it. Thus, I don't fully recall what piece of clothing Saynday needed. I wish I could ask her as I write this in the fall of 2022. Unfortunately, to my everlasting sorrow, she passed away in the summer of 2020 from leukemia. This is why Saynday's confusion makes sense to me. I still miss Jenny very much.

5. Erdoes and Ortiz state that such modesty was unnecessary back in the day. "It should be noted, too, that there are no 'dirty' words in Indian languages. A penis is a penis, not a 'dick' or a 'peter,' and a vulva is just that, not a 'twat' or a 'snatch.'" Erdos and Ortiz, *Trickster Tales*, 21.

Chapter 1

1. Sydney L. Harring, *Crow Dog's Case: American Indian Sovereignty, Tribal Law, and United States Law in the Nineteenth Century* (New York: Cambridge University Press, 1994), 109.

2. Ibid., 108–9.

3. Ibid., 110.

4. Ibid.

5. See "Chapter 5—The Allotment Era," in *Federal Indian Law and Policy: An Introduction*, by Keith Richotte, Jr. (St. Paul, MN: West Academic Publishing, 2020), 93–112.

6. Ibid.

7. Richard H. Pratt, "The Advantages of Mingling Indians with Whites," in *Americanizing the American Indian: Writings by the Friends of the Indians, 1880–1900*, ed. Francis Paul Prucha (Cambridge, MA: Harvard University Press, 1973), 261.

8. This is why civil law is sometimes referred to as "private law" and criminal law is sometimes referred to as "public law." It is also why suits between private parties are titled something like *Smith v. Jones* while criminal cases are often titled *[Name of a state] v. Johnson* or *The People v. Edwards*.

9. Harring, *Crow Dog's Case*, 110.

10. Ibid., 115.

11. Ibid., 118–26.

12. Vine Deloria Jr. and Clifford M. Lytle, *American Indians, American Justice* (Austin: University of Texas Press, 1983), 168–69. Sydney L. Harring, the foremost historian of this incident, acknowledges this story but does cast some doubt upon its veracity. Harring, *Crow Dog's Case*, 125.

13. Harring, *Crow Dog's Case*, 115.

14. As Harring has noted, "The dispute between Spotted Tail and Crow Dog cannot be understood in contemporary U.S. cultural terms." Ibid., 107.

15. Richotte, *Federal Indian Law*, 123.

16. I leave it up to you to decide which system is more civilized.

17. *Nix v. Hedden*, 149 U.S. 304 (1893).

18. 109 U.S. 556 (1883).

19. Ibid. at 557–58.

20. In 1871 Congress "ended" treaty making with tribal nations with a small rider buried deep within a much larger appropriations bill. Appropriations Act of March 3, 1871, 16 Stat. 544, 566 (codified as amended at 25 U.S.C. § 71). Despite the ostensible demise of treaties, the federal government continued to negotiate "agreements" with tribal nations for several decades after the 1871 rider. Agreements functioned in much the same way as treaties, with the only real difference being that agreements required passage in both houses of Congress whereas treaties required approval only in the Senate. Vine Deloria Jr. and David E. Wilkins, *Tribes, Treaties, and Constitutional Tribulations* (Austin:

University of Texas Press, 1999), 60. See also Vine Deloria Jr. and Raymond J. DeMallie, *Documents of American Indian Diplomacy, Vols. 1 and 2* (Norman: University of Oklahoma Press, 1999). Consequently, the 1868 treaty and the 1877 agreement considered in this dispute functioned in the same manner.

21. *Ex Parte Crow Dog* at 567.

22. Harring, *Crow Dog's Case*, 132–33.

23. *Ex Parte Crow Dog* at 569.

24. Ibid. at 571.

25. Ibid.

26. Ibid.

27. *U.S. Statutes at Large*, 23:385.

28. As of today the Major Crimes Act covers over thirty offenses. Felix S. Cohen, *Handbook of Federal Indian Law (2012 ed.)* (San Francisco: LexisNexis, 2012), 750.

29. Obviously I don't know if you took your high school civics class in the tenth grade or another grade or if you took it at all. To be honest, I don't recall in which grade I took it. But I'm on a roll here, so let's not let this insignificant detail distract us from the larger point.

30. Sidney L. Harring, "The Distorted History That Gave Rise to the 'So Called' Plenary Power Doctrine: The Story of *United States v. Kagama*," in *Indian Law Stories*, ed. Carole Goldberg, Kevin K. Washburn, and Philip P. Frickey (New York: Thompson Reuters/Foundation Press, 2011), 157.

31. Ibid., 155–56. The irony was further compounded by the fact that the Allotment Act, the legislation with which the federal government undertook the allotment process on many tribal lands, was still a year away from passage and the agent on the reservation had taken it upon himself to begin allotting lands of his own accord. Allotment Act, *U.S. Statutes at Large*, 24:388–91. Harring suggests that the Indian agent may have taken this premature step to protect tribal interests. Harring, "Distorted History," 155–56. Nonetheless, that this tool of civilization would provoke the killing offers evidence that allotment lacked the curative powers that reformers of the day expected it to have.

32. Harring, "Distorted History," 157, 169.

33. *United States. v. Kagama*, 118 U.S. 375 (1886).

34. U.S. Constitution, art. I, sec. 2, cl. 3; and 14th Am., sec. 2.

35. David E. Wilkins, *American Indian Sovereignty and the U.S. Supreme Court: The Masking of Justice* (Austin: University of Texas Press, 1997), 70–71.

36. *Kagama* at 378–79.

37. Ibid. at 378.

38. Or maybe I am less of a ham and just more of a dork. Whatever. Your labels mean nothing to me. Besides, this example works, so I am going to keep using it.

39. *Kagama* at 381.

40. Miller's opinion has been described by one prominent source as "not known for its coherence or clarity." Cohen, *Handbook (2012 ed.)*, 390.

41. *Kagama* at 379.

42. Ibid. at 380.

43. Ibid. at 384.

44. Ibid. at 382.

45. Ibid. at 383.

46. Ibid. at 384.

47. Ibid. at 384–85.

48. As discussed later in this chapter, *Kagama* is the first of three cases from the Allotment Era that significantly broadened the Plenary Power Doctrine. See also *Lone Wolf v. Hitchcock*, 187 U.S. 553 (1903); and *United States v. Sandoval*, 231 U.S. 28 (1913).

49. As Deloria and Wilkins put it, "The final analysis of the *Kagama* case, a conclusion that most lawyers and federal officials are reluctant to draw, is that somehow the Supreme Court held a federal statute applying to Indians to be constitutional while rejecting every possible constitutional clause and phrase that would render it so." Deloria and Wilkins, *Tribes, Treaties*, 79.

50. For a brief history of the development and persistence of race and racism in the United States, see David R. Roediger, *How Race Survived U.S. History: From Settlement and Slavery to the Obama Phenomenon* (London: Verso, 2008).

51. As Philip P. Frickey aptly describes it, "*Kagama* was the first case in which the Supreme Court essentially embraced the doctrine that Congress has plenary power over Indian affairs. Its apparent inconsistency with the most fundamental of constitutional principles—the *McCulloch* understanding that Congress ordinarily possesses only that authority delegated to it in the Constitution—is an embarrassment of constitutional theory. Its slipshod method of bootstrapping a congressional plenary power over Indian affairs is an embarrassment of logic. Its holding, which intimates that congressional power over Indian affairs is limitless, is an embarrassment of humanity." Philip P. Frickey, "Domesticating Federal Indian Law," *Minnesota Law Review* 81, no. 1 (November 1996): 35.

52. According to the tribal nation's website, the reservation is "just a 30-minute ferry ride away from Downtown Seattle." "Frequently Asked Questions," Suquamish Tribe, 2024, https://suquamish.nsn.us/home/about-us/faqs/.

53. Sarah Krakoff, "Mark the Plumber v. Tribal Empire, or Non-Indian Anxiety v. Tribal Sovereignty? The Story of *Oliphant v. Suquamish Indian Tribe*," in Goldberg, Washburn, and Frickey, eds., *Indian Law Stories*, 264, 270.

54. Ibid., 271.

55. Ibid.

56. 435 U.S. 191 (1978). Concerning *Oliphant*'s scholarly reception, one noteworthy professor, Robert Williams, has written, "*Oliphant* is one of the most

important Indian law decisions issued by the Supreme Court in the post-*Brown* era, and it unembarrassedly perpetuates the Marshall model's overarching principle of white racial supremacy contained in the European colonial-era doctrine of discovery. It does so through a particularly virulent mode of rights-destroying, jurispathic transmission. *Oliphant*, as written by Rehnquist, cites, quotes, and relies upon racist nineteenth-century beliefs and stereotypes to justify an expansive, rights-destroying, present-day interpretation of the Marshall model. According to *Oliphant*, Indian tribes, as lawless and uncivilized savage peoples, were implicitly divested of any asserted rights that might conflict with the superior sovereign interests of the United States under the discovery doctrine." Robert A. Williams Jr., *Like a Loaded Weapon: The Rehnquist Court, Indian Rights, and the Legal History of Racism in America* (Minneapolis: University of Minnesota Press, 2005), 97–98. Williams may be alone in his distinctive writing style, but he is hardly without compatriots in his critique of the case.

57. As John H. Vinzant puts it, "The Court, in the 1970's, began to make a distinction between geographical sovereignty and member based sovereignty. Member based sovereignty meant tribes only wielded power over tribal members in certain instances. The task for the Court was determining the boundaries of this power." John H. Vinzant, *The Supreme Court's Role in American Indian Policy* (El Paso, TX: LFB Scholarly Publishing, 2009), 133.

58. Stephen L. Pevar, *The Rights of Indians and Tribes*, 4th ed. (New York: Oxford University Press, 2012), 131–32.

59. *Oliphant* at 208.

60. "We recognize that some Indian tribal court systems have become increasingly sophisticated and resemble in many respects their state counterparts. We also acknowledge that with the passage of the Indian Civil Rights Act of 1968, which extends certain basic procedural rights to anyone tried in Indian tribal court, many of the dangers that might have accompanied the exercise by tribal courts of criminal jurisdiction over non-Indians only a few decades ago have disappeared. Finally, we are not unaware of the prevalence of non-Indian crime on today's reservations which the tribes forcefully argue requires the ability to try non-Indians. But these are considerations for Congress to weigh in deciding whether Indian tribes should finally be authorized to try non-Indians. They have little relevance to the principles which lead us to conclude that Indian tribes do not have inherent jurisdiction to try and to punish non-Indians." Ibid. at 211–12.

61. As noted by N. Bruce Duthu about *Oliphant*, "The Court, drawing mostly from nineteenth-century precedents, revived the assimilation-era doctrine of *United States v. Kagama*." N. Bruce Duthu, *American Indians and the Law* (New York: Viking, 2008), 21.

62. As Williams notes, "In its efforts to reconstruct *Crow Dog* as a color-

blind application of the principle that it is unfair to subject one race of people to the alien laws and penalties of another race, something important has been left out of *Oliphant*'s text. Rehnquist's careful elision of *Crow Dog*'s extensive nineteenth-century catalog of negative racial stereotypes of Indians obscures the full extent of the discriminatory, racist meanings of what Matthews is really saying in *Crow Dog*." Williams, *Like a Loaded Weapon*, 109.

63. 495 U.S. 676 (1990).

64. Bethany R. Berger, "*United States v. Lara* as a Story of Native Agency," *Tulsa Law Review* 40, no. 1 (Fall 2004): 11.

65. *Duro* at 679.

66. Ibid. at 688.

67. Ibid.

68. Ibid. at 693.

69. Ibid.

70. See "Chapter 10—The Self-Determination Era," in Richotte, *Federal Indian Law*, 193–213.

71. 25 U.S.C.A. § 1301(2).

72. "Nor shall any person be subject for the same offence to be twice put in jeopardy of life or limb." U.S. Constitution, 5th Am.

73. Consequently, as your criminal law professor is likely to tell you, should you be foolish enough to go to law school, if a person is acquitted of a crime, the person could walk out to the courthouse steps and confess to the crime immediately after the verdict and the government couldn't do anything about it. This is, of course, an overly simplistic example, and if one government (say, a state government) couldn't do anything about it, then perhaps another (say, the federal government) could. In addition, the Double Jeopardy Clause does not protect against charges for a different or a subsequent crime. Nonetheless, this example gets the point across.

74. Berger, "*United States v. Lara*," 11–12.

75. 25 U.S.C. § 1301 et seq.

76. The limited options for punishments under the Indian Civil Rights Act create a perverse disincentive for tribal nations to prosecute significant crimes and to further invest in tribal criminal justice systems. But that is a conversation for a different book.

77. Berger, "*United States v. Lara*," 13–14.

78. Richotte, *Federal Indian Law*, 388–89.

79. *United States v. Lara*, 541 U.S. 193 (2004).

80. Ibid. at 200.

81. Ibid. at 202.

82. Ibid.

83. Ibid. at 200.

84. Ibid.

85. Ibid.

86. I don't actually believe that I am the cleverest Indian law scholar in the world. But I do think I have a shot at being the funniest.

87. At least that's how the dictionary app on my computer defines it.

88. "Crusaders were offered a plenary indulgence by the Pope" is the sentence the dictionary app on my computer offers. I didn't say the sentence was always useful, just that it was often provided.

89. It is possible to parse "plenary' in more than two ways. For example, two prominent scholars have offered three different definitions: as an exclusive power, as a preemptive power, and as an unlimited and absolute power. They argue that their first two understandings of plenary power in Indian law are valid and appropriate, and the third is not. See Chapter 3, "'Such an Outrage': The Doctrine of Plenary Power," in *Uneven Ground: American Indian Sovereignty and Federal Law,* by David E. Wilkins and K. Tsianina Lomawaima (Norman: University of Oklahoma Press, 2001), 98–116. In limiting my discussion to two definitions, I do not mean to suggest that the scholars who identify more than two versions of plenary power are wrong. Rather, for the purposes of this project it is less useful to identify all the ways plenary power could be understood than it is to define the big categories under which all of the more minute definitions might fall.

90. 31 U.S. 515 (1832).

91. 21 U.S. 543 (1823).

92. 30 U.S. 1 (1831).

93. You might start with the following: Lindsay G. Robertson, *Conquest by Law: How the Discovery of America Dispossessed Indigenous Peoples of Their Lands* (New York: Oxford University Press, 2005); Blake A. Watson, *Buying America from the Indians:* Johnson v. McIntosh *and the History of Native Land Rights* (Norman: University of Oklahoma Press, 2012); and Jill Norgren, *The Cherokee Cases: Two Landmark Federal Decisions in the Fight for Sovereignty* (Norman: University of Oklahoma Press, 2003).

94. *Worcester* at 557.

95. Ibid. at 561.

96. Ibid.

97. Ibid. at 559.

98. States were generally not respectful of the borders—geographical, legal, political, or otherwise—ostensibly established in *Worcester* and routinely grabbed authority over Native peoples and spaces. See Deborah A. Rosen, *American Indians and State Law: Sovereignty, Race, and Citizenship, 1790–1880* (Lincoln: University of Nebraska Press, 2007). The federal government did push back on a number of these efforts—seemingly primarily to protect its own interests in the federalism model and secondarily to protect tribal interests—but not with nearly enough vigor to seriously discourage state intrusions let

alone eliminate them. In a pivotal 1959 case, *Williams v. Lee*, the Supreme Court echoed the basic understanding in *Worcester* but acknowledged a retreat from its holding. "Over the years this Court has modified these principles in cases where essential tribal relations were not involved and where the rights of Indians would not be jeopardized, but the basic policy of *Worcester* has remained." *Williams v. Lee*, 358 U.S. 217 (1959), 219. By the early twenty-first century the Supreme Court had moved far enough from *Worcester*'s holding that it could claim, "State sovereignty does not end at a reservation's border." *Nevada v. Hicks*, 533 U.S. 353 (2001), 361.

99. For a useful articulation of the Allotment Era, see Fredrick H. Hoxie, *A Final Promise: The Campaign to Assimilate the Indians, 1880–1920* (Lincoln: University of Nebraska Press, 1984).

100. As Petra A. Shattuck and Jill Norgren point out, "While the 'plenary' character of federal power with respect to Indian tribes had originally been understood to demarcate the exclusive nature of the federal authority over Indian affairs against competing state laws and private deals, the reach of the government's plenary power came to be understood as 'nearly absolute' with respect to the tribes themselves by the end of the nineteenth century." Petra A. Shattuck and Jill Norgren, *Partial Justice: Federal Indian Law in a Liberal Constitutional System* (New York: Berg, distributed exclusively in the United States and Canada by St. Martin's Press, 1991), 121.

101. See Blue Clark, Lone Wolf v. Hitchcock: *Treaty Rights and Indian Law at the end of the Nineteenth Century* (Lincoln: University of Nebraska Press, 1994); Angela R. Riley, "The Apex of Congress' Plenary Power over Indian Affairs: The Story of *Lone Wolf v. Hitchcock*," in Goldberg, Washburn, and Frickey, eds., *Indian Law Stories*, 189–228.

102. *Lone Wolf* at 565.

103. Ibid. at 566. As Vine Deloria Jr. noted, "That decision slammed the door on the question of morality and justice. It was like appointing a fox to guard the chicken coop." Vine Deloria Jr., *Custer Died for Your Sins: An Indian Manifesto* (New York: Macmillan, 1969), 37.

104. See Gerald Torres, "Who Is an Indian? The Story of *United States v. Sandoval*," in Goldberg, Washburn, and Frickey, eds., *Indian Law Stories*, 109–45.

105. *Sandoval* at 48.

106. It was also a time, as we will explore in greater detail in Chapter 3, when American courts were developing parallel articulations of plenary power against immigrants and American colonies. See Natsu Taylor Saito, *From Chinese Exclusion to Guantánamo Bay: Plenary Power and the Prerogative State* (Boulder: University of Colorado Press, 2007).

107. *Morton v. Mancari*, 417 U.S. 535, 555 (1974).

108. On rare occasions, the Supreme Court has struck down parts of federal legislation concerning Native peoples based on violations of specific constitu-

tional provisions. For example, in 1996 the Court found that a portion of the Indian Gaming Regulatory Act (IGRA) was unconstitutional under the 11th Amendment. See *Seminole Tribe of Florida v. Florida*, 517 U.S. 44 (1996). However, it is fair to ask about the extent to which these limitations affect plenary power over Native peoples. For example, the offending part of IGRA in *Seminole Tribe* concerned a waiver of state sovereign immunity. Moreover, neither plenary power itself nor the Indian Commerce Clause has been the basis to find an act of Congress concerning Native peoples unconstitutional.

109. This assumes, of course, that he would ever want to talk about it again.

110. U.S. Constitution, art. VI. Truthfully, this end note feels kind of redundant, but it's better to be safe than sorry I guess.

111. 142 S. Ct. 2228 (2022).

112. 410 U.S. 113 (1973).

113. As acknowledged in note 108 of this chapter, while on rare occasion the Supreme Court has found that some aspect of legislation that touches upon Native America might be invalid under the U.S. Constitution, neither plenary power itself nor the Indian Commerce Clause has been the basis to find an act of Congress concerning Native peoples unconstitutional. The authority that has been exercised under plenary power has been frighteningly extensive and far beyond our traditional understanding of the limits of governmental authority. For a particularly egregious example, see *United States v. Clapox*, 35 F. 575 (1888).

114. *Lone Wolf* at 564.

115. *Sandoval* at 39.

116. We will wrestle with this conundrum in greater detail in Chapter 4.

117. *Lara* at 200.

118. As Sarah H. Cleveland has noted, "The Supreme Court has spent much of the past century repackaging the inherent powers doctrines into traditional enumerated categories without significant change to the underlying holdings. Rationales that allowed the exercise of governmental power based on doctrines of inherent powers and international law now parade as enumerated text without any recognition either of the international law origins of the principles or the racist, illiberal ideology on which they are based." Sarah H. Cleveland, "Powers Inherent in Sovereignty: Indians, Aliens, Territories, and the Nineteenth Century Origins of Plenary Power over Foreign Affairs," *Texas Law Review* 81, no. 1 (November 2002): 278.

119. Early in life, in part because of these meetings, I decided that I was not going to be a drinker. I have stuck to my decision and can truthfully say that, while I have indulged in the occasional sip of this or that, I have never been drunk (or all that close). Nonetheless, because of these experiences with my father, I have long contended that I have been to more AA meetings than most alcoholics.

Chapter 2

1. It also feels unnecessarily provocative, and maybe even dangerous, to describe something as a "conspiracy" as I write these words in 2023, as a number of truly bizarre and hardly benign conspiracy theories have snuck into enough mainstream thought to have significantly altered the landscape in which we live.

2. I'm going to go ahead and presume that you have read Chapter 1, so I'm not going to rehash why it is important to solve this mystery right now. If you haven't read Chapter 1, I encourage you to do so and can't help wondering why you are reading this book out of order. Did a professor of yours assign only this chapter in this book? You should tell that professor to assign the whole book.

3. *Lara* at 200.

4. Seriously, just go read Chapter 1 right now if you haven't already.

5. I promise that this will be the last "meta."

6. The Declaration actually uses the words "all men" when making reference to the universality of rights among individuals. Such language offers a telling glimpse into the scope of peoples whom the signers of the Declaration sought to include and exclude in their understanding of who could claim the rights they sought to claim for themselves. For the limited purpose of constructing a usable theory of American governance for this chapter, I am utilizing more generous language than is found in the original document. If you are (understandably) troubled by this choice, I ask for your patience. We will be addressing the less inclusive aspects of the exercise of federal power in short order. Declaration of Independence.

7. Ibid.

8. Ibid.

9. As described by Deloria and Wilkins, "The freedom of individual sovereignty thus meant an absolute power of control over person and property. The social contract occurred when the individual surrendered part of this absolute right to control and protect their person and property to the group and received in return its protection." Vine Deloria Jr. and David E. Wilkins, *The Legal Universe: Observations on the Foundations of American Law* (Golden, CO: Fulcrum Publishing, 2011), 6.

10. 10th Am., U.S. Constitution.

11. As Thurman Lee Hester Jr. noted, "Thus the states are said to be sovereign though their power is severely limited by the Federal Government. This is because the power of both the state and Federal Governments are derived from the same source: the people. The United States government, through the Constitution, is founded on the principle of popular sovereignty." Thurman Lee Hester Jr., *Political Principles & Indian Sovereignty* (New York: Routledge, 2001), 95–96. Although political scientists would likely bristle at such a statement, for our purposes we can roughly equate Hester's description of "popular sovereignty" with our understanding of the social contract.

12. Put more sophisticatedly, Maggie Blackhawk reminds us, "At the heart of constitutional law is the question of how best to constitute, distribute, and limit government power." Maggie Blackhawk, "Federal Indian Law as Paradigm Within Public Law," *Harvard Law Review* 132, no. 7 (May 2019): 1791.

13. Matthew Fletcher takes it a step further, arguing that "consent theory is of course a pure fiction, in that no one person has ever 'consented' to the American federal government's authority except in symbolic or meaningless ways." Matthew L. M. Fletcher, "Tribal Consent," *Stanford Journal of Civil Rights & Civil Liberties* 8, no. 1 (April 2012): 45–122, 50. I do not disagree with this assertion, yet I still find utility in engaging with the concepts of consent, the social contract, and their ilk on their own terms for reasons that I hope are made clear later in this chapter.

14. Richard B. Collins puts it this way: "That governments derive 'their just powers from the consent of the governed' is among the Declaration's self-evident truths." Richard B. Collins, "Indian Consent to American Government," *Arizona Law Review* 31, no. 2 (1989): 370.

15. A number of Indian law scholars have noted that this basic understanding is foundational to theories of American governance. For example, T. Alexander Aleinikoff stated, "The idea of popular sovereignty is that a contract has been formed among the members to establish a state and to delegate to it powers to act on their behalf." T. Alexander Aleinikoff, *Semblances of Sovereignty: The Constitution, the State, and American Citizenship* (Cambridge, MA: Harvard University Press, 2002), 5. Wilkins and Lomawaima reminded us, "'Consent of the governed' is a treasured democratic principle." Wilkins and Lomawaima, *Uneven Ground*, 110. Early in one of his most prominent articles, Robert N. Clinton noted, "Specifically, this essay suggests that application of the Supreme Court's historically-based, originalist methodology to those portions of the Constitution dealing with federal power over Indian affairs compels the need to reexamine several basic Indian law doctrines, most notably the so-called federal Indian plenary power doctrine. It also suggests that such scrutiny is consistent with perhaps the most revered principle of the United States Constitution—namely, that all legitimate governmental authority derives from the consent of the people who have chosen to delegate only certain limited powers to the federal government (a theory often called 'popular delegation' or 'popular sovereignty')." Robert N. Clinton, "There Is No Federal Supremacy Clause for Indian Tribes," *Arizona State Law Journal* 34, no. 1 (Spring 2002): 113–260, 115.

16. For example, the extent to which it is realistic to believe that one can move to another state or country because one is discontented with the politics of where one currently resides is worthy of question, particularly for those facing economic, educational, or other socioeconomic disadvantages. And this is to say nothing of the challenges faced and still facing those who were

excluded from the social contract at the time of the founding of the United States. Matthew Fletcher argues that "the Framers were slaveholders and Indian-haters. They wrote a Constitution designed to maintain slavery and destroy Indians." Matthew L. M. Fletcher, *The Ghost Road: Anishinaabe Responses to Indian-Hating* (Wheat Ridge, CO: Fulcrum Publishing, 2020), 6. Obviously a lot has changed in the United States and with the U.S. Constitution since their inceptions. Have those changes been enough to make legitimate claims to the consent of those groups (and others excluded at the founding) to American governance presumed by social contract theory and the U.S. Constitution itself?

17. Others, of course, have made this point as well. Perhaps most forcefully, American Civil Liberties Union staff attorney and Indian law scholar Stephen L. Pevar wrote, "The United States controls Indian tribes because it has the military power to do so. The ultimate source of the federal government's power over Indians is its military strength. Other justifications are given besides this one, but the fact is that if the United States were not militarily more powerful, Indian tribes today would exercise the same sovereignty they did prior to the arrival of the Europeans." Pevar, *The Rights of Indians*, 56. Echoing this basic sentiment, Philip P. Frickey has stated about Indian law as a whole, "If there is any bedrock principle in the field at all, it is that might makes right." Philip P. Frickey, "Adjudication and Its Discontents: Coherence and Conciliation in Federal Indian Law," *Harvard Law Review* 110, no. 8 (June 1997): 1754–84, 1754–55.

18. The cynic in me has been especially emboldened ever since I was granted tenure.

19. Also, the cynic in me has yet to advance an argument on how I can convince a publisher to print a book with 150 blank pages.

20. See Robert A. Williams Jr., *The American Indian in Western Legal Thought: The Discourses of Conquest* (New York: Oxford University Press, 1990).

21. There isn't a definitive list of the sources of authority for plenary power that the Supreme Court has cited to which those of us who are concerned about such things agree. But I promise you that we are going to cover pretty much all of the ones that anyone might point to.

22. For example, see David J. Silverman, *This Land Is Their Land: The Wampanoag Indians, Plymouth Colony, and the Troubled History of Thanksgiving* (New York: Bloomsbury Publishing, 2019); James W. Baker, *Thanksgiving: The Biography of an American Holiday* (Durham: University of New Hampshire Press, 2009).

23. This is a typical first step for colonizers. One of the earliest and most famous attempts to justify the colonial presence in the Americas was the *Requerimiento*, a Spanish legal document that was intended to be read to the inhabitants of the "New World" and that ostensibly outlined the rights and obligations of the various parties under an international order. For a brief his-

tory of the development and implementation of the *Requerimiento*, see David Boucher, "Invoking a World of Ideas: Theory and Interpretation in the Justification of Colonialism," *Theoria: A Journal of Social and Political Theory* 63, no. 2 (2016): 8–11.

24. 10 U.S. 87 (1810).

25. For a brief detailing of the case, see C. F. Hobson, "The Yazoo Lands Sale Case: *Fletcher v. Peck* (1810)," *Journal of Supreme Court History* 42 (November 2017): 239–55.

26. In an important article, Howard R. Berman noted, "One of the central elements of this case was whether the State of Georgia had the power to convey a property interest in western lands that were in part held under 'Indian title.'" However, "in the majority opinion written by John Marshall, the Court in large part ignored the pleadings as to the nature of the Indian title." Howard R. Berman, "The Concept of Aboriginal Rights in the Early Legal History of the United States," *Buffalo Law Review* 27, no. 4 (Fall 1978): 638, 640.

27. *Fletcher v. Peck* at 142–43.

28. As Berman noted, "Remarkably, in this one phrase, Marshall was able to recognize the existence of the Indian title, reaffirm the role of the United States as the sovereign entity empowered to extinguish that title, and give the paramount property right to the lands in question to the State of Georgia. The Court thus validated the disputed covenant of the land conveyance, but at the expense of any clear definition of the nature of the Indian title." Berman, "Concept of Aboriginal Rights," 641.

29. The astoundingly ridiculous story of how this case came to be, as well as many other critical facets of the case that we will not be concentrating on in this chapter, is much better documented in two particularly noteworthy texts. See Robertson, *Conquest by Law*; and Watson, *Buying America*. Since I already cited these books in Chapter 1, I will also point you to a slightly more concise yet still powerful description of the case and its consequences. See Lindsay G. Robertson, "The Judicial Conquest of Native America: The Story of *Johnson v. M'Intosh*," in Goldberg, Washburn, and Frickey, eds., *Indian Law Stories*, 29–59.

30. As Marshall put it early in his opinion, "The inquiry, therefore, is, in a great measure, confined to the power of Indians to give, and of private individuals to receive, a title which can be sustained in the Courts of this country." *Johnson* at 571.

31. Which seems to be an increasingly challenging prospect for folks nowadays, but I hope that you'll play along.

32. Although it is worthy of note that what colonizing nations thought they were accomplishing with treaties was not always what tribal nations thought was being accomplished. See Robert A. Williams Jr., *Linking Arms Together: American Indian Treaty Visions of Law and Peace, 1600–1800* (New York: Oxford University Press, 1997).

33. I also always apologize for making them do this. Interestingly, there is apparently one of John Marshall's chairs in the library of one of the law schools where I have taught my Indian Law course (I note "apparently" because I have only heard about it and have never bothered to see it myself). Thus, for those students I get to tell them that they can imagine sitting in that chair. OK fine, maybe this wasn't that interesting.

34. Lindsay Robertson argues quite powerfully that John Marshall was perhaps not as thoughtful about this case as my approach in my course gives him credit for. Noting that the decision in *Johnson v. McIntosh* was handed down eight days after it was argued, Robertson stated, "I think the opinion offers an instructive picture of how intelligent people can sometimes unthinkingly create catastrophic problems they find themselves powerless to fix." Even so, Robertson also acknowledges that subsequent justices have forged that which John Marshall laid down into the basis for American claims to tribal lands that suited the ends of the colonizer. Robertson, *Conquest by Law*, xiii. Consequently, I believe that it is still worthy of conceptualizing the issue in the manner presented because it allows one to see how this construction of tribal rights is dominant and how, as will soon to be explained in this chapter, it led to American claims to plenary power over Native America.

35. *Johnson* at 572.

36. Ibid. at 573.

37. I must confess that the way that I teach this case in my course probably leaves the impression that John Marshall invented the Doctrine of Discovery out of thin air (I also suspect that I'm not the only professor who might leave this impression with her/his students). Nonetheless, as Marshall's own words attest, the Doctrine was well established by the time that *Johnson v. McIntosh* was decided. See Robert J. Miller, "The Doctrine of Discovery: The International Law of Colonialism," *Indigenous Peoples' Journal of Law, Culture, and Resistance* 5, no. 1 (2019): 36–37. Interestingly, Justice William Johnson's dissent in *Fletcher v. Peck* made reference to the Doctrine. "What, then, practically is the interest of the states in the soil of the Indians within their boundaries? Unaffected by particular treaties, it is nothing more than what was assumed at the first settlement of the country, to wit, a right of conquest or of purchase, exclusively of all competitors within certain defined limits." *Fletcher* at 147.

38. "This principle was, that discovery gave title to the government by whose subjects, or by whose authority, it was made, against all other European governments. . . . It was a right with which no Europeans could interfere. It was a right which all asserted for themselves, and to the assertion of which, by others, all assented." *Johnson* at 573.

39. Ibid. at 587.

40. Ibid. at 574.

41. Ibid.

42. Ibid.

43. It is worthy of note that the ruling of this case turns a basic rule of property law—one that you already know even if you haven't had any legal training—on its head. For example, let's say that I am selling a yacht (I mean, if we are going to make up examples, let's go big). Let's also say that at 10 a.m. I sell the yacht to person A. Then at 11 a.m. I sell the yacht to person B. Who owns the yacht? Again, you don't have to have had any legal training to know that A owns the yacht. I don't own the yacht because I sold it. B doesn't own it because I no longer had the right to sell the yacht. A owns the yacht because A bought it first. However, in *Johnson v. McIntosh* the Court decided that the second purchaser owned the property. In other words, the Supreme Court completely disrupted a simple principle of property law. Why? Well, hopefully the rest of this chapter offers a more fulsome explanation, but basically it's because American law goes crazy and folds over onto itself whenever Native peoples are involved.

44. Ibid. at 588.

45. Ibid. at 589.

46. Ibid.

47. Ibid. at 590.

48. Ibid.

49. Ibid. at 591.

50. Ibid.

51. "The absolute ultimate title has been considered as acquired by discovery, subject only to the Indian title of occupancy, which title the discoverers possessed the exclusive right of acquiring." Ibid. at 592.

52. As Berman puts it, Marshall "presented what might be termed a political standard based on the creation of a myth of conquest that was rooted in the judicial power to define, rather than in historical reality. It is on this point that the opinion becomes confusing and occasionally incoherent." Berman, "Concept of Aboriginal Rights," 647.

53. "However this restriction may be opposed to natural right, and to the usages of civilized nations, yet, if it be indispensable to that system under which the country has been settled, and be adapted to the actual condition of the two people, it may, perhaps, be supported by reason, and certainly cannot be rejected by Courts of justice." *Johnson* at 591–92.

54. Once established, this idea caught on quickly. Writing in 1835, Justice Henry Baldwin stated, "Subject to this right of [Native] possession, the ultimate fee was in the crown and its grantees, which could be granted by the crown or colonial legislatures while the lands remained in possession of the Indians, though possession could not be taken without their consent." *Mitchel v. United States*, 34 U.S. 711, 745–46 (1835). A year later, Baldwin wrote about tribal land claims, "This subject was so fully and ably considered in *M'Intosh*

v. Johnson, that we have only to refer to the language of the court to show that every European government claimed and exercised the right of granting lands, while in the occupation of the Indians." *United States v. Fernandez*, 35 U.S. 303, 304 (1836). Writing in 1840, Justice John McLean stated, "The Indian title being only a right of occupancy, the state of North Carolina had the power to grant fee in the lands, subject to this right." *Lessee of Lattimer v. Poteet*, 39 U.S. 4, 14 (1840).

55. *Scott v. Sandford*, 60 U.S. 393 (1857).

56. According to Taney, peoples of African descent were "considered as a subordinate and inferior class of beings, who had been subjugated by the dominant race, and, whether emancipated or not, yet remained subject to their authority, and had no rights or privileges but such as those who held the power and the Government might choose to grant them." Ibid. at 404–5.

57. *United States v. Rogers*, 45 U.S. 567 (1846).

58. Ibid. at 571.

59. Ibid. at 573.

60. Ibid. at 572.

61. As Williams described it, "Taney justified Congress's unlimited jurisdictional power over Indian affairs by reprising the Marshall model's rendition of the rights-destroying, jurispathic effects of the doctrine of discovery upon the Indian tribes of the continent." Williams, *Loaded Weapon*, 74.

62. "The situation of [peoples of African descent] was altogether unlike that of the Indian race. The latter, it is true, formed no part of the colonial communities, and never amalgamated with them in social connections or in government. But although they were uncivilized, they were yet a free and independent people, associated together in nations or tribes, and governed by their own laws. Many of these political communities were situated in territories to which the white race claimed the ultimate right of dominion. But that claim was acknowledged to be subject to the right of the Indians to occupy it as long as they though [*sic*] proper, and neither the English nor colonial Governments claimed or exercised any dominion over the tribe or nation by whom it was occupied, nor claimed the right to the possession of the territory, until the tribe or nation consented to cede it. These Indian Governments were regarded and treated as foreign Governments, as much so as if an ocean had separated the red man from the white; and their freedom has constantly been acknowledged, from the time of the first emigration to the English colonies to the present day, by the different Governments which succeeded each other. Treaties have been negotiated with them, and their alliance sought for in war; and the people who compose these Indian political communities have always been treated as foreigners not living under our Government." *Scott v. Sandford* at 403–4.

63. *United States Use of Mackey v. Coxe*, 59 U.S. 100, 103 (1856).

64. As Nell Jessup Newton put it, "The more the government's interest was

characterized as an ownership interest, the more it became possible to regard the ownership of land alone as giving the government power to govern Indians." Nell Jessup Newton, "Federal Power over Indians: Its Sources, Scope, and Limitations," *University of Pennsylvania Law Review* 132, no. 2 (January 1984): 209.

65. Quoting Marshall, "The Indian territory is admitted to compose a part of the United States. In all our geographical treatises, histories, and laws it is so considered." Quoting Taney, "We think it too firmly and clearly established to admit of dispute that the Indian tribes residing within the territorial limits of the United States are subject to their authority, and where the county occupied by them is not within the limits of one of the States Congress may, by law, punish any offence committed there, no matter whether the offender be a white man or an Indian." *The Cherokee Tobacco*, 78 U.S. 616, 619 (1870).

66. Ibid.

67. *Kagama* at 379. Of *Kagama*, Wilkins writes, "The court relied on geography as the basis for power. . . . In other words, 'ownership in the country' vested in the federal, not state, government, the virtually unreviewable plenary power of the Congress to do whatever it deemed essential to civilize and control Native peoples." David E. Wilkins, *Hollow Justice: A History of Indigenous Claims in the United States* (New Haven, CT: Yale University Press, 2013), xvi.

68. I am well aware that pretty much no human being has or ever will be described as a "casual reader of Supreme Court opinions," but I am trying to make a point here, so just go with me on this one.

69. For example, Marshall appears to have wanted to mitigate (although not entirely undo) the damage he did in *Johnson v. McIntosh* in the third case of his Trilogy, *Worcester v. Georgia*, noting the Doctrine of Discovery "regulated the right given by discovery among the european discoverers; but could not affect the rights of those already in possession, either as aboriginal occupants, or as occupants by virtue of a discovery made before the memory of man. It gave the exclusive right to purchase, but did not found that right on a denial of the right of the possessor to sell." *Worcester* at 544. Writing for the Court a few years after *Worcester*, Justice Henry Baldwin stated, "The merits of this case do not make it necessary to inquire whether the Indians within the United States had any other rights of soil or jurisdiction; it is enough to consider it as a settled principle, that their right of occupancy is considered as sacred as the fee simple of the whites." *Mitchel* at 747. "Fee simple" is a term of property law that denotes the strongest form of landownership. On several subsequent occasions American courts have described tribal occupancy rights as "sacred as the fee."

70. *Shoshone Tribe of Indians v. United States*, 299 U.S. 476, 496 (1937).

71. *United States v. McGowan*, 302 U.S. 535, 539 (1938).

72. "The line of cases adjudicating Indian rights on American soil leads to the conclusion that Indian occupancy, not specifically recognized as ownership

by action authorized by Congress, may be extinguished by the Government without compensation." *Tee-Hit-Ton Indians v. United States*, 348 U.S. 272, 288–89 (1955). This sentence immediately precedes the most infamous sentence of the case, which we will get to later in this chapter.

73. *Oliphant* at 208–9.

74. Ibid. at 209.

75. Ibid.

76. "The Congress shall have Power to dispose of and make all needful Rules and Regulations respecting the Territory or other Property belonging to the United States; and nothing in this Constitution shall be so construed as to Prejudice any Claims of the United States, or of any particular State." U.S. Constitution, art. IV, sec. 3, cl. 2. On rare occasion, the Supreme Court has suggested that this clause is the basis for federal plenary power over Native peoples. For example, in *United States v. Celestine*, Justice David J. Brewer wrote, "By the second clause of § 3, Art. IV, of the Constitution, to Congress, and to it alone, is given 'power to dispose of and make all needful rules and regulations respecting the territory or other property belonging to the United States.' From an early time in the history of the Government it has exercised this power, and has also been legislating concerning Indians occupying such territory." *United States v. Celestine*, 215 U.S. 278, 284 (1909). However, this reading of this section of the U.S. Constitution has not garnered much traction and has been critiqued close to as much as it has been offered. See *Federal Power Commission v. Tuscarora Indian Nation*, 262 U.S. 99, 129 (1960) (Black, J., dissenting).

77. As Hester notes, "Without harkening back to feudalism, it is hard to see how the United States could claim something like plenary power on the basis of the doctrine of discovery." Hester, *Political Principles*, 104.

78. For example, Article 10 of an 1838 removal treaty between the Miami and the United States noted, "And when the said tribe shall have emigrated, the United States shall protect the said tribe and the people thereof, in their rights and possessions, against the injuries, encroachments and oppressions of any person or persons, tribe or tribes whatsoever." Treaty with the Miami, November 6, 1838, 7 Stat. 569, Art. 10. Article 14 of an 1854 treaty stated, "The Shawnees acknowledge their dependence on the Government of the United States, and invoke its protection and care." Treaty with the Shawnee, May 10, 1854, 10 Stat. 1053, Art. 14. Article 1 of a post–Civil War treaty stated, "The Seminoles also agree to remain at peace with all other Indian tribes and themselves. In return for these pledges of peace and friendship, the United States guarantee them quiet possession of their country, and protection against hostilities on the part of other tribes." Treaty with the Seminole, March 21, 1866, 14 Stat. 755, Art. 1. These few examples illustrate the general trend in the language of many treaties in which the United States pledged protection to tribal nations.

79. "Despite the importance of the federal-Indian trust relationship, it is not always easy to clearly identify the origin of the federal obligation. Specific treaties can be identified as the source of some tribes. For others, executive agreements, legislation, and court decisions create the trust relationship." Institute for the Development of Indian Law, *Old Problems, Persistent Issues: Nine Essays on American Indian Law* (Washington, DC: Institute for the Development of Indian Law, 1979), 3.

80. As Matthew Fletcher notes, "This weakness and dependency language was about the source of federal power more than it was about actual Indian people." Fletcher, *Ghost Road*, 58.

81. For example, the famous (in Indian studies circles at least) Northwest Ordinance of 1787 stated, "The utmost good faith shall always be observed toward the Indians. . . . Laws founded in justice and humanity shall from time to time be made, for preventing wrongs being done to them, and for preserving peace and friendship with them." *Journals of the Continental Congress* 32:340–41. Also, as noted previously, many treaties contained language about protection.

82. As William C. Canby Jr. noted, "While Marshall's reference was perhaps more literary than legal and did not attempt to spell out the incidents of the guardian-ward relationship, his statement served as a conceptual basis for further evolution of the doctrine." William C. Canby Jr., *American Indian Law in a Nutshell*, 7th ed. (St. Paul, MN: West Academic Publishing, 2020), 41.

83. *Johnson v. McIntosh* at 591.

84. Ibid.

85. *Cherokee Nation* at 17.

86. Ibid.

87. Unsurprisingly, Native peoples did not regard familial terms in the same manner. As Williams noted, "Kinship terms were used in treaty making for a variety of purposes. Besides determining many of the minor protocols of council diplomacy, kinship terms were used to define the expected forms of behavior among treaty partners." Williams, *Linking Arms Together*, 71. As Williams also noted, for Native peoples, the designation of "father" in treaty relations had more to do with the obligations of the "father" than the subsummation of the rights of the "children." Ibid., 107–8.

88. "This principle, acknowledged by all Europeans, because it was the interest of all to acknowledge it, gave to the nation making the discovery, as its inevitable consequence, the sole right of acquiring the soil and of making settlements on it. It was an exclusive principle which shut out the right of competition among those who had agreed to it; not one which could annul the previous rights of those who had not agreed to it. It regulated the right given by discovery among the european discoverers; but could not affect the rights of those already in possession, either as aboriginal occupants, or as occupants by virtue of a discovery made before the memory of man. It gave the exclusive

right to purchase, but did not found that right on a denial of the right of the possessor to sell." *Worcester* at 544.

89. Ibid. at 552, 561.

90. *Parks v. Ross*, 52 U.S. 362, 374 (1851).

91. *Chouteau v. Molony*, 57 U.S. 203, 237–38 (1854).

92. *Scott v. Sandford* at 404.

93. *United States v. Forty-Three Gallons of Whiskey*, 93 U.S. 188, 194 (1876).

94. 95 U.S. 517 (1877).

95. Ibid. at 525.

96. Ibid. As Cleveland notes, "Like Justice Taney in *Rogers* . . . Justice Field reasoned that only internal conscience, rather than legal constraint, limited congressional authority in regulating Indian land rights. . . . Nothing in the opinion suggested any constitutional source of authority for this power or any constraint on its exercise." Cleveland, "Powers Inherent," 53–54.

97. *Elk v. Wilkins*, 112 U.S. 94, 99 (1884).

98. Stephen D. Bodayla, "'Can An Indian Vote?': *Elk v Wilkins*, a Setback for Indian Citizenship," *Nebraska History* 67 (1986): 373; Wilkins, *American Indian Sovereignty*, 119–20.

99. *Elk v. Wilkins* at 99. He also cited *Scott v. Sandford* to fortify his ruling. Ibid. at 100–101.

100. *Scott v. Sandford* at 106–7.

101. Of this era of legal history Shattuck and Norgren wrote, "Regardless of how Native Americans saw themselves, in the United States the status and position of the tribes had changed from that of independent nations to dependent wards of the federal government." Shattuck and Norgren, *Partial Justice*, 124. Clinton stated, "In the late nineteenth century, as the attention of the federal government increasingly turned toward colonialist expansion of political hegemony over the tribes, the trusteeship doctrine reemerged. This time, though, the doctrine was used as an affirmative source of federal authority, rather than merely as a description of legal status. Thus, in cases like *Kagama*, *Lone Wolf*, and *Sandoval*, the Court justified the emergence of the plenary power doctrine not on any textual source of authority derived from the Constitution but, rather, on the basis of the assumed obligation of the federal government as trustee to shoulder the white man's burden of leading its indigenous charges toward a more 'enlightened' way of life." Robert N. Clinton, "Redressing the Legacy of Conquest: A Vision Quest for a Decolonized Federal Indian Law," *Arkansas Law Review* 46, no. 1 (1993), 131–32.

102. *Kagama* at 383.

103. Succinctly summarizing how Miller's opinion relied on both of the major justifications for plenary power that we are tracing in this chapter, Milner S. Ball noted, "The grounds conjured by Miller to uphold Congress's power are that the federal government 'owns' the country and that Indians

are weak and helpless." Milner S. Ball, "Constitution, Court, Indian Tribes," *American Bar Foundation Research Journal* 12, no. 1 (Winter 1987): 52.

104. *Kagama* at 384. As the original Cohen *Handbook* notes, "Thus in *United States v. Kagama* the Supreme Court found that the protection of the Indians constituted a national problem and referred to the practical necessity of protecting the Indians and the nonexistence of such a power in the states." Felix S. Cohen, *Handbook of Federal Indian Law* (Washington, DC: USGPO, 1942), 90.

105. *Lone Wolf* at 564.

106. "In one of the cited cases it was clearly pointed out that Congress possessed a paramount power over the property of the Indians, by reason of its exercise of guardianship over their interests, and that such authority might be implied, even though opposed to the strict letter of a treaty with the Indians." Ibid. at 565.

107. Ibid. at 566.

108. *Sandoval* at 46.

109. Ibid. at 48.

110. "The recognized relation between the parties to this controversy, therefore, is that between a superior and an inferior, whereby the latter is placed under the care and control of the former. . . . The parties are not on an equal footing." *Choctaw Nation v. United States*, 119 U.S. 1, 28 (1886); "From the beginning of the government to the present time, they have been treated as 'wards of the nation,' 'in a state of pupilage,' 'dependent political communities.'" *Cherokee Nation v. Southern Kan. Ry. Co.*, 135 U.S. 641, 653 (1890); "The Indians of the country are considered as the wards of the nation, and whenever the United States set apart any land of their own as an Indian reservation, whether within a State or Territory, they have full authority to pass such laws and authorize such measures as may be necessary to give to these people full protection in their persons and property, and to punish all offences committed against them or by them within such reservations." *United States v. Thomas*, 151 U.S. 577, 585 (1894); "We repeat that in the view of the paramount authority of Congress over the Indian tribes, and of the duties imposed on the Government by their condition of dependency, we cannot say that Congress could not empower the Dawes Commission to determine, in the manner provided, who were entitled to citizenship in each of the tribes and make out correct rolls of such citizens, an essential preliminary to effective action in promotion of the best interests of the tribes." *Stephens v. Cherokee Nation*, 174 U.S. 445, 488 (1899); "The Indian tribes within the limits of the United States are not foreign nations; though distinct political communities, they are in a dependent condition; and Chief Justice Marshall's description, that 'they are in a state of pupilage' and 'their relations to the United States resembles that of a ward to his guardian,' has become more and more appropriate as they have grown less powerful and more dependent." *Jones v. Meehan*, 175 U.S. 1, 10 (1899); "While the

Cherokee Nation and other Indian tribes domiciled within the United States had been recognized by the United States as separate communities, and engagements entered into with them by means of formal treaties, they were yet regarded as in a condition of pupilage or dependency, and subject to the paramount authority of the United States." *Cherokee Nation v. Hitchcock*, 187 U.S. 294, 305 (1902); "These Indians are yet wards of the Nation, in a condition of pupilage or dependency, and have not been discharged from that condition. . . . These suggestions entirely ignore the relation existing between the United States and the Indians. It is not a relation simply of contract, each party to which is capable of guarding his own interests, but the Indians are in a state of dependency and pupilage, entitled to the care and protection of the Government. When they shall be let out of that state is for the United States to determine without interference by the courts or by any State." *United States v. Rickert*, 188 U.S. 432, 437, 442–43 (1903); "In a general way it may be said that the recognized relation between the Government and the Indians is that of a superior and an inferior, whereby the latter is placed under the care and control of the former." *In re Heff*, 197 U.S. 488, 497–98 (1905); "The Government cannot be supposed to have abandoned merely for a moment and for a secondary matter its general attitude towards the Indians as wards over whom and whose property it retained unusual powers, so long as they remained set apart from the body of the people." *Conley v. Ballinger*, 216 U.S. 84, 90 (1910); "We must remember in considering this subject that the Congress of the United States has undertaken from the earliest history of the Government to deal with the Indians as dependent people and to legislate concerning their property with a view to their protection as such." *Tiger v. Western Inv. Co.*, 221 U.S. 286, 310 (1911); "During the continuance of this guardianship, the right and duty of the Nation to enforce by all appropriate means the restrictions designed for the security of the Indians cannot be gainsaid. . . . Out of its peculiar relation to these dependent peoples sprang obligations to the fulfillment of which the national honor has been committed." *Heckman v. United States*, 224 U.S. 413, 437 (1912); "As in the instance of other tribal Indians, the members of this tribe were wards of the United States, which was fully empowered, whenever it seemed wise to do so, to assume full control over them and their affairs, to determine who were such members, to allot and distribute the tribal lands among them, and to terminate the tribal government." *Gritts v. Fisher*, 224 U.S. 640, 642–43 (1912); "It must be remembered that the fundamental consideration is the protection of a dependent people." *United States v. Pelican*, 232 U.S. 442, 450 (1914); "The trust period has not expired, nor has the tribal relation of the Indians been dissolved. An agent or superintendent remains in charge of their affairs and they are still wards of the Government." *Perrin v. United States*, 232 U.S. 478, 481 (1914); "The Quapaws are still under national tutelage. . . . The guardianship of the United States continues, notwithstanding the citizenship conferred upon the allottees." *United States v. Noble*, 237 U.S. 74, 79 (1915); "The provisions of the Allotment Act must be construed in light of the policy they were obviously intended to execute. It was a policy relating to the welfare of Indians,—wards of the United States." *Levindale Lead & Zinc Min. Co. v. Coleman*, 241 U.S. 432, 437 (1916); "Before dealing with its interpretation, it is necessary to have in mind certain matters which are well settled by the previous decisions of this court. The tribal Indians are wards of the Government, and as such under its guardianship. It rests with Congress to determine the time and extent of emancipation. Conferring citizenship is not inconsistent with the continuation of such guardianship, for it has been held that even after the Indians have been made citizens the relation of guardian and ward for some purposes may continue. On the other hand, Congress may relieve the Indians from such guardianship and control, in whole or in part, and may, if it sees fit, clothe them with full rights and responsibilities concerning their property or give them a partial emancipation if it thinks that course better for their protection." *United States v. Waller*, 243 U.S. 452, 459–60 (1917); "As in other instances, the wish of the ward had to yield to the will of the guardian. And Congress was free to exert this guardianship in any manner which it deemed appropriate, and to adjust its action to new or changing conditions, so long as no fundamental right was violated." *United States v. Rowell*, 243 U.S. 464, 468 (1917); "It is thoroughly established that Congress has plenary authority over the Indians and all their tribal relations, and full power to legislate concerning their tribal property. The guardianship arises from their condition of tutelage or dependency; and it rests with Congress to determine when the relationship shall cease; the mere grant of rights of citizenship not being sufficient to terminate it." *Winton v. Amos*, 255 U.S. 373, 391–92 (1921); "The contention that the United States was without authority to maintain the suit in the capacity of guardian for these Indians is without merit. In [*Kagama*] the general doctrine was laid down by the Court that the Indian tribes are wards of the nation, communities dependent on the United States. . . . This duty of protection and power extend [*sic*] to individual Indians, even though they may have become citizens." *Cramer v. United States*, 261 U.S. 219, 232 (1923); "Such power rests upon the dependent character of the Indians, their recognized inability to safely conduct business affairs, and the peculiar duty of the Federal Government to safeguard their interests and protec [*sic*] them against the greed of others and their own improvidence." *Sunderland v. United States*, 266 U.S. 226, 233–34 (1924); "At the outset the bill shows that the Indians although citizens of the State, are in many respects, and particularly in their relations to the matter here in controversy, under the guardianship of the United States and entitled to its aid and protection." *United States v. Minnesota*, 270 U.S. 181, 193–94 (1926); "The Indians of the pueblo are wards of the United States and hold their lands subject to the restriction that the same cannot be alienated in any-wise without its consent."

United States v. Candelaria, 271 U.S. 432, 443 (1926); "The guardianship of the United States over the Osage Indians has not been abandoned; they are still the wards of the nation, and it rests with Congress alone to determine when that relationship shall cease." *United States v. Ramsey*, 271 U.S. 467, 469 (1926); "We have had frequent occasion to point out the duty of the United States to protect its wards, the Indians, and the consequent broad extent of its power over then and their affairs." *United States v. Jackson*, 280 U.S. 183, 190 (1930); "In [*Sandoval*] this Court, after full examination of the subject, held that the status of the Indians of the several pueblos in New Mexico is that of dependent Indian tribes under the guardianship of the United States and that by reason of this status they and their lands are subject to the legislation of Congress enacted for the protection of tribal lands and their property. . . . We then pointed out that neither their citizenship, if they are citizens, nor their communal ownership of the full title in fee simple is an obstacle to the exercise of such guardianship over them and their property." *United States v. Chavez*, 290 U.S. 357, 362–63 (1933); "The fundamental consideration of both Congress and the Department of the Interior in establishing this colony has been the protection of a dependent people. . . . Congress alone has the right to determine the manner in which this country's guardianship over the Indians shall be carried out." *United States v. McGowan* at 538–39; "Also, it is immaterial that respondents are citizens, because it is settled that the grant of citizenship to the Indians is not inconsistent with their status as wards whose property is subject to the plenary control of the federal government. It rests with Congress to determine when the guardianship relation shall cease." *Board of Com'rs of Creek County v. Seber*, 318 U.S. 705, 718 (1943); "The federal Government's power over Indians is derived . . . from the necessity of giving uniform protection to a dependent people." *Williams v. Lee* at 219 FN 4. Just to name a few. Do you believe me now?

111. Why not a few more? "And, of course, the long-accepted concept of a guardian-ward relationship between the United States and its Indians, with all the requirements of fair dealing and protection that this involves, means that the Indians are not free to treat their lands as wholly their own." *Federal Power Commission* at 130 (1960) (Black, J., dissenting); "The power of Congress . . . gained breadth by reason of historic experiences that induced Congress to treat Indians as wards of the Nation." *Mescalero Apache Tribe v. Jones*, 411 U.S. 145, 159 (1973) (Douglas, J., dissenting); "Resolution of the instant issue turns on the unique legal status of Indian tribes under federal law and upon the plenary power of Congress, based on a history of treaties and the assumption of a 'guardian-ward' status, to legislate on behalf of federally recognized Indian tribes." *Mancari* at 551; "These limitations rest on the fact that the dependent status of Indian tribes within our territorial jurisdiction is necessarily inconsistent with their freedom independently to determine their external

relations." *United States v. Wheeler*, 435 U.S. 313, 326 (1978); "This interpretive principle is a response to the unique relationship between the Federal Government and the Indian people, 'who are wards of the nation, dependent upon its protection and good faith.'" *Washington v. Confederated Bands and Tribes of Yakima Indian Nation*, 439 U.S. 463, 502–3 (1979) (Marshall, J., dissenting); "This statute was enacted against the backdrop of a relationship between the United States and the Indian tribes that had long been considered to '[resemble] that of a ward to his guardian.'" *United States v. Mitchell*, 445 U.S. 535, 548 (1980) (White, J., dissenting); "These limitations rest on the fact that the dependent status of Indian tribes within our territorial jurisdiction is necessarily inconsistent with their freedom independently to *determine their external relations.*" *Montana v. United States*, 450 U.S. 544, 564 (1981) (emphasis in original); "In contrast to when Congress acts with respect to the States, when Congress acts with respect to the Indian tribes, it generally does so pursuant to . . . its superior position over the tribes." *Merrion v. Jicarilla Apache Tribe*, 455 U.S. 130, 155 FN 21 (1982); "Thus, the Court accords an Indian tribe, whose sovereignty 'exists only at the sufferance of Congress and is subject to complete defeasance,' greater immunity from state taxes than is enjoyed by the sovereignty of the United States on whom it is dependent." *Ramah Navajo School Bd., Inc. v. Bureau of Revenue of New Mexico*, 458 U.S. 832, 856–57 (1982) (Rehnquist, J., dissenting); "The question we must answer is whether the sovereignty retained by the tribes in their dependent status within our scheme of government includes the power of criminal jurisdiction over nonmembers." *Duro* at 684; "These limitations rest on the fact that the dependent status of Indian tribes within our territorial jurisdiction is necessarily inconsistent with their freedom independently to *determine their external relations.*" *Hicks* at 378 (Souter, J., concurring) (emphasis in original); "As dependents, the tribes are subject to plenary control by Congress." *Michigan v. Bay Mills Indian Cmty.*, 572 U.S. 782, 788 (2014). Boy, I really did read a lot of cases for this book. Perhaps I should take a cue from Saikrishna Prakash and put it this succinctly: "To this day, some courts continue to cite this wardship theory as a basis for plenary power over Indian tribes." Saikrishna Prakash, "Against Tribal Fungibility," *Cornell Law Review* 89, no. 5 (July 2004): 1078.

112. In short, a guardian has greater control over a ward, including the authority to make significant life choices for the ward. A trustee, on the other hand, has control over a trust (often consisting of money or property or other items of significant value) for the benefit of a beneficiary. However, the trustee does not otherwise have the authority to make significant life choices for the beneficiary. For example, a guardian will likely be able to make medical decisions for a ward while a trustee will not be able to make medical decisions for a beneficiary.

113. "Furthermore, this Court has recognized the distinctive obligation of

trust incumbent upon the Government in its dealings with these dependent and sometimes exploited people. In carrying out its treaty obligations with Indian tribes, the Government is something more than a mere contracting party. Under a humane and self imposed policy which has found expression in many acts of Congress and numerous decisions of this Court, it has charged itself with moral obligations of the highest responsibility and trust. Its conduct, as disclosed in the acts of those who represent it in dealings with the Indians, should therefore be judged by the most exacting fiduciary standards." *Seminole Nation v. United States*, 316 U.S. 286, 296–97 (1942).

114. *Creek Nation v. United States*, 318 U.S. 629, 642 (1943) (Murphy, J., dissenting).

115. According to the Matthew Fletcher, "The Supreme Court began to use the metaphor of a guardianship, a metaphor that quickly infiltrated American Indian affairs' political discussion and rhetoric. Under this metaphor, the United States served as a 'guardian' to its Indian 'wards,' akin to children who were incompetent to determine their own affairs. The guardian-ward metaphor still infuses much of Indian affairs policy and judicial decisionmaking. Eventually, by the 1970s, the federal government thoroughly rejected the old metaphors in favor of a trust relationship." Matthew L. M. Fletcher, *Principles of Federal Indian Law* (St. Paul, MN: West Academic Publishing, 2017), 123.

116. *United States v. Mitchell*, 463 U.S. 206, 225 (1983).

117. *Oneida County, N.Y. v. Oneida Indian Nation of New York State*, 470 U.S. 226, 247 (1985).

118. *Mountain States Tel. & Tel. Co. v. Pueblo of Santa Ana*, 472 U.S. 237, 276 (1985) (Brennan, J., dissenting).

119. "One of the basic principles of Indian law is that the federal government has a trust or special relationship with Indian tribes. . . . Today the trust doctrine is one of the cornerstones of Indian law." Cohen, *Handbook (2012 ed.)*, 412.

120. Often American courts employ what are called "canons of construction" to read challenging legal documents. Canons are not laws unto themselves but interpretive tools that aid judges and promote consistency. The canons of construction that have developed in Indian law are particularly important, as the history of treaty relations utilized words and produced language—such as "protection"—that did not always capture the spirit of what tribal signatories understood themselves to be agreeing to. For a brief description of the Indian canons of construction, see Pevar, *Rights of Indians*, 51–52. For more on the promise, weakness, and malleability of the canons, see Samuel E. Ennis, "Implicit Divestiture and the Supreme Court's (Re)Construction of the Indian Canons," *Vermont Law Review* 35, no. 3 (Spring 2011): 623–88; and Jill De La Hunt, "The Canons of Indian Treaty and Statutory Construction: A Proposal for Codification," *University of Michigan Journal of Law Reform* 17, no. 3 (Spring 1984): 681–712.

121. As Irene K. Harvey noted, "When the law deals with Indians, then, it deals not with persons but with dependents and wards designated as such by time-honored legal processes." Irene K Harvey, "Constitutional Law: Congressional Plenary Power over Indian Affairs: A Doctrine Rooted in Prejudice," *American Indian Law Review* 10, no. 1 (1982): 145.

122. "The second clause of the third section of the fourth article of the constitution is equally convincing. 'The congress shall have power to dispose of, and make all needful regulations and rules respecting the territory of the United States.' What that territory was, the rights of soil, jurisdiction, and sovereignty claimed and exercised by the states and the old congress, has been already seen. It extended to the formation of a government whose laws and process were in force within its whole extent, without a saving of Indian jurisdiction." *Cherokee Nation v. Georgia* at 40 (Johnson, J., concurring). "By the second clause of § 3, Art. IV, of the Constitution, to Congress, and to it alone, is given 'power to dispose of and make all needful rules and regulations respecting the territory or other property belonging to the United States.' From an early time in the history of the Government it has exercised this power, and has also been legislating concerning Indians occupying such territory." *Celestine* at 284. "Congress must be deemed to have known, as this Court held in *Federal Power Comm'n v. Oregon* that the licensing power, 'in relation to public lands and reservations of the United States springs from the Property Clause' of the Constitution." *Federal Power v. Tuscarora* at 113. The 1982 edition of the Cohen *Handbook* also noted, "The power of Congress under the Property Clause to dispose of and regulate 'the Territory or other Property belonging to the United States' has been considered an additional source of authority over Indian affairs." Felix S. Cohen, *Handbook of Federal Indian Law (1982 ed.)* (Charlottesville, VA: Michie Bobbs-Merrill, 1982), 209.

123. Deloria and Wilkins allude to the interconnectedness of the Territory Clause and the Doctrine of Discovery, stating, "Although it never seems to play a prominent role in the deliberations of either Congress or the federal courts when they deal with Indian matters, an analysis of critical decisions of the Supreme Court seems to suggest that the property clause, and/or the fact that American claims to legal title to lands in North America under the doctrine of discovery, plays an important part in determining the posture and actions of the United States toward Indians." Deloria and Wilkins, *Tribes, Treaties*, 80.

124. Whose "occupation was war" according to John Marshall. *Johnson* at 590.

125. U.S. Constitution, art. II, sec. 2, cl. 2. "[The Constitution] confers on congress the powers of war and peace; of making treaties and of regulating commerce with foreign nations, and among the several states, and with the Indian tribes. These powers comprehend all that is required for the regulation of our intercourse with the Indians." *Worcester* at 559; "The Tribes have been

regarded as dependent nations, and treaties with them have been looked upon not as contracts, but as public laws which could be abrogated at the will of the United States." *Choate v. Trapp*, 224 U.S. 665, 671 (1912); "Originally the Indian tribes were separate nations within what is now the United States. Through conquest and treaties they were induced to give up complete independence and the right to go to war in exchange for federal protection, aid, and grants of land." *Williams v. Lee* at 218; "The source of federal authority over Indian matters has been the subject of some confusion, but it is now generally recognized that the power derives from federal responsibility for regulating commerce with Indian tribes and for treaty making." *McClanahan v. State Tax Commission of Arizona*, 441 U.S. 164, 172 FN 7 (1973); The plenary power of Congress to deal with the special problems of Indians is drawn both explicitly and implicitly from the Constitution itself. . . . [The Treaty Clause] gives the President the power, by and with the advice and consent of the Senate, to make treaties. This has often been the source of the Government's power to deal with the Indian tribes." *Mancari* at 551–52; "The treaty power does not literally authorize Congress to act legislatively, for it is an Article II power authorizing the President, not Congress, 'to make Treaties.' But, as Justice Holmes pointed out, treaties made pursuant to that power can authorize Congress to deal with 'matters' with which otherwise 'Congress could not deal.' And for much of the Nation's history, treaties, and legislation made pursuant to those treaties, governed relations between the Federal Government and the Indian tribes." *Lara* at 201. In addition, the 2012 edition of the Cohen *Handbook* states, "The treaty clause, granting the power to the President to negotiate treaties subject to the ratification by the Senate, has been a principal foundation for federal power in Indian affairs." Cohen, *Handbook (2012 ed.)*, 386.

126. For example, in note 120 of this chapter we have already noted that American courts have developed canons of construction to read Indian treaties. Thus, one might ask when and how the canons should be applied. Other factors include, but are certainly not limited to, the fact that Congress "ended" treaty making with tribal nations in 1871. *U.S. Statutes at Large*, 16:566. The process of negotiations between the United States and tribal nations continued after 1871 and resulted in "agreements," which function in much the same way as treaties. Furthermore, Congress was careful to note in the small rider in a larger appropriations bill that "ended" treaty making that "nothing herein contained shall be construed to invalidate or impair the obligation of any treaty heretofore lawfully made or ratified with any such Indian nation or tribe." Ibid. Thus, among the many questions one might ask is how should we read treaties in the present day since they are not subject to renegotiation? Also, Native peoples are now regarded as American citizens. Indian Citizenship Act, *U.S. Statutes at Large*, 43:253. How should a court of law regard a treaty between the United States and a different political entity whose citizens—whether they

consented to it or not—are now understood to also be U.S. citizens? Finally (since these notes are getting a little long), the Supreme Court has held that a treaty can grant the federal government authority beyond what is granted in the U.S. Constitution. *See Missouri v. Holland*, 252 U.S. 416 (1920). Thus, one might ask what authority over a specific tribal nation a specific treaty grants to the United States. For a useful primer on the Treaty Power in general, see Oona A. Hathaway et al., "The Treaty Power: Its History, Scope and Limits," *Cornell Law Review* 98, no. 2 (January 2013): 239–326. As is obvious, questions about treaties can get pretty complicated pretty quickly. However, just because questions about treaties can get complicated does not suggest or imply that the Treaty Power grants plenary power over Native America.

127. As Ann Tweedy puts it, "To the extent the Treaty Clause can be construed to be applicable to the issue of plenary power, it would appear to authorize, at most, federal good faith negotiation with tribes regarding their continued political existence, not unilateral annihilation of tribes as legal entities." Ann E. Tweedy, "Connecting the Dots Between the Constitution, the Marshall Trilogy, and *United States v. Lara*: Notes Toward a Blueprint for the Next Legislative Restoration of Tribal Sovereignty," *University of Michigan Journal of Law Reform* 42, no. 3 (Spring 2009): 662.

128. For example, some light internet research suggests that Canada spends only about 3 percent of what the United States does on defense. "Military Power of USA and Canada," ArmedForces.eu, 2019, https://armedforces.eu/compare/country_USA_vs_Canada; "List of Countries with Highest Military Expenditures," Wikipedia, last edited March 16, 2024, https://en.wikipedia.org/wiki/List_of_countries_by_military_expenditures. Again, this was some very light internet research. But if you've got some reliable information that Canada actually spends so much more on defense (not just, say, 15 percent versus 3 percent) that it refutes the larger point I am trying to make, I am willing to consider it.

129. "Since Johnson v. McIntosh, decided in 1823, gave rationalization to the appropriation of Indian lands by the white man's government, the extinguishment of Indian title by that sovereignty has proceeded, as a political matter, without any admitted legal responsibility in the sovereign to compensate the Indian for his loss. Exclusive title to the lands passed to the white discoverers, subject to the Indian title with power in the white sovereign alone to extinguish that right by 'purchase or conquest.' The whites enforced their claims by the sword and occupied the lands as the Indians abandoned them." *Northwestern Bands of Shoshone Indians v. United States*, 324 U.S. 335, 339 (1945); "Every American schoolboy knows that the savage tribes of this continent were deprived of their ancestral ranges by force and that, even when the Indians ceded millions of acres by treaty in return for blankets, food, and trinkets, it was not a sale but the conquerors' will that deprived them of their land." *Tee-Hit-Ton*

at 289–90; "Originally the Indian tribes were separate nations within what is now the United States. Through conquest and treaties they were induced to give up complete independence and the right to go to war in exchange for federal protection, aid, and grants of land." *Williams v. Lee* at 218.

130. Jill Gustafson, 78 Am Jur 2d War § 118. Interestingly, the positionality of conquered peoples and lands in American law appears to have shifted as a result of a treaty. According to the 2nd Circuit Court of Appeals, "The nineteenth century American view that military conquest completely displaced the sovereignty of the prior possessor was substantially modified by the Regulations respecting the Laws and Customs of War on Land, ratified by the United States as an annex to the Fourth Hague Convention of 1907. Since the adoption of these Regulations it is generally agreed that the occupant does not succeed to sovereignty over the occupied territory, but has only limited administrative authority." *State of Netherlands v. Federal Reserve Bank*, 201 F.2d 455, 461 (1953). Admittedly, both citations in this note outline the rights of a conqueror within conquered territory. Nonetheless, the limited scope of rights attributed to the conqueror necessarily implies the presence of rights for the conquered.

131. "But this power of Congress to organize territorial governments, and make laws for their inhabitants, arises not so much from the clause in the Constitution in regard to disposing of and making rules and regulations concerning the Territory and other property of the United States, as from the ownership of the country in which the Territories are, and *the right of exclusive sovereignty which must exist in the National Government, and can be found nowhere else. Kagama* at 380 (emphasis added); "Moreover, 'at least during the first century of America's national existence . . . Indian affairs were more an aspect of military and foreign policy than a subject of domestic or municipal law.' Insofar as that is so, Congress' legislative authority would rest in part, not upon 'affirmative grants of the Constitution,' but upon the Constitution's adoption of preconstitutional powers necessarily inherent in any Federal Government, namely powers that this Court has described as 'necessary concomitants of nationality.'" *Lara* at 201.

132. The case that everyone cites for the general proposition that there are federal powers beyond the U.S. Constitution that are inherent in sovereignty is *United States v. Curtiss-Wright Export Corp.*, 299 U.S. 304 (1936). For one of the many critiques of *Curtiss-Wright*, see Louis Fisher, "The Staying Power of Erroneous Dicta: From *Curtiss-Wright* to *Zivotofsky*," *Constitutional Commentary* 31, no. 2 (Summer 2016): 149–220. See also Cleveland, "Powers Inherent"; and Matthew L. M. Fletcher, "Preconstitutional Federal Power," *Tulane Law Review* 82, no. 2 (December 2007): 509–66.

Chapter 3

1. I mean, you've already read this far. Why not indulge me for just five more pages?

2. *Worcester* at 561.

3. *Kan. Indians*, 72 U.S. 737, 757 (1867).

4. *Rickert* at 437.

5. "But these Indians are within the geographical limits of the United States. The soil and the people within these limits are under the political control of the Government of the United States, or of the States of the Union. There exist within the broad domain of sovereignty but these two." *Kagama* at 379.

6. Ibid. at 384.

7. Sec. 6, Allotment Act.

8. *Board of Com'rs of Jackson County v. U.S.*, 308 U.S. 343, 353–54 (1939) (Black, J., concurring).

9. "Despite bitter criticism and the defiance of Georgia which refused to obey this Court's mandate in Worcester the broad principles of that decision came to be accepted as law. Over the years this Court has modified these principles in cases where essential tribal relations were not involved and where the rights of Indians would not be jeopardized, but the basic policy of Worcester has remained. . . . Essentially, absent governing Acts of Congress, the question has always been whether the state action infringed on the right of reservation Indians to make their own laws and be ruled by them." *Williams v. Lee* at 219–20.

10. *See Oklahoma v. Castro-Huerta*, 597 U.S. ___, 142 S. Ct. 2486 (2022). See also Stacy Leeds et al., "*Oklahoma v. Castro-Huerta*—Rebalancing Federal-State-Tribal Power," *Journal of Appellate Practice and Process* 23, no. 1 (Winter 2023): 47–104.

11. The second definition of Plenary Power did not emerge fully developed from *Kagama*. As Deloria and Wilkins note, "Many passages from *Kagama* are sprinkled through *Lone Wolf* and give every indication that *Lone Wolf* was the fully matured child of *Kagama*, the dicta of the former becoming the doctrines of the latter." Deloria and Wilkins, *The Legal Universe*, 162.

12. *Thomas v. Gay*, 169 U.S. 264, 274 (1898).

13. *Stephens* at 488.

14. *Cherokee Nation v. Hitchcock* at 306.

15. *Sizemore v. Brady*, 235 U.S. 441, 447 (1914).

16. Also, didn't we basically make this same point in Chapter 1?

17. Treaty of Peace between the United States of America and the Kingdom of Spain, December 10, 1898, 30 Stat. 1754.

18. For a significantly more thorough and reasonable articulation of the Spanish-American War, see Ivan Musicant, *Empire by Default: The Spanish-American War and the Dawn of the American Century* (New York: H. Holt, 1998).

19. *Downes v. Bidwell*, 182 U.S. 244, 279 (1901).

20. For example, the question in *Balzac v. Porto Rico* was to what extent the U.S. Constitution's guarantee to jury trials applied to the territories. Writing for the majority, Chief Justice (and former president) William Howard Taft stated, "It is well settled that these provisions for jury trial in criminal and civil cases apply to the Territories of the United States. But it is just as clearly settled that they do not apply to territory belonging to the United States which has not been incorporated into the Union. It was further settled in *Downes v. Bidwell* . . . that neither the Philippines nor Porto Rico was territory which had been incorporated in the Union or become a part of the United States, as distinguished from merely belonging to it." *Balzac v. Porto Rico*, 258 U.S. 298, 304–5 (1922). As succinctly stated by Christina Duffy Ponsa-Kraus, "[The Supreme Court] invented, out of whole cloth, the distinction between incorporated territories, which were on their way to statehood, and unincorporated territories, which might never become states, and placed these newly annexed territories in the latter category." Christina Duffy Ponsa-Kraus, "The *Insular Cases* Run Amok: Against Constitutional Exceptionalism in the Territories," *Yale Law Journal* 131, no. 8 (June 2022): 2449–2541.

21. *Downes* at 279.

22. Ibid. at 279–80.

23. As Aleinikoff stated, "In short, in the *Insular Cases*—as in the Indian cases—the logic of territoriality ran into the impossibility of full membership for 'savage peoples.' The Court found a middle position that neither sacrificed the Constitution nor unduly hindered American empire building. The possessions could be 'subject to the jurisdiction of the United States, [but] not *of* the United States.'" Aleinikoff, *Semblances of Sovereignty*, 23.

24. "Large powers must necessarily be entrusted to Congress in dealing with these problems, and we are bound to assume that they will be judiciously exercised." *Downes* at 283.

25. As Ponsa-Kraus put it, "The distinction between incorporated and unincorporated territories thus served as the cornerstone of a racially motivated imperialist legal doctrine: the idea of the unincorporated territory gave sanction to indefinite colonial rule over majority-nonwhite populations at the margins of the American empire." Ponsa-Kraus, "*Insular Cases*," 2454.

26. The Supreme Court recently declined to overrule the *Insular Cases* in a dispute that many felt was well suited to that very purpose. See *Fin. Oversight & Mgmt. Bd. for P.R. v. Aurelius Inv., LLC*, 140, S. Ct. 1649 (2020).

27. Isn't it fun to hope! I can't possibly imagine anything spoiling the good feelings I have right now!

28. Art. V, Treaty with China, July 28, 1868, 16 Stat. 739.

29. Cleveland, *Powers Inherent*, 115–16.

30. "Whenever in the opinion of the Government of the United States, the

coming of Chinese laborers to the United States, or their residence therein, affects or threatens to affect the interests of that country, or to endanger the good order of the said country or of any locality within the territory thereof, the Government of China agrees that the Government of the United States may regulate, limit, or suspend such coming or residence, but may not absolutely prohibit it. The limitation or suspension shall be reasonable and shall apply only to Chinese who may go to the United States as laborers, other classes not being included in the limitations. Legislation taken in regard to Chinese laborers will be of such a character only as is necessary to enforce the regulation, limitation, or suspension of immigration, and immigrants shall not be subject to personal maltreatment or abuse." Art. I, Treaty-China, November 17, 1880, 22 Stat. 826.

31. For a much more thorough retelling of this history, see Andrew Gyory, *Closing the Gate: Race, Politics, and the Chinese Exclusion Act* (Chapel Hill: University of North Carolina Press, 1998).

32. 130 U.S. 581 (1889).

33. "The appeal involves a consideration of the validity of the act of Congress of October 1, 1888, prohibiting Chinese laborers from entering the United States who had departed before its passage, having a certificate issued under the act of 1882 as amended by the act of 1884, granting them permission to return. The validity of the act is assailed as being in effect an expulsion from the country of Chinese laborers, in violation of existing treaties between the United States and the government of China, and of rights vested in them under the laws of Congress." Ibid. at 589.

34. If you didn't pick up on this right away, don't worry about it. You're still astute! Believe me, I recognize that there have been a lot of cases and a lot of law and a lot of lawyerly gobbledygook thrown at you. So, again, if you didn't see it right away, don't tie yourself up in a knot. It's on me, not you. Keep your chin up and keep reading!

35. *Lone Wolf* at 566.

36. I mean it. I think you are awesome! Keep reading!

37. "By the Constitution, laws made in pursuance thereof and treaties made under the authority of the United States are both declared to be the supreme law of the land, and no paramount authority is given to one over the other." *Chae Chan Ping* at 600.

38. "In either case the last expression of the sovereign will must control." Ibid.

39. "It will not be presumed that the legislative department of the government will lightly pass laws which are in conflict with the treaties of the country; but that circumstances may arise which would not only justify the government in disregarding their stipulations, but demand in the interests of the country that it should do so, there can be no question. Unexpected events

may call for a change in the policy of the country. Neglect or violation of stipulations on the part of the other contracting party may require corresponding action on our part. When a reciprocal engagement is not carried out by one of the contracting parties, the other may also decline to keep the corresponding engagement." Ibid. at 600–601.

40. Ibid. at 603.

41. "The competition steadily increased as the laborers came in crowds on each steamer that arrived from China, or Hong Kong, an adjacent English port. They were generally industrious and frugal. Not being accompanied by families, except in rare instances, their expenses were small; and they were content with the simplest fare, such as would not suffice for our laborers and artisans. The competition between them and our people was for this reason altogether in their favor, and the consequent irritation, proportionately deep and bitter, was followed, in many cases, by open conflicts, to the great disturbance of the public peace." Ibid. at 594–95.

42. Ibid. at 595.

43. Ibid.

44. Ibid.

45. Ibid. at 606.

46. "It matters not in what form such aggression and encroachment come, whether from the foreign nation acting in its national character or from vast hordes of its people crowding in upon us. The government, possessing the powers which are to be exercised for protection and security, is clothed with authority to determine the occasion on which the powers shall be called forth; and its determination, so far as the subjects affected are concerned, are necessarily conclusive upon all its departments and officers. If, therefore, the government of the United States, through its legislative department, considers the presence of foreigners of a different race in this country, who will not assimilate with us, to be dangerous to its peace and security, their exclusion is not to be stayed because at the time there are no actual hostilities with the nation of which the foreigners are subjects." Ibid.

47. Ibid.

48. To be absolutely clear, this is a version of silliness that lacks any humor whatsoever.

49. "In exercising the great power which the people of the United States, by establishing a written Constitution as the supreme and paramount law, have vested in this court, of determining, whenever the question is properly brought before it, whether the acts of the legislature or of the executive are consistent with the Constitution, it behooves the court to be careful that it does not undertake to pass upon political questions, the final decision of which has been committed by the Constitution to the other departments of the government." *Fong Yue Ting v. United States*, 149 U.S. 698, 712 (1893).

50. As D. Carolina Nunez has noted, "Since the era of Chinese exclusion, the Court has never had an opportunity to again address a categorical bar on entry so blatantly based on criteria now heavily scrutinized under the law. Never again has Congress categorically barred individuals from entry based on race or national origin. And Congress has never barred individuals from entry based on religion. But the Court *has* reaffirmed the broad plenary power established in *The Chinese Exclusion Case* to uphold other legislation that would be held unconstitutional if applied to citizens in the United States. Indeed, '[the] Court has repeatedly emphasized that "over no conceivable subject is the legislative power of Congress more complete than it is over" the admission of aliens.' Plenary power has insulated Congress's immigration-related laws from substantive and procedural due process, equal protection, First Amendment, and Fourth Amendment norms. Although the scope of plenary power has certainly eroded over time, it continues to exist today (to the dismay of numerous immigration law scholars and commentators)." D. Carolina Nunez, "Dark Matter in the Law," *Boston College Law Review* 62, no. 5 (May 2021): 1558–59.

51. For a good place to start, see Saito, *From Chinese Exclusion*.

52. As Russel Lawrence Barsh and James Youngblood Henderson put it, "The nineteenth century was the heyday of European imperialism and the debut of the white man's burden." Russel Lawrence Barsh and James Youngblood Henderson, *The Road: Indian Tribes and Political Liberty* (Berkeley: University of California Press, 1980), 86.

53. *Kagama* at 384.

54. *Downes* at 279–80.

55. *Chae Chan Ping* at 595.

56. "Because of the local ill feeling, the people of the States where they are found are often their deadliest enemies. From their very weakness and helplessness, so largely due to the course of dealing of the Federal Government with them and the treaties in which it has been promised, there arises the duty of protection, and with it the power." *Kagama* at 379.

57. "We are also of opinion that the power to acquire territory by treaty implies not only the power to govern such territory, but to prescribe upon what terms the United States will receive its inhabitants." *Downes* at 279.

58. "To preserve its independence, and give security against foreign aggression and encroachment, is the highest duty of every nation, and to attain these ends nearly all other considerations are to be subordinated." *Chae Chan Ping* at 606.

59. Mark R. Killenbeck, "A Prudent Regard to Our Own Good? The Commerce Clause, in Nation and States," *Journal of Supreme Court History* 38, no. 3 (November 2013): 284–85.

60. For example, in the late twentieth century the Supreme Court famously curtailed congressional authority under what is called the Interstate Com-

merce Clause. *See United States v. Lopez*, 514 U.S. 549 (1995); and *United States v. Morrison*, 529 U.S. 598 (2000).

61. Writing about not just the Commerce Clause but Section 8 (which includes the Commerce Clause) as a whole, Garrett Epps has noted, "The economic powers granted in Section Eight can also be read to form a seamless whole. This might be called *the power to create an economic system*, complete with money, credit, transport, and communications; to operate within the states to create 'post offices and post roads' as a means of knitting the country into one economy; and to prescribe rules for commerce between any of the actors, inside the country or outside. Congress seems to be not only the arbiter but the creator of the new economic unit, not only the center but the spinner of the web" (emphasis in original). Garrett Epps, *American Epic: Reading the U.S. Constitution* (Oxford: Oxford University Press, 2013), 22.

62. And make no mistake, we do still debate this.

63. As Thurman Lee Hester Jr. noted, "If mere mention in the Constitution is sufficient to place a group 'under the Constitution' and give Congress plenary power over the group, then the same Commerce Clause would give the U.S. Congress plenary power over every foreign nation." Hester, *Political Principles*, 99.

64. As Curtis G. Berkey put it, "The idea that the authority of the federal government would include the power to violate the sovereignty of Indian nations by exercising powers over them would have been preposterous to most of the delegates. . . . Rather, the exclusive authority of Congress and the president was understood to extend only to those matters necessary to conduct foreign, or external relations with Indian tribes." Curtis G. Berkey, "United States—Indian Relations: The Constitutional Basis," in *Exiled in the Land of the Free: Democracy, Indian Nations, and the U.S. Constitution*, ed. John C. Mohawk and Oren R. Lyons (Santa Fe, NM: Clear Light Publishers, 1992), 190–91.

65. Stop snickering.

66. 1790 Trade and Intercourse Act, Sec. 7, *U.S. Statutes at Large*, 1:137–38.

67. 1834 Trade and Intercourse Act, *U.S. Statutes at Large*, 4:729–35.

68. Francis Paul Prucha, *American Indian Policy in the Formative Years: The Indian Trade and Intercourse Acts, 1790–1834* (Cambridge, MA: Harvard University Press, 1962), 45.

69. 1790 Trade and Intercourse Act, Sec. 1.

70. Ibid. at Sec. 4.

71. Ibid. at Sec. 5.

72. Of the original Trade and Intercourse Act, Prucha writes, "These laws, which were originally designed to implement the treaties and enforce them against obstreperous whites, gradually came to embody the basic features of federal Indian policy. . . . The law first of all provided for the licensing of traders and established penalties for trading without a license. Then it struck

directly at the current frontier difficulties. To prevent the steady eating away at the Indian Country by individuals who privately acquired lands from the Indians, it declared the purchase of lands from the Indians invalid unless made by a public treaty with the United States. To put a stop to the outrages committed on the Indians by whites who aggressively invaded the Indian Country, the act made provision for the punishment of murder and other crimes committed by whites against the Indians in Indian Country." Prucha, *American Indian Policy*, 45–46.

73. Once again, Prucha is instructive. "The laws were not 'Indian' laws; they touched the Indian only indirectly, as they limited him in his trade and his sale of land. The legislation was, rather, directed against the lawless whites on the frontier and sought to restrain them from violating the sacred treaties made with the Indians." Ibid. at 48.

74. 1834 Trade and Intercourse Act, Sec. 17.

75. Ibid.

76. "And if such nation or tribe shall neglect or refuse to make satisfaction, in a reasonable time, not exceeding twelve months, it shall be the duty of such superintendent, agent, or sub-agent, to make return of his doings to the commissioner of Indian affairs, that such further steps may be taken as shall be proper, in the opinion of the President, to obtain satisfaction for the injury; and, in the mean time, in respect to the property so taken, stolen or destroyed, the United States guaranty, to the party so injured, an eventual indemnification." Ibid.

77. Ibid.

78. Certainly treaties are manifestations of consent between tribal nations and the federal government. But treaties are acts of consent to a specific set of circumstances and conditions rather than a general consent to be governed under the U.S. Constitution in the manner recognized by social contract theory. Even in the heart of the Allotment Era, the Supreme Court recognized that tribal sovereignty originates outside the U.S. Constitution. See *Talton v. Mayes*, 163 U.S. 376 (1896). Consequently, tribal nations do not fit into the constitutional order in any manner that makes the application of social contract theory to tribal nations under the U.S. Constitution obvious or seamless. In fact—and I suspect that you have already picked up on this as you are, as we have established, an astute reader—much of the purpose of what we have been doing in this book to this point is to demonstrate how claims to federal power over Native America are disconnected to claims to federal power elsewhere that are more fully supported under a social contract theory.

79. *Worcester* at 592 (McLean, J., concurring).

80. *Forty-Three Gallons* at 194.

81. As put by Gregory Ablavsky, "The Supreme Court routinely invokes the [Indian Commerce] Clause to justify plenary power, but this assertion does

not find support either in text or in any discussion of tribes' constitutional status in the Clause's sparse drafting and adoption history." Gregory Ablavsky, "Beyond the Indian Commerce Clause," *Yale Law Journal* 124, no. 4 (January–February 2015): 1053.

82. The 1924 Indian Citizenship Act is, in this nerd's opinion, a fascinating moment in Native legal history that is still understudied. It was regarded by federal policy makers at the time as the closing of a loophole, as it was estimated that two-thirds of the Native population were already American citizens through other means, such as under the Allotment Act and its progeny, through intermarriage, through treaty stipulations, and so on. See U.S. Congress, House, Committee on Indian Affairs, Unpublished Hearings, May 19, 1924. Yet, it also reflects the tenor of the dying-yet-still-in-force Allotment Era of federal policy in that it was an imposition that at least some Native peoples did not welcome. As noted by New York Representative Homer P. Snyder, a member of the House Committee on Indian Affairs, "The New York Indians are very much opposed to [the Citizenship Act], but I am perfectly willing to take the responsibility if the committee sees fit to agree to this." Ibid. Do you see why this is fascinating? It feels like we should know more about this moment. Of course, this is not to say that we don't know anything. If you would like a concise, helpful understanding of the Indian Citizenship Act and its surrounding circumstances, see Kevin Bruyneel, "Challenging American Boundaries: Indigenous People and the 'Gift' of U.S. Citizenship," *Studies in American Political Development* 18, no. 1 (April 2004): 30–43.

83. For a useful articulation of one pocket of resistance to the imposition of colonial citizenship, see Sheryl R. Lightfoot, "Decolonizing Self-Determination: Haudenosaunee Passports and Negotiated Sovereignty," *European Journal of International Relations* 27, no. 4 (December 2021): 971–94.

84. In fact, dual citizenship has been on the rise across the world. See Tanja Brøndsted Sejersen, "'I Vow to Thee My Countries—the Expansion of Dual Citizenship in the 21st Century," *International Migration Review* 42, no. 3 (September 2008): 623–49.

85. I'm not going to tell you how astute you are again, because I fear that you will start thinking I am being insincere. But please know that I trust you as a reader and a thinker if you have decided to engage with this book and that I truly believe that at some point in the last two and a half chapters you really did come to understand that this was a going to be a more difficult endeavor than it would appear at first glance. Unless, of course, you are Oswald F. Johnson of Zap, North Dakota. There is no way he got it. That guy is a total idiot.

86. *Brown v. Board of Education*, 347 U.S. 483 (1954).

87. Specifically about the 14th Amendment—one of the amendments to emerge directly out of the American Civil War—Justice Henry Billings Brown stated, "The object of the amendment was undoubtedly to enforce the ab-

solute equality of the two races before the law, but in the nature of things it could not have been intended to abolish distinctions based upon color, or to enforce social, as distinguished from political equality, or a commingling of the two races upon terms unsatisfactory to either. Laws permitting, and even requiring, their separation in places where they are liable to be brought into contact do not necessarily imply the inferiority of either race to the other, and have been generally, if not universally, recognized as within the competency of the state legislatures in the exercise of their police power. The most common instance of this is connected with the establishment of separate schools for white and colored children, which has been held to be a valid exercise of the legislative power even by courts of States where the political rights of the colored race have been longest and most earnestly enforced." *Plessy v. Ferguson*, 163 U.S. 537, 544 (1896).

88. *Brown* at 495.

89. For example, in 1995 Robert Clinton wrote in a footnote about the footnote in question, "The modem Supreme Court nominally repudiated the extra-constitutional source of power it created in the notion of trusteeship by announcing that all federal power in Indian affairs is derived from the Indian Commerce Clause and the power to make treaties. Nevertheless, the Court continues to adhere to the plenary power doctrine, albeit under the guise of the Indian Commerce Clause, which did not constitute its historical roots." Robert N. Clinton, "The Dormant Indian Commerce Clause," *Connecticut Law Review* 27, no. 4 (Summer 1995): 1166n324. In 2002 he wrote that "the Supreme Court, not surprisingly, no longer overtly acknowledges notions of wardship, racial superiority and dominance at the source of the Indian plenary power doctrine. This subtle change probably occurred in a footnote in the Supreme Court's decision in *McClanahan v. Arizona State Tax Commission*. . . . Thus, in a footnote, the Court in passing glossed over the colonialist, racially-based wardship origins of the Indian plenary power doctrine. It purported to ground the federal Indian plenary power doctrine in part on precisely the ground that *Kagama*, the cornerstone case, rejected—the Indian Commerce Clause. . . . Rather, the federal judiciary simply continues to espouse an Indian plenary power doctrine, albeit now grounding it on the Indian Commerce Clause, rather than the racially-tainted colonialist wardship theory under which it first developed." Clinton, "No Federal Supremacy Clause," 195–96. Citing *McClanahan* in a footnote, Sarah Cleveland stated, "The Court, however, also began to bring the doctrine within the folds of the Constitution and gradually relocated the power to the Constitution's enumerated clauses. . . . The Court also relaxed the Indian Commerce Clause doctrine in the post-*Schechter Poultry* era, and in 1974, the Court rejected any extraconstitutional basis of the authority, holding that the power was 'drawn both explicitly and implicitly from the Constitution itself.' By 1989, the Court confirmed that 'the central function of the Indian Commerce Clause

is to provide Congress with plenary power to legislate in the field of Indian affairs." Cleveland, "Powers Inherent," 78. Also making direct reference to *McClanahan*, Nathan Speed stated, "The modern Supreme Court continues to utilize the plenary power doctrine. The Court has, however, lessened its reliance on the 'ward' theory in favor of textualism. [Directly quoting *McClanahan*] This is a remarkable statement, especially given that *Kagama* expressly rejected the Indian Commerce Clause as a justification for plenary power." Nathan Speed, "Examining the Interstate Commerce Clause Through the Lens of the Indian Commerce Clause," *Boston University Law Review* 87, no. 2 (April 2007): 484.

90. *McClanahan* at 172 FN 7.

91. I'm sure that you picked up on the fact that Thurgood Marshall cited not just the Indian Commerce Clause but the Treaty Clause as well. As we went over in Chapter 2, the Treaty Clause unto itself as a basis for plenary power is unconvincing. That being noted, we will turn our attention to it again later in this chapter.

92. As N. Bruce Duthu has noted, "Repeated iterations of the government's self-proclaimed plenary power in Indian affairs became more commonplace in the twentieth century but even through the early 1980s, the Court's Indian law cases continued to reflect ambiguity as to the precise source of this massive federal authority." N. Bruce Duthu, *Shadow Nations: Tribal Sovereignty and the Limits of Legal Pluralism* (New York: Oxford University Press, 2013), 150.

93. *Mackey v. Coxe* at 103.

94. To be perfectly fair to McLean, he did also write that "it is refreshing to see the surviving remnants of the races which once inhabited and roamed over this vast country as their hunting-grounds, and as the undisputed proprietors of the soil, exchanging their erratic habits for the blessings of civilization." Ibid. So at least the Cherokee have that going for them.

95. Ibid.

96. *Choctaw Nation* at 27.

97. *Talton v. Mayes* at 382.

98. *United States v. Jackson* at 191.

99. *Board v. Seber* at 715.

100. "In the exercise of the war and treaty powers, the United States overcame the Indians and took possession of their lands, sometimes by force, leaving them an uneducated, helpless and dependent people, needing protection against the selfishness of others and their own improvidence. Of necessity, the United States assumed the duty of furnishing that protection, and with it the authority to do all that was required to perform that obligation and to prepare the Indians to take their place as independent, qualified members of the modern body politic. This was classically summarized in *United States v. Kagama*." Ibid.

101. *United States v. Antelope*, 430 U.S. 641, 648 (1977).

102. Ibid.

103. *Castro-Huerta* at 2493.

104. Ibid.

105. "Today the Court rules for Oklahoma. In doing so, the Court announces that, when it comes to crimes by non-Indians against tribal members within tribal reservations, Oklahoma may 'exercise jurisdiction.' But this declaration comes as if by oracle, without any sense of the history recounted above and unattached to any colorable legal authority. Truly, a more ahistorical and mistaken statement of Indian law would be hard to fathom." Ibid. at 2511 (Gorsuch, J., dissenting).

106. I mean you made it this far, right? Why not see if I can redeem myself?

107. Perhaps I shouldn't put words into your mouth. You are obviously free to decide for yourself whether there is any point to reading this. I will request, however, that you read to the end before you make up your mind. Trust me, I am building toward something here.

108. Is it still foreshadowing when I announce it like that?

109. Research suggests that not only do Native peoples actually drink less than other groups, but the belief that Native peoples have some sort of genetic disposition toward alcoholism might lead to greater alcohol abuse when they do drink. See James K. Cunningham, Teshia A. Solomon, and Myra L. Muramoto, "Alcohol Use Among Native Americans Compared to Whites: Examining the Veracity of the 'Native American Elevated Alcohol Consumption' Belief," *Drug and Alcohol Dependence* 160, no. 1 (March 2016): 65–75; and Vivian M. Gonzalez and Monica C. Skewes, "Belief in the Myth of an American Indian/Alaska Native Biological Vulnerability to Alcohol Problems Among Reservation-Dwelling Participants with a Substance Use Problem," *Alcoholism: Clinical and Experimental Research* 45, no. 11 (November 2021): 2309–21.

110. See Jill E. Martin, "'The Greatest Evil': Interpretations of Indian Prohibition Laws, 1832–1953," *Great Plains Quarterly* 23, no. 1 (Winter 2003): 35–53.

111. Ibid. at 37.

112. 1802 Trade and Intercourse Act, *U.S. Statutes at Large,* 2:139–46.

113. Today tribal nations have much more, although not complete, say over the regulation of liquor on their lands. See 18 U.S.C. § 1161. See also Chapter 13, "Federal Indian Liquor Laws," in Cohen, *Handbook (2012 ed).*

114. Prucha, *American Indian Policy,* 104.

115. *Forty-Three Gallons* at 194.

116. Davis continued, "Their peculiar habits and character required this; and the history of the country shows the necessity of keeping them 'separate, subordinate, and dependent.'" Ibid.

117. *Sandoval* at 45–46.

118. See Mark Tushnet, "Willis Van Devanter: The Person," *Journal of Supreme Court History* 45, no. 3 (November 2020): 308–27; and William D. Bader and

Frank J. Williams, "Chapter XIII—Willis Van Devanter," in *Unknown Justices of the United States Supreme Court* (Buffalo, NY: William S. Hein, 2011), 117–19.

119. Wilkins, *American Indian Sovereignty*, 125–27.

120. *Perrin* at 482.

121. *United States v. Nice*, 241 U.S. 591, 597 (1916).

122. Ibid.

123. *Williams v. Lee* at 219 FN 4.

124. *Mazurie* at 554 (1975).

125. Ibid. at 554–55.

126. *Antelope* at 645.

127. Seemingly every piece of scholarship that engages with the Interstate Commerce Clause relates the same basic historical trajectory. John Marshall opened the door to a potentially expansive reading of the clause in *Gibbons v. Ogden*, 22 U.S. (9 Wheat.) 1 (1824); in the late nineteenth and early twentieth centuries the Supreme Court was reluctant to find federal authority under the Interstate Commerce Clause; during the New Deal Era and for a long time thereafter, the Supreme Court reversed course and never overturned any federal effort as an overextension of the Interstate Commerce Clause; in the late twentieth and twenty-first centuries the Supreme Court has retreated from its exclusively deferential position, but the significant authority of the federal government under the Interstate Commerce clause remains. For some useful examples of this narrative, see Robert J. Pushaw Jr. and Grant S. Nelson, "The Likely Impact of National Federation on Commerce Clause Jurisprudence," *Pepperdine Law Review* 40, no. 4 (2013): 980–85; and David M. Crowell, "*Gonzales v. Raich* and the Development of Commerce Clause Jurisprudence: Is the Necessary and Proper Clause the Perfect Drug?," *Rutgers Law Journal* 38, no. 1 (Fall 2006): 254–83.

128. Grant S. Nelson and Robert J. Pushaw Jr., "Rethinking the Commerce Clause: Applying First Principles to Uphold Federal Commercial Regulations but Preserve State Control over Social Issues," *Iowa Law Review* 85, no. 1 (October 1999): 79–88; Pushaw and Nelson, "Likely Impact," 982n44.

129. See Richard A. Cortner, *Civil Rights and Public Accommodations: The* Heart of Atlanta Motel *and* McClung *Cases* (Lawrence: University Press of Kansas, 2001).

130. *Mescalero Apache* at 159 (Douglas, J., dissenting).

131. 78 Stat. 241. Cortner noted, "The public accommodations provisions of Title II . . . had from the beginning been considered the heart of the Civil Rights Act," and also, "the public accommodations provisions of Title II were . . . primarily based on the power of Congress under the Commerce Clause to regulate interstate and foreign commerce." Cortner, *Civil Rights*, 17.

132. "The Senate Commerce Committee made it quite clear that the fundamental object of Title II was to vindicate 'the deprivation of personal dignity that surely accompanies denials of equal access to public establishments.' At

the same time, however, it noted that such an objective has been and could be readily achieved 'by congressional action based on the commerce power of the Constitution.' Our study of the legislative record, made in the light of prior cases, has brought us to the conclusion that Congress possessed ample power in this regard." *Heart of Atlanta Motel v. United States*, 379 U.S. 241, 250 (1964). See also *Katzenbach v. McClung*, 379 U.S. 294 (1964).

133. For a useful recounting of how the Indian Civil Rights Act came to be, see Donald L. Burnett Jr., "An Historical Analysis of the 1968 Indian Civil Rights' Act," *Harvard Journal on Legislation* 9, no. 4 (1971–72): 557–626. See also Michael Reese, "The Indian Civil Rights Act: Conflict Between Constitutional Assimilation and Tribal Self-Determination," *Southeastern Political Review* 20, no. 1 (June 1992): 29–61. To better understand the impact of the Indian Civil Rights Act, see Kristen A. Carpenter, Matthew L. M. Fletcher, and Angela R. Riley, eds., *The Indian Civil Rights Act at Forty* (Los Angeles: UCLA American Indian Studies Center, 2012).

134. U.S. Congress, Senate, Committee on the Judiciary, Hearings Before the Subcommittee on Constitutional Rights, *Constitutional Rights of the American Indian, Aug. 29, 30, 31, and Sep. 1*, 87th Congress, 1st sess. (Washington, DC: USGPO, 1962), 3.

135. U.S. Congress, Senate, Committee on the Judiciary, *Protecting the Rights of the American Indian*, Report No. 841, 90th Congress, 1st sess. (Washington, DC: USGPO, 1967), 7. By the way, I do recognize that the "although" in that sentence makes it unnecessarily confusing. But the gist of the statement remains—lots of parts of the U.S. Constitution allow the federal government to interfere with the inner workings of a tribal nation, and interfere it has!

136. U.S. Congress, House, Committee on Interior and Insular Affairs, Subcommittee on Indian Affairs, *Rights of Members of Indian Tribes Hearing, Mar. 29, 1968*, 90th Congress, 2nd sess. (Washington, DC: USGPO, 1968), 106, 107.

137. U.S. Congress, Senate, Committee on the Judiciary, Subcommittee on Constitutional Rights, *Constitutional Rights of the American Indian, Committee Print*, 89th Congress, 2nd sess. (Washington, DC: USGPO, 1966), 1.

138. Ibid. at FN 4. The other clauses were the "warmaking power" (art. I, sec. 8, cl. 11), the "treatymaking power" (art. II, sec. 2, cl. 2), the "power to govern and dispose of territory and other property held by the United States" (art. IV, sec. 3, cl. 2), and the "power to tax and spend" (art. I, sec. 8, cl. 1).

139. Burnett, "Historical Analysis," 604–14. As Burnett puts it, "In the angry clash of black and white, North and South, Indian law was made." Ibid., 614.

140. See "Chapter 9—The Termination Era," in Richotte, *Federal Indian Policy*, 173–92.

141. For a very useful study of the Termination Era, see Donald L. Fixico, *Termination and Relocation: Federal Indian Policy, 1945–1960* (Albuquerque: University of New Mexico Press, 1986).

142. According to one study, termination legislation—bills intended to end the political relationship between the federal government and tribal nations and redefine tribal lands—affected only 3 percent of tribal citizens and 3.2 percent of tribal lands. Charles F. Wilkinson and Eric R. Biggs, "The Evolution of Termination Policy," *American Indian Law Review* 5, no. 1 (1977): 151.

143. Lyndon B. Johnson, "Special Message to the Congress on the Problems of the American Indian: 'The Forgotten American,'" online by Gerhard Peters and John T. Woolley, The American Presidency Project, March 6, 1968, https://www.presidency.ucsb.edu/node/237467.

144. Richard Nixon, "Special Message to the Congress on Indian Affairs," online by Gerhard Peters and John T. Woolley, The American Presidency Project, July 8, 1970, https://www.presidency.ucsb.edu/node/240040.

145. See "Chapter 10—The Self-Determination Era," in Richotte, *Federal Indian Policy*, 193–213.

146. For example, writing in dissent in 1982, William Rehnquist stated, "Thus, the Court accords an Indian tribe, whose sovereignty 'exists only at the sufferance of Congress and is subject to complete defeasance,' greater immunity from state taxes that is enjoyed by the sovereignty of the United States on whom it is dependent." *Ramah* at 856–57 (Rehnquist, J., dissenting). More recently, Justice Elena Kagan has written that "Indian tribes are 'domestic dependent nations' that exercise 'inherent sovereign authority.' As dependents, the tribes are subject to plenary control by Congress." *Bay Mills* at 788.

147. This sentiment seems to have only grown in the years since. Writing in 2023, Justice Amy Coney Barrett stated, "A power unmoored from the Constitution would lack both justification and limits. So like the rest of its legislative powers, Congress's authority to regulate Indians must derive from the Constitution, not the atmosphere." *Haaland v. Brackeen*, 599 U.S. ___, 11, 143 S. Ct. 1609, 1627 (2023).

148. *Antelope* at 645 FN 6. In another footnote, Berger also stated, "It should be noted, however, that this Court has consistently upheld federal regulations aimed solely at tribal Indians, as opposed to all persons subject to federal jurisdiction. Indeed, the Constitution itself provides support for legislation directed specifically at the Indian tribes," while citing back to footnote 6 and thus the Indian Commerce Clause. Ibid. at 649 FN 11.

149. *United States v. John*, 437 U.S. 634, 653 (1978).

150. *White Mountain Apache Tribe v. Bracker*, 448 U.S. 136, 142 (1980).

151. *Montana v. Blackfeet Tribe of Indians*, 471 U.S. 759, 764, 765 (1985).

152. Other than, of course, the Apportionment Clauses, but we went over that in Chapter 1.

153. Put slightly differently by Thurman Lee Hester Jr., "The labyrinth of Indian law is necessary to hide the fact that the United States is violating its most fundamental principles." Hester, *Political Principles*, 110.

154. *Lara* at 200.

155. Ibid.

156. Of course you do! After all, I've already mentioned it three other times in this chapter. How could anyone ever forget?

157. *Brackeen* at 1628.

158. "Second, Congress, with this Court's approval, has interpreted the Constitution's 'plenary' grants of power as authorizing it to enact legislation that both restricts and, in turn, relaxes those restrictions on tribal sovereign authority." *Lara* at 202.

159. "Third, Congress' statutory goal . . . is not an unusual legislative objective." Ibid. at 203.

160. "Fourth, Lara points to no explicit language in the Constitution suggesting a limitation on Congress' institutional authority to relax restrictions on tribal sovereignty previously imposed by the political branches." Ibid. at 204.

161. "Fifth, the change at issue here is a limited one." Ibid.

162. "Sixth, our conclusion that Congress has the power to relax the restrictions imposed by the political branches on the tribes' inherent prosecutorial authority is consistent with our earlier cases." Ibid. at 205.

163. As Taylor Ledford has noted, "The Court in *Lara* decided that the best path to resolve the tensions between inherent tribal sovereignty and Congress's plenary authority was to pretend as though Congress's authority was never extra-constitutional." Taylor Ledford, "Foundations of Sand: Justice Thomas's Critique of the Indian Plenary Power Doctrine," *American Indian Law Review* 43, no. 1 (2018): 169.

164. *Brackeen* at 1629.

165. During the academic year of 2022–23, when I began drafting this book in earnest, things have only gotten more intense. First, there were increasing revelations about Thomas's wife, Ginni, and her involvement in attempts to overturn the 2020 presidential election results. Jo Becker and Danny Hakim, "Ginni Thomas Urged Arizona Lawmakers to Overturn Election," *New York Times*, May 20, 2022, updated September 29, 2022, https://www.nytimes.com/2022/05/20/us/politics/ginni-thomas-election-trump.html?action=click&module=RelatedLinks&pgtype=Article. Then there were revelations about Clarence Thomas's financial involvement with a wealthy Republican donor. Joshua Kaplan, Justin Elliott, and Alex Mierjeski, "Clarence Thomas and the Billionaire," *ProPublica*, April 6, 2023, https://www.propublica.org/article/clarence-thomas-scotus-undisclosed-luxury-travel-gifts-crow; Joshua Kaplan, Justin Elliott, and Alex Mierjeski, "Billionaire Harlan Crow Bought Property from Clarence Thomas. The Justice Didn't Disclose the Deal," *ProPublica*, April 13, 2023, https://www.propublica.org/article/clarence-thomas-harlan-crow-real-estate-scotus; Joshua Kaplan, Justin Elliott, and Alex Mierjeski, "Clarence

Thomas Had a Child in Private School. Harlan Crow Paid the Tuition," *ProPublica*, May 4, 2023, https://www.propublica.org/article/clarence-thomas-harlan-crow-private-school-tuition-scotus. The conversations over the dinner table in the Thomas house must be fascinating.

166. *Lara* at 214, 244 (Thomas, J., concurring). He further cited *Kagama* to note, "At one time, the implausibility of this assertion at least troubled the Court, and I would be willing to revisit the question." Ibid. at 244. He also noted, "The treaty power does not, as the Court seems to believe, provide Congress with free-floating power to legislate as it sees fit on topics that could potentially implicate some unspecified treaty. Such an assertion is especially ironic in light of Congress' enacted prohibition on Indian treaties." Ibid. at 225.

167. Ibid. at 226. He continued, "Such an acknowledgement might allow the Court to ask the logically antecedent question *whether* Congress (as opposed to the President) has this power. A cogent answer would serve as the foundation for the analysis of the sovereignty issues posed by this case. We might find that the Federal Government cannot regulate the tribes through ordinary domestic legislation and simultaneously maintain that the tribes are sovereigns in any meaningful sense. But until we begin to analyze these questions honestly and rigorously, the confusion that I have identified will continue to haunt our cases." Ibid (emphasis in original). As Frank Pommersheim has noted about this concurrence, "Justice Thomas's opinion possesses a certain unassailable, even severe, logic. The Indian Commerce Clause and the treaty-making clauses of the Constitution do not confer the plenary authority routinely ascribed to them." Frank Pommersheim, *Broken Landscape: Indians, Indian Tribes, and the Constitution* (New York: Oxford University Press, 2009), 253.

168. *Adoptive Couple v. Baby Girl*, 570 U.S. 637, 659 (2013) (Thomas, J., concurring).

169. *United States v. Bryant*, 579 U.S. 140, 160 (2016) (Thomas, J., concurring).

170. *Upstate Citizens for Equal, Inc. v. United States*, 140 S. Ct. 2587, 2588 (2017) (Thomas, J., dissenting).

171. *Brackeen* at 1670 (Thomas, J., dissenting). He continued, "Because the Constitution contains one Indian-specific power, there is simply no reason to think that there is some sort of free-floating, unlimited power over all things related to Indians." Ibid.

172. For a brief recounting of the dismissive attitude that some Supreme Court justices have held toward Indian law cases, see Peter D'Errico, "Scalia's Death: Will It Affect Indian Country?," ICTNews.org, February 18, 2016, updated September 12, 2018, https://ictnews.org/archive/scalias-death-will-it-affect-indian-country.

173. As stated by Matthew Fletcher, "The Supreme Court has continued to recognize congressional plenary power in the modern era without theorizing the justifications of such authority in great detail, and without delving

into whether congressional authority extends into the *internal affairs* of Indian tribes." Fletcher, "Tribal Consent," 91.

174. "The Supreme Court has always sidestepped the question of the extent and source of the authority of Congress and the Executive branch to deal with Indian affairs." Fletcher, "Preconstitutional," 564.

Chapter 4

1. As William J. Hynes and William G. Doty noted, "Anyone attempting to study tricksters faces significant methodological issues. For example, at one extreme one finds colleagues trained in Jungian psychology talking about the *the* [*sic*, emphasis in original] trickster as a universal archetype to be encountered within each of us and in most belief systems. At the other extreme, some anthropologists have called for the elimination of the term 'trickster' altogether because it implies that a global approach to such a figure is possible whereas they find it appropriate to focus only upon one tribal national group at a time." William J. Hynes and William G. Doty, "Introducing the Fascinating and Perplexing Trickster Figure," in *Mythical Trickster Figures: Contours, Contexts, and Criticisms*, ed. William J. Hynes and William G. Doty (Tuscaloosa: University of Alabama Press, 1993), 4–5.

2. It's probably also necessary to point out that, as Lewis Hyde notes, tricksters tend to be dudes. "I have been speaking of the trickster as 'he' because all the regularly discussed figures are male. There is no shortage of tricky women in this world, of course, or of women in myth fabled for acts of deception, but few of these have the elaborated career of deceit that tricksters have." Lewis Hyde, *Trickster Makes This World: Mischief, Myth, and Art* (New York: Farrar, Straus and Giroux, 2010), 8. Hyde offers his understanding of why this is. Ibid., 335–43. I will leave it up to you to decide if you find the argument convincing. I will merely note that I haven't found more theorizing on this point, and perhaps we could use some. So, are you looking for a dissertation topic?

3. Speaking to the breadth of trickster stories across the globe, one prominent collection of essays noted of its survey of the genre, "This book presents a variety of tricksters set within their specific sociocultural settings across a wide variety of cultures. Some of the tricksters to be encountered include the African Ananse, Eshu, and Legba; Western tricksters such as Hermes, Saint Peter, and Herschel; Native American figures such as Coyote, Wakdjunkaga, and Manabozo; and such Asian tricksters as Susa-no-o, Sun Wak'ung, Agu Tampa, and Horangi. Readers will find many examples of trickster episodes in this book, appearing across a wide range of contexts." Hynes and Doty, *Mythical Trickster Figures*, 2.

4. As Lewis Hyde notes, "Tricksters are regularly honored as creators of culture. They are imagined not only to have stolen certain essential goods from heaven and given them to the race but to have gone on and helped shape this

world so as to make it a hospitable place for human life. . . . In the Greek tradition, Hermes doesn't simply acquire fire, he invents and spreads a method, a *techne,* for making fire, and when he steals cattle from the gods he is simultaneously presenting the human race with the domestic beasts whose meat that fire will cook. A whole complex of cultural institutions around killing and eating cattle are derived from the liar and thief, Hermes." Hyde, *Trickster Makes This World,* 8–9.

5. As Herald McKinley put it, "Almost every culture around the world tells stories about the mischief-makers. These crafty tricksters defy divine authority, the laws of nature, and accepted rules of behavior. The trickster can be both good and evil, clever and stupid, sacred and comical." Herald McKinley, *Myths of the Native Americans* (New York: Cavendish Square, 2016), 63. Admittedly, this is a work of "juvenile literature," as mentioned previously. However, it is still very much possible for those of us who are no longer "juvenile" to learn from these texts, especially since they are often tasked with explaining complex things in simple, understandable ways.

6. Noting a number of Native trickster figures, Erdoes and Ortiz state that "Iktomi, the Sioux Spider Man, and Rabbit Boy are complicated culture heroes. We certainly see them, in classic Trickster style, being clever and foolish at the same time, smart-asses who outsmart themselves. But they are much more than that. Iktomi is a supernatural character with broad powers; Rabbit Boy stars in important creation myths, as the creator. Iktomi is powerful as well as powerless; he is a prophet, a liar who sometimes tricks by using the truth. He is a spider but transforms himself into a man, bigger than life and smaller than a pea. He is a clown, often with a serious message. Like Coyote and Veeho, he has a strong amorous streak and at times seems completely driven by sex." Erdoes and Ortiz, *Trickster Tales,* xiv.

7. Reflecting different dialects and other nuances, there are several ways to spell and pronounce the name of the Anishinaabe trickster figure. As Alethea K. Helbig wrote, Anishinaabe peoples "have known this mythological figure by such names as Nanibojo, Manabus, Wenibojo, and Wisakejak, among others. Among the Ojibwa themselves, one of the largest tribes north of Mexico, pronunciations have varied, but the version Nanabozhoo is frequently found." Alethea K. Helbig, *Nanabozhoo: Giver of Life* (Brighton, MI: Green Oak Press, 1987), 2. Frances Densmore stated of the Anishinaabe trickster figure that "Winabojo is the same personage as Nanabush and Nanabojo, being known by several unrelated names among Algonquian tribes." Frances Densmore, *Chippewa Customs* (Washington, DC: Smithsonian Institution, 1929; St. Paul: Minnesota Historical Society Press, 1979), 97. Citations are to the Minnesota Historical Society Press edition. I use the spelling Nanaboozhoo because that is how I learned it and how this trickster's name sounds to me.

8. Versions of this story can be found in Helbig, *Nanabozhoo,* 168; and, Victor

Barnouw, *Wisconsin Chippewa Myths & Tales: And Their Relation to Chippewa Life* (Madison: University of Wisconsin Press, 1977), 46. As is the prerogative of the storyteller of a trickster story, I am telling (or, more correctly, writing) my version to achieve my goals. The differences that exist between my version and the versions in the citations (which also differ slightly from each other) hold, at least in my mind, no particular significance. I am merely writing in my own voice, much as I would tell the story in my own way if I were relating it orally.

9. A version of this story can be found in Helbig, *Nanabozhoo*, 173–75. As in the previous story, I am exercising the prerogative of the storyteller by telling (or, more correctly, writing) my version to achieve my goals. The differences that exist between my version and the version in the citation hold, at least in my mind, no particular significance. I am merely writing in my own voice, much as I would tell the story in my own way if I were relating it orally.

10. Is there any way this dusty, old story can relate to the modern world in which we live today? Hmmm, I wonder . . .

11. As Victor Barnouw described it, "[Nanaboozhoo] seems to be neither a human being nor a god, but something of both." Barnauw, *Wisconsin Chippewa*, 51. Another storyteller described it this way: "As for [Nanaboozhoo], we only know that he was a man like ourselves. Yet he had more power than any other Indian; he could speak to the water and make it stop and to the wind and make it talk. He called the animals his brothers; men he called his uncles; women and trees and all that grows and all that flies he called his brothers and sisters." Homer H. Kidder, recorder, and Arthur P. Bourgeois, ed., *Ojibwa Narratives of Charles and Charlotte Kawbawgam and Jacques LePique, 1893–1895* (Detroit, MI: Wayne State University Press, 1994), 30.

12. Basil Johnston, *The Manitous: The Spiritual World of the Ojibway* (St. Paul: Minnesota Historical Society Press, 2001), xxii–xxiii.

13. As Lewis Hyde put it, "In short, trickster is a boundary-crosser. Every group has its edge, its sense of in and out, and trickster is always there, at the gates of the city and the gates of life, making sure there is commerce. . . . Trickster is the creative idiot, therefore, the wise fool, the gray-haired baby, the cross-dresser, the speaker of sacred profanities." Hyde, *Trickster Makes This World*, 7.

14. Helbig, *Nanabozhoo*, 55–57.

15. Ibid., 58–76.

16. Frances Densmore is instructive. "Stories concerning [Nanaboozhoo] are told and retold by the old people around the winter fire, and as many of them are amusing there has arisen an impression that [Nanaboozhoo] was a fantastic deity. This, however, is a popular misunderstanding, as [Nanaboozhoo] in the mind of the old Indian was the master of life—the source and impersonation of the lives of all sentient things, human, faunal, and floral. He endowed these with life and taught each its particular ruse for deceiving its

enemies and prolonging its life. His 'tricks' were chiefly exhibitions of his ability to outwit the enemies of life. He was regarded as the master of ruses, but he also possessed great wisdom in prolonging of life. It was he who gave the Indians their best remedies for treating the sick and who taught the animals the varied forms of protective disguise by which their lives can be extended. His own inherent life was so strong that when he apparently had been put to death he reappeared in the same or a different form." Densmore, *Chippewa Customs*, 97–98.

17. Helbig, *Nanabozhoo*, 128–29, 153–54, 171–72.

18. Barnouw, *Wisconsin Chippewa*, 38–40; Kidder, *Ojibwa Narratives*, 29; Helbig, *Nanabozhoo*, 93–95.

19. Barnouw, *Wisconsin Chippewa*, 85.

20. About tricksters in general Lewis Hyde noted, "When [the trickster] lies and steals, it isn't so much to get away with something or get rich as to disturb the established categories of truth and property and, by so doing, open the road to possible new worlds." Hyde, *Trickster Makes This World*, 13.

21. Obviously this is a much more detailed story than how I am telling it, and there was no one single individual who brought the smartphone into existence. That being acknowledged, the larger point stands. Tricksters are creators who spark our own creativity.

22. There are plenty of stories about Nanaboozhoo dressing in what has traditionally been regarded as female clothing. See Helbig, *Nanabozhoo*, 206–8. All of which is to note that I don't think Nanaboozhoo would be all that concerned with what others wear or how they understand and identify themselves.

23. I suppose that I have to admit that if your starting point is that there actually is something inferior about Native peoples, then this line of reasoning is logical. However, if that is your starting point, I am not sure we will ever find enough common ground to engage with each other, and I am surprised that you are reading this book in the first place. I would also ask you to consider why that is your starting point and leave it at that for now.

24. I have previously defined "tribal advocate" as "any person or entity that seeks to expand tribal sovereignty and benefit the lives of Native peoples. The term is not meant to exclude any person or thing on the basis of race or tribal affiliation. Rather, it is meant to be a broadly inclusive term that encompasses, but is not limited to, lawyers, legal historians, other academics, and, of course, tribal nations and tribal members." Keith Richotte, Jr., "A Legal Pluralist Approach to Tribal Constitutions," *William Mitchell Law Review* 36, no. 2 (2010): 447n1.

25. Conference of Western Attorneys General, *American Indian Law Deskbook, 2022 edition* (St. Paul, MN: Thomson Reuters, 2022, 13.

26. Cohen, *Handbook (2012 ed.)*, 383.

27. David H. Getches et al., *Cases and Materials on Federal Indian Law*, 7th ed. (St. Paul, MN: West Academic Publishing, 2017), 339.

28. Angelique Wambdi Eaglewoman and Stacy L. Leeds, *Mastering American Indian Law*, 2nd ed. (Durham, NC: Carolina Academic Press, 2019), 22.

29. These are just a few of many examples. "Even if the Commerce Clause confers an Indian affairs power on Congress, at first glance, it is not clear that this power can justify the regulation of the purely internal affairs of the Indians." Stephen Andrews, "In Defense of the Indian Commerce Clause," *American Indian Law Journal* 9, no. 2 (2020–21): 186; "The federal government's assertion of unrestricted authority over Indian nations, particularly their land and governments, rests on a flimsy legal foundation. It is said to arise, almost mythically, from an amalgamation of judicial decisions, federal statutes, and administrative rulings. Although the juridical basis for this so-called plenary authority has not been persuasively established, most courts and many lawyers accept uncritically such power." Berkey, "United States," 190; "*Lone Wolf*'s proposal that Congress's plenary power over Indians is a nonreviewable political question has not prevailed. But the ideas that Congress's power is plenary in the sense that it is total power over tribes and that this power is grounded in superiority are very much alive and well. *Kagama* and *Lone Wolf* lead directly to Justice Thurgood Marshall's statement in the 1982 case of *Merrion v. Jicarilla Apache Tribe* about the derivation of Congress's authority from its 'superior position' over the tribes. Justice Marshall did not there cite *Kagama* and *Lone Wolf*, but those cases and their reasoning are the source of the idea." Ball, "Constitution," 54; "Significantly, while recent cases, like *Cotton Petroleum*, incorrectly ascribe the origins of the plenary power doctrine to the Indian Commerce Clause, it should be recalled that the *Kagama* case, from which both the trusteeship power and its concomitant plenary power doctrine sprang, expressly rejected the Indian Commerce Clause as a broad source of federal authority over Indian affairs. The plenary power doctrine, therefore, represents a relic of Indian law's colonialist past, rather than a well-grounded, historically rooted constitutional doctrine whose legitimacy can be traced either to intentionally broad constitutional text or some original understanding of the framers." Clinton, "Redressing," 120; "While the labels may have changed as to the source of federal power in Indian affairs, the Supreme Court has not abandoned the sweeping claims to federal colonialist authority over Indian tribes developed under the colonialist wardship theory." Clinton, "Federal Supremacy," 196; "Declaring that the United States has plenary power in certain areas of law is an illocutionary legal act: it brings this power into being by calling it forth, and finding its limit there. Indeed, efforts by the Supreme Court to locate the source of plenary power quickly take them past the Constitution, the source of their authority, and in search of some power that inheres in sovereignty itself." Susan Bibler Coutin, Justin Richland, and Véronique Fortin, "Routine

Exceptionality: The Plenary Power Doctrine, Immigrants, and the Indigenous Under U.S. Law," *University of California Irvine Law Review* 4, no. 1 (2014): 103; "In theory, Congress should have no greater power over Indian nations than it does over states, but in historical practice such has not been the case." Deloria, "The Application of the Constitution," 287; "The commerce clause was the only source of explicit power claimed by the federal government. In theory, this clause should not have extended to Congress any greater authority over Native nations that it exercises over states. In both historical and contemporary practice, however, such has not been the case. As indigenous dominion waned during the nineteenth and twentieth centuries, the federal government used the commerce clause (and other self-generated powers) to justify many new assertions of national authority over Native peoples." Deloria and Wilkins, *Legal Universe*, 128; "The problem with relying on the Indian Commerce Clause is apparent. The Court has held that the plenary power authorizes congressional regulation even of the internal affairs of Indian tribes and the private transactions of individual Indians. That requires an expansive understanding of the word 'Commerce'—an understanding far more expansive than the Court has allowed for the same word in the Interstate Commerce Clause." Michael Doran, "The Equal-Protection Challenge to Federal Indian Law," *University of Pennsylvania Journal of Law and Public Affairs* 6, no. 1 (2020–21): 16; "Indeed, an attribute of discrimination is its power to legitimate and sustain the inferiority of a group." Harvey, "Constitutional Law," 145; "In addition, of course, there is no constitutional provision that grants Congress plenary power in Indian affairs but rather only the ability to regulate 'trade with Indians' and make treaties with Indians." Pommersheim, *Broken Landscape*, 136; "Despite its lack of constitutional roots, this power nevertheless proclaims extensive—even limitless—power over tribes in blatant contradiction of the Lockean notion of limited government sovereignty. The plenary power doctrine appears to be extraconstitutional in its origins and extravagant in its placement of unlimited authority in the hands of the Congress at the expense of tribal sovereignty." Frank Pommersheim, "Is There a (Little or Not So Little) Constitutional Crisis Developing in Indian Law? A Brief Essay," *University of Pennsylvania Journal of Constitutional Law* 5, no. 2 (January 2003): 287; "The legal consequences of the metamorphosis of the plenary power concept in the course of the nineteenth century was to legitimize the exercise of unilateral and *standardless* power by the United States over Indian tribes whose lack of recourse was confirmed by this one-sided allocation of power." Shattuck and Norgren, *Partial Justice*, 127 (emphasis in original); "Yet, most scholars agree that the Commerce Clause is insufficient by itself to grant Congress plenary power over the internal affairs of Indian tribes." Alex Tallchief Skibine, "Constitutionalism, Federal Common Law, and the Inherent Powers of Indian Tribes," *American Indian Law Review* 39, no. 1 (2014–15): 116; "Starting with the Indian Commerce Clause, the textual authorization to regulate commerce with tribes cannot be logically interpreted to authorize the legislative annihilation of tribes' political existence sanctioned in *Wheeler*. Even the broadest Commerce Clause cases outside of the Indian law context require that there be some nexus between commerce and the regulated activity, despite the 'plenary' quality of federal Commerce power. Moreover, the Court has required stronger nexuses in recent years." Tweedy, "Connecting the Dots," 661; "Although some commentators, most notably Felix S. Cohen, have suggested that Congress's commerce clause power is *over* tribes and that this power is 'much broader' over tribes than is the Congress's power over interstate commerce, there is nothing in the Constitution to support such an interpretation." Wilkins and Lomawaima, *Uneven Ground*, 102–3.

30. Encapsulating a division that continues to this day, David E. Wilkins has noted, "There is also considerable disagreement among scholars on whether plenary power is a necessary congressional power which protects tribes, or whether it is an abhorrent and undemocratic concept because it entails the congressional exercise of wide political authority over tribes." David E. Wilkins, "The U.S. Supreme Court's Explication of 'Federal Plenary Power': An Analysis of Case Law Affecting Tribal Sovereignty, 1886–1914," *American Indian Quarterly* 18, no. 3 (Summer 1994): 349.

31. Christine Bolt described those who led the way in the Assimilation Era as such: "The new Indian reformers, like their predecessors, encompassed active Protestants, including missionaries and clergymen and their wives from a range of sects. Among their number were humanitarians interested in other reform activities such as freedman's aid, women's rights, pacifism and temperance, as well as journalists and writers, educators, lawyers, businessmen, anthropologists and federal government employees. Geographically the movement was concentrated in the eastern states, though there were some members from the Midwest and the West, and politically Republicans were well represented. The reformers were middle-class individuals who did not take up the cause with a view to making money out of it and who welcomed to their gatherings educated and atypical Indian apostles of the white way. Members of the three main Indian reform organizations—and there were many lesser ones—attended and reported each other's meetings, giving credit where credit was due and creating in their proceedings a certain air of self-satisfaction which is only slightly less repellent to the unregenerate than reformer bickering. Since the gap between East and West, Republican and Democrat, and reformer and administrator over the conduct of Indian affairs had narrowed by the 1880s, and the humanitarians aimed at change through legislation, a conciliatory approach to legislators and bureau officials was sensible. Less sensible was their conviction that Indians could be quickly turned into white men." Christine Bolt, *American Indian Policy and American Reform* (London: Allen & Unwin, 1987), 93.

32. As Frederick E. Hoxie has noted, "The singularity of Indian assimilation is less striking when one recalls that the goal . . . was not a blending of Indian and white societies but Anglo conformity: the alteration of native culture to fit a 'civilized' model. Reformers insisted that Indians should follow the 'white man's road.' The expression is significant, for it indicates the kind of future being planned for Native Americans. . . . Moreover, both scholars and politicians believed the incorporation process could occur quicky and contribute to the general good." Hoxie, *A Final Promise*, 33.

33. This is just an observation, not advice for any would-be despots, warlords, or other sundry villains.

34. David Wallace Adams, perhaps the foremost authority on boarding schools, identified five goals of education for the reformers of this era, each of which was intended to further the goal of assimilation: "The first priority was to provide the Indian child with the rudiments of an academic education, including the ability to read, write, and speak the English language. . . . Second, Indians needed to be individualized. . . . The third aim of education was to reconstruct Indigenous conceptions of home and family. . . . The fourth aim of Indian education was Christianization. . . . The fifth aim of Indian schooling was citizenship training." David Wallace Adams, *Education for Extinction: American Indians and the Boarding School Experience, 1875–1928*, 2nd ed. rev. and exp. (Lawrence: University Press of Kansas, 2020), 25, 25, 27, 28, 28.

35. As Margaret D. Jacobs noted, "Through the removal of Indian children to distant boarding schools, along with the individual allotment of communally held land and the suppression of native religious practices, reformers and officials hoped American Indians would be assimilated into the mainstream of society. 'There is but one policy possible if we are to do the Indians any good,' editorialized one newspaper in Illinois, 'and that is to divide them up and get one Indian family away from another and get them mixed up with white people.'" Margaret D. Jacobs, *White Mother to a Dark Race: Settler Colonialism, Maternalism, and the Removal of Indigenous Children in the American West and Australia, 1880–1940* (Lincoln: University of Nebraska Press, 2009), 26–27.

36. Jacobs described the basic concepts of governmental efforts at education in the Allotment Era. "The Bureau of Indian Affairs (BIA) established a network of institutions, starting with day schools on reservations for the youngest children, who would then ideally graduate to on-reservation boarding schools, and then attend off-reservation boarding schools. Usually government authorities aimed to remove the children from the ages of eight to ten for a period of five to ten years, when they would normally be educated into the ways of their own people, and socialize them instead in Christian, middle-class, white mores." Ibid., 30–31.

37. Adams, *Education for Extinction*, 61–62; Jacobs, *White Mother*, 31. Jacobs also noted, "By 1902 the BIA had established 154 boarding schools (includ-

ing twenty-five off-reservation schools) and 154 day schools for about 21,500 Native American children. Of these children, about 17,700 attended some sort of boarding school. There were also still a number of mission schools operated by various religious organizations that contracted with the federal government to carry out the government's educational mission." Jacobs, *White Mother*, 31.

38. Adams, *Education for Extinction*, 126–31; Hoxie, *A Final Promise*, 60–61.

39. Adams, *Education for Extinction*, 137–49, 122–26, 250–65.

40. I would, of course, encourage you to start with the texts that I have cited over the last few pages. I would also encourage you to see Brenda J. Child, *Boarding School Seasons: American Indian Families, 1900–1940* (Lincoln: University of Nebraska Press, 1998).

41. As noted by Frederick E. Hoxie, "By the early 1900s, it was almost impossible for a family to avoid sending its children away for an education, the principal goal of which was to separate the children from their traditions and their past." Frederick E. Hoxie, "From Prison to Homeland: The Cheyenne River Indian Reservation Before World War I," in *The Plains Indians of the 20th Century*, ed. Peter Iverson (Norman: University of Oklahoma Press, 1985), 59.

42. Which is why Nevada is famous for, among other things, drive-thru wedding chapels and easy-to-obtain divorces, whereas other states generally have more requirements to complete either a marriage or a divorce.

43. As Margaret D. Jacobs noted, "The BIA devised a solution in 1958 that appealed to both federal cost cutters and cash-strapped state agencies: the Indian Adoption Project. This project promoted the placement of Indian children in non-Indian adoptive families; it looked to the ultimate private sector to take over the expense of raising Indian children and assimilating them once and for all. Reducing the costs of care for Indian children served as their priority, but BIA and state bureaucrats justified the Indian Adoption Project as a caring program that would rescue supposedly forgotten Indian children and find them permanent homes." Margaret D. Jacobs, *A Generation Removed: The Fostering and Adoption of Indigenous Children in the Postwar World* (Lincoln: University of Nebraska Press, 2014), 6–7.

44. "Disturbingly, most bureaucrats by the late 1950s rarely imagined a solution to the care of Indian children that involved strengthening Indian families and keeping Indian children within their homes. Most government officials deemed Indian families inherently and irreparably unfit, and so they ignored the proposition of funding preventative and rehabilitative services to Indian families. Ultimately they regarded this path as too costly and out of step with the overarching policy goals of the period: to terminate Indian tribes and de-Indigenize Indian people. Policymakers now used new terms and strategies, but the primary settler colonial goal of eliminating American Indian people remained unchanged. Indian children and Indian families suffered as a result." Ibid., 7.

45. U.S. Congress, House, Hearings Before a Subcommittee on Indian Affairs and Public Lands, February 9 and March 9, 1978, 85th Congress, 2nd sess., S. 1214, 29.

46. Ibid.

47. Ibid.

48. Ibid.

49. 92 Stat. 3069, 25 U.S.C. § 1901 et seq. As stated by Carol L. Tebben, "ICWA is a rejoinder to the longstanding and concerted legal effort that had been effectuated in the United States to influence the children of tribal nations to abandon their tribal heritage." Carol L. Tebben, "In Defense of ICWA: The Constitution, Public Policy, and Pragmatism," in *Facing the Future: The Indian Child Welfare Act at 30*, ed. Matthew L. M. Fletcher, Wenona T. Singel, and Kathryn E. Fort (East Lansing: Michigan State University Press, 2009), 273.

50. There tends to be much confusion on this point in those instances when ICWA flares up in the public consciousness. There seems to be the misunderstanding that ICWA mandates that Native children stay among Native peoples or that tribal courts always decide in the best interests of the tribal nation rather than the best interests of the child. However, this is not the case. ICWA merely authorizes tribal courts to determine what is in the best interests of the child in child placement proceedings. Often this means keeping the child within the community, but sometimes it doesn't. The belief that tribal courts are unwilling or unable to ever rule in the favor of a non-Native party seems more based on the assumptions of non-Native non-specialists than on evidence.

51. In 2016 the Department of the Interior issued binding regulations about the application of ICWA in state courts in large part because of this issue. According to the regulations, "some State court interpretations of ICWA have essentially voided Federal protections for groups of Indian children to whom ICWA clearly applies. And commenters provided numerous anecdotal accounts where Indian children were unnecessarily removed from their families and placed in non-Indian settings; where the rights of Indian children, their parents, or their Tribes were not protected; or where significant delays occurred in Indian child-custody proceedings due to disputes or uncertainty about the interpretation of the Federal law." Department of the Interior, Bureau of Indian Affairs, "Indian Child Welfare Act Proceedings; Final Rule," *Federal Register* 81, no. 114 (June 14, 2016): 38779, https://www.govinfo.gov/content/pkg/FR-2016-06-14/pdf/2016-13686.pdf.

52. "ICWA's requirements remain vitally important today. Although ICWA has helped to prevent the wholesale separation of Tribal children from their families in many regions of the United States, Indian families continue to be broken up by the removal of their children by non-Tribal public and private agencies. Nationwide, based on 2013 data, Native American children are rep-

resented in State foster care at a rate 2.5 times their presence in the general population. This disparity has *increased* since 2000. In some States, including numerous States with significant Indian populations, Native American children are represented in State foster-care systems at rates as high as 14.8 times their presence in the general population of that State." Ibid. at 38783–84 (emphasis in original).

53. Brief of Casey Family Programs and twenty-six other child welfare and adoption organizations as *Amici Curiae* in Support of Federal and Tribal Defendants, *Haaland v. Brackeen*, Nos. 21-376, 21-377, 21-378, 21-380, August 19, 2022, On writs of certiorari to the United States Court of Appeals for the Fifth Circuit, Supreme Court of the United States: 17–18.

54. Brief for the States of California, Arizona, Colorado, Connecticut, Idaho, Illinois, Iowa, Maine, Massachusetts, Michigan, Minnesota, Nevada, New Jersey, New Mexico, New York, North Carolina, Oregon, Pennsylvania, Rhode Island, South Dakota, Utah, Washington, and Wisconsin, and the District of Columbia, as *Amici Curiae* in Support of Federal and Tribal Defendants, *Haaland v. Brackeen*, Nos. 21-376, 21-377, 21-378, 21-380, August 19, 2022, On writs of certiorari to the United States Court of Appeals for the Fifth Circuit, Supreme Court of the United States: 4–10.

55. Casey Family Programs, *Child and Family Services Practice Model: A Safe and Permanent Family for Every Youth*, March 2021, https://www.casey.org/media/101-Practice-Model.pdf, 8.

56. As argued by a part of the coalition, "ICWA's separate child-placement scheme for 'Indian children' violates the Constitution's guarantee of equal protection." Brief for individual petitioners, *Haaland v. Brackeen*, Nos. 21-376, 21-377, 21-378, 21-380, May 26, 2022, On writs of certiorari to the United States Court of Appeals for the Fifth Circuit, Supreme Court of the United States: 14. Marcia Zug has noted, "Many of these lawsuits are brought by the Goldwater Institute, an organization unapologetically dedicated to eliminating the ICWA. . . . Goldwater's aggressive anti-ICWA tactics have also been adopted by other ICWA litigants." Marcia Zug, "ICWA's Irony," *American Indian Law Review* 45, no. 1 (2020–21): 30. To understand more about how ICWA is often portrayed outside Indian country, see Sarah Deer, Elise Higgins, and Thomas White, "Editorializing ICWA: 40 Years of Colonial Commentary," *Indigenous Peoples' Journal of Law, Culture and Resistance* 7 (2022): 27–58.

57. Both of my anonymous readers made mention of this, and I thank them for making me think more fully about it. The peer review process works! At least some of the time!

58. 92 Stat. 3069, Title II, Sec. 201(a).

59. *Brackeen* at 1628.

60. For example, the brief for the tribal defendants in *Brackeen* states that "'an unbroken current of judicial decisions,' based on 'long continued legisla-

tive and executive usage,' have recognized Congress's broad 'power and the duty' to 'exercis[e] a fostering care and protection over' Indians, 'whether within or without the limits of a state.'" Brief for tribal defendants, *Haaland v. Brackeen*, Nos. 21-376, 21-377, 21-378, 21-380, On writs of certiorari to the United States Court of Appeals for the Fifth Circuit, Supreme Court of the United States: 19. To be fair, this brief does evidence an understanding of the different versions of plenary power, at one point making the more nuanced statement that "Congress's multiple Indian-affairs powers . . . all confirm that Congress may regulate intercourse between Indians and non-Indians to protect Indians from harm." Ibid. To that end, my purpose is not to excoriate the lawyers for tribal interests or the tribal nations themselves. Rather, it is to point out that the way the Supreme Court (dis)regards plenary power forces tribal advocates into making bigger statements about plenary power than they should have to.

61. Kathryn Fort, perhaps the foremost expert on ICWA at the time *Brackeen* was handed down, described it as "a massive win." Kathryn Fort, "A Quick Brackeen Opinion Post," *Turtle Talk*, June 15, 2023, https://turtletalk.blog/2023/06/15/a-quick-brackeen-opinion-post/.

62. *Brackeen* at 1627.

63. Ibid.

64. Ibid at 1627–28.

65. Ibid.

66. Ibid. at 1628.

67. Ibid. at 1629.

68. Natsu Taylor Saito has noted both that plenary power is "a legal theory designed to protect explicit assertions of colonial authority" and that "contemporary legal decisions may employ more sanitized language and count on layers of precedent to mask their underlying reasoning, but the judiciary's continued reliance on the plenary power doctrine puts us on notice that only the 'principles of natural justice inherent in the Anglo-Saxon character' stand between those deemed Other and 'manifestly hostile' state action. The government may choose to extend certain rights or privileges when politically expedient, but it does so only as an exercise of its own prerogative, not because it recognizes an obligation to do so." Natsu Taylor Saito, *Settler Colonialism, Race, and the Law: Why Structural Racism Persists* (New York: NYU Press, 2020), 154–55, 157–58.

69. *Brackeen* at 1629–30.

70. Brief for tribal defendants, 18–19.

71. Brief of the American Bar Association as *Amicus Curiae* in Support of Petitioners in 21-376 and 21-377, and in Support of Respondents in 21-378 and 21-380, *Haaland v. Brackeen*, Nos. 21-376, 21-377, 21-378, 21-380, August 18, 2022, On writs of certiorari to the United States Court of Appeals for the Fifth Circuit, Supreme Court of the United States: 18–19.

72. Brief of *Amicus Curiae*, Senator James Abourezk, in Support of Federal and Tribal Parties, *Haaland v. Brackeen*, Nos. 21-376, 21-377, 21-378, 21-380, August 18, 2022, On writs of certiorari to the United States Court of Appeals for the Fifth Circuit, Supreme Court of the United States: 12.

73. Indian Self-Determination and Education Assistance Act, 25 U.S.C. §§ 5301–5423; American Indian Religious Freedom Act, 92 Stat. 469; Indian Arts and Crafts Act of 1990, 104 Stat. 4662.

74. 25 U.S.C.S. §1901(1). Frank Pommersheim has noted, "The ICWA expressly rests on Congress's authority under the Indian Commerce Clause, plenary power, and its 'responsibility for the protection and preservation of Indian tribes and their resources.'" Pommersheim, *Broken Landscape*, 243.

75. As Vine Deloria Jr. and Clifford Lytle have noted, "Attorneys thus 'make' federal Indian law in a very fundamental way that cannot be compared to their function with respect to any other body of law." Deloria and Lytle, *American Indians*, 141. Robert Odawi Porter has further illuminated this point: "American-trained lawyers have a tremendous impact on tribal sovereignty if they operate from the assumption that decisions of the U.S. Supreme Court and the entire body of American federal law apply to the Indian nations. It is a basic premise of the American legal system that federal law reigns supreme and that the Supreme Court holds the final word on matters of American constitutional and federal law. American-trained lawyers instinctively know this to be true. By accepting this premise, however, lawyers working for Indian nations must necessarily accept the application of the full panoply of Indian subjugation doctrines developed by the Court over the years such as the Doctrine of Discovery, the Plenary Power Doctrine, the Trust Responsibility Doctrine, and the concept of Domestic Dependent Nationhood. Now, this is not to say that lawyers representing Indian nations *accept* these cases, or even believe them to be *right*, but it is true that these lawyers generally behave as if these cases are *relevant* and that they thus must *apply* to the Indian nations." Robert Odawi Porter, "The Inapplicability of American Law to the Indian Nations," *Iowa Law Review* 89, no. 5 (May 2004): 1616 (emphasis in original).

76. As an added bonus, not only do I have the utmost respect for these people, but I can still tolerate most of them! On the other hand, the people I can no longer tolerate, in alphabetical order, are . . . You know what, I probably shouldn't have even included this note.

77. *Lara* at 215 (Thomas, J., concurring).

78. Ibid. at 218.

79. "The ICWA asserts that the Indian Commerce Clause, Art. I, §8, cl. 3, and 'other constitutional authority' provide Congress with 'plenary power over Indian affairs.' The reference to 'other constitutional authority' is not illuminating, and I am aware of no other enumerated power that could even arguably support Congress' intrusion into this area of traditional state authority.

The assertion of plenary authority must, therefore, stand or fall on Congress' power under the Indian Commerce Clause. Although this Court has said that the 'central function of the Indian Commerce Clause is to provide Congress with plenary power to legislate in the field of Indian affairs,' neither the text nor the original understanding of the Clause supports Congress' claim to such 'plenary' power." *Adoptive Couple* at 658–59 (Thomas, J., concurring).

80. "I join the Court's opinion in full but write separately to explain why constitutional avoidance compels this outcome. Each party in this case has put forward a plausible interpretation of the relevant sections of the Indian Child Welfare Act (ICWA). However, the interpretations offered by respondent Birth Father and the United States raise significant constitutional problems as applied to this case. Because the Court's decision avoids those problems, I concur in its interpretation." Ibid. at 656.

81. "On the one hand, the only reason why tribal courts had the power to convict Bryant in proceedings where he had no right to counsel is that such prosecutions are a function of a tribe's core sovereignty. . . . On the other hand, the validity of Bryant's ensuing federal conviction rests upon a contrary view of tribal sovereignty. . . . Thus, even though tribal prosecutions of tribal members are purportedly the apex of tribal sovereignty, Congress can second-guess how tribes prosecute domestic abuse perpetrated by Indians against other Indians on Indian land by virtue of its 'plenary power' over Indian tribes." *Bryant* at 158–59 (Thomas, J., concurring).

82. Ibid. at 161.

83. As Matthew L. M. Fletcher succinctly put it, "Undermining the theoretical foundations of federal plenary power might serve to limit federal authority over Indian affairs, but it might also destroy much of what Indian people and tribes relied upon as their best hopes for a remedy." Fletcher, "Preconstitutional," 524. Philip P. Frickey's statement to the same effect evidences that this has been a long-standing concern. "Indeed, there is a substantial risk that any diminution of congressional plenary power over Indian affairs in the near future will be rooted in an impulse to mainstream the field—and thus will come at the expense of the tribes, rather than for their benefit." Frickey, "Domesticating," 49.

84. Others have been less generous. "In short, lawyers who are supposed to be representing the Indian position have repeatedly *conceded* that the United States government has virtually unchecked political power over Indians, Indian governments and Indian property. It is not likely that these concessions have been authorized by the Indian peoples whose cases were being heard, and they certainly have not been authorized by all other Indian tribes who find the concessions used as precedents to deny their rights as well." Steven Tullberg and Robert T. Coulter, "The Failure of Indian Rights Advocacy: Are Lawyers to Blame?," in *Rethinking Indian Law*, comp. and ed. National Lawyers Guild, Com-

mittee on Native American Struggles (New York: National Lawyers Guild, Committee on Native American Struggles, 1982): 51 (emphasis in original). I make my own viewpoint clear in this paragraph, and I tend to think that this was probably a much more valid critique during the time that it was written than perhaps now. Nonetheless, I leave it to you to decide for yourself how to regard those who work in the trenches of this area of law.

85. As Robert A. Williams Jr. described the issue, "The problem with any approach to protecting Indian rights that relies upon the principle of racial discrimination perpetuated by the Marshall model is that those rights are never really safe under the Supreme Court's Indian law." Williams, *Loaded Weapon*, 151.

Chapter 5

1. Go ahead and look at the Bibliography. We've done a lot together. You've been a real trooper. I'm proud of you!

2. Of course, the benefits of plenary power in the present for tribal nations are generally just responses to the destruction that the doctrine has wrought in the past. The Indian Child Welfare Act is a perfect example. Would we need ICWA if not for the legacy of "lawfully" removing Native children from Native families in the Allotment Era and beyond? Understood in this light, it is obvious that plenary power remains a net negative for tribal nations and peoples.

3. For example, Robert N. Clinton stated, "Any effort to decolonize federal Indian law, therefore, must begin with a rejection of the plenary power doctrine in favor of legally enforceable doctrines far more protective of the sovereignty of Indian tribes." Clinton, *Redressing*, 121.

4. "From the very beginning, international law strongly shaped indigenous rights in North America. . . . In short, the international legal realm was a primary source for defining tribal rights in the United States. . . . Given this dynamic interaction, our domestic law should logically keep pace with international norms on indigenous issues. . . . This should be especially true in the United States, where customary international law forms a part of the federal common law and where the United States has long held a leadership role in the protection of human rights." Walter R. Echo-Hawk, *In the Light of Justice: The Rise of Human Rights in Native America and the U.S. Declaration of the Rights of Indigenous Peoples* (Golden, CO: Fulcrum Publishing, 2013), 63–64.

5. "Paradoxically, I shall argue that the domestication of federal Indian law may require internationalizing the way we think about the field—and the way we think about how the Constitution works in this unique area of law. For I shall contend that, properly understood, plenary power in federal Indian law, like that in immigration law, arose from conceptions of the inherent sovereignty of nations under international law." Frickey, "Domesticating," 36–37; "The postcolonial approach to Indian rights that I argue for tells the justices to

turn to the heretofore neglected fifth element of the Marshall model and to use the contemporary international law of indigenous peoples' human rights as an interpretive backdrop for aiding judicial understanding of Indian rights claims in America. . . . In other words, the precedent established by the Marshall Trilogy would support these justices in their use of contemporary international law principles in a present-day Court decision on Indian rights. These justices would just be following the judicial example set by Marshall himself in these foundational early-nineteenth-century Indian rights opinions for the Court." Williams, *Loaded Weapon*, 171, 173.

6. "Federal Indian law is not related to or consistent with international law, even though it finds its most defensible context in that setting. Nor is it related to American domestic law based on the Constitution and its amendments. . . . Indians in their tribal relations and Indian tribes in their relation to the federal government hang suspended in a legal no-man's-land. The solution to this problem—the means to bring a sense of coherent, logical consistency and historical accuracy and precedent to this subject—would be to return tribes to their political status as it existed prior to the prohibition against treaty making in 1871." Deloria and Wilkins, *Tribes, Treaties*, 158–59; "The limit on Indian affairs power requires the resuscitation of tribal treaty-making, which will restore constitutional separation of powers, continue recent legal trends toward self-determination, overturn a hundred and fifty years of colonialism, and capture the present moment of creative disruption in racial relations by bequeathing to the tribes their own *Brown v. Board of Education* crowning achievement for tribal sovereignty." Lorianne Updike Toler, "The Missing Indian Affairs Clause," *University of Chicago Law Review* 88, no. 2 (March 2021): 486.

7. "The current Supreme Court created these plenary doctrines and is therefore an unlikely source to disavow them. Congress, for its part, has shown little inclination to get involved. As a result, the foundational principles of Indian law are gravely at risk as both promise and law. In the short run, Congress must be persuaded to use its extensive legislative authority to curb these denigrations of tribal sovereignty that are contrary to the long-standing congressional and executive policy of meaningful self-determination. Yet, in the long run, only a constitutional amendment can truly guarantee and vouchsafe an essential and enduring tribal sovereignty." Pommersheim, *Broken Landscape*, 301.

8. "Race and Ethnicity in the United States: 2010 Census and 2020 Census," United States Census, August 12, 2021, https://www.census.gov/library/visualizations/interactive/race-and-ethnicity-in-the-united-state-2010-and-2020-census.html.

9. It continued, "Their lands and property shall never be taken from them without their consent; and in their property, rights and liberty, they never shall be invaded or disturbed, unless in just and lawful wars authorized by

Congress, but laws founded in justice and humanity shall from time to time be made, for preventing wrongs being done to them, and for preserving peace and friendship with them." Northwest Ordinance, 32:240–41.

10. A prominent congressional commission from the earlier days of the Self-Determination Era expressed a remarkably similar sentiment. "The relationship should be thought of not only in terms of moral and legal duty, but also as a partnership agreement to ensure that Indian tribes have available to them the tools and resources to survive as distinct political and cultural groups." American Indian Policy Review Commission, *Final Report, Submitted to Congress, May 17, 1977* (Washington, DC: USGPO, 1977), 127.

11. "The standard of review most recently expressed is that the legislative judgment should not be disturbed '[a]s long as the special treatment can be tied rationally to the fulfillment of Congress' unique obligation toward the Indians.'" *Delaware Tribal Business Committee v. Weeks*, 430 U.S. 73, 85 (1977).

12. "The Court developed what is now known as the Implicit Divestiture Doctrine under which upon incorporation into the United States, Indian tribes were implicitly divested of any sovereign power inconsistent with their status as domestic dependent nations." Skibine, "Constitutionalism," 78.

13. "Relying on the claimed supremacy of federal law created by the Indian plenary power doctrine, the federal judiciary has unilaterally exercised judicial plenary power over Indian affairs, assisted by opponents of Indian sovereignty, and sometimes by the tribes themselves, who continue to present and argue such cases to the federal courts." Clinton, "Federal Supremacy," 214.

14. "While the precise source and scope of the federal government's power in Indian affairs has been the subject of significant debate, the very fact of a government-to-government relationship is beyond question." Sarah Krakoff, "They Were Here First: American Indian Tribes, Race, and the Constitutional Minimum," *Stanford Law Review* 69, no. 2 (February 2017): 527.

15. "The wide-scale use of treaties indicates that the federal government was interested in regulating Native American affairs, but realized that the constitutionally proper method for creating such regulations was through bilateral treaties rather than unilateral congressional action." Speed, "Examining," 485.

16. "In 1871, Congress enacted a statute ending the treaty-making process with Indian tribes. . . . Little remarked anywhere is the fact that the statute is probably unconstitutional. This is so because the primary effect of the statute is to strip the president of his Art. II, § 2 power to enter into treaties with Indian tribes. Under the Constitution, treaty making is an executive power, not a congressional power. Congress has no authority to limit the constitutional authority of any coordinate branch of the federal government, including that of the chief executive. This is the quintessence of checks and balances and the separation of powers doctrine. Yet perhaps, as elsewhere, basic constitutional principles do not appear to have much traction in Indian law." Pommer-

sheim, *Broken Landscape*, 64–65. Also, we got into a bit more detail about the end of treaty making in note 20 in Chapter 1 if it is helpful.

17. All right, fine. Maybe this isn't "as simply as possible," but it's pretty good and I am on a roll here, so let's not get too bent out of shape about it.

18. "It is obvious that there may be matters of the sharpest exigency for the national well being that an act of Congress could not deal with but that a treaty followed by such an act could." *Missouri v. Holland* at 433.

19. Well, OK, maybe just a little bit.

20. A prominent casebook has identified all of the basic elements of this argument. "Modern day constitutional theory normally requires some grounding in the constitutional text for any assertion of congressional power. So long as federal power was based upon tribal consent through treaty-making, a constitutional source for the exercise of that power was readily available. Basic American constitutional law recognizes that a treaty 'may endow Congress with a source of legislative authority independent of the power enumerated in Article I (although, of course, still limited by the Constitution's explicit constraint on federal action).'" Carole E. Goldberg et al., *American Indian Law: Native Nations and the Federal System, Cases and Materials*, 7th ed. (New Providence, NJ: LexisNexis, 2015), 494.

21. "To the 'Courts of the conqueror,' Indian tribes are all the same. . . . In a case of strange bedfellows, some Indian law scholars also treat Indian tribes as if they were fungible." Prakash, "Against Tribal Fungibility," 1071.

22. *Cherokee Nation* at 25 (Johnson, J., concurring).

23. *Bryant* at 159 (Thomas, J., concurring).

24. The full quotation is, "It is one of the happy incidents of the federal system that a single courageous State may, if its citizens choose, serve as a laboratory; and try novel social and economic experiments without risk to the rest of the country." *New State Ice Co. v. Liebmann*, 285 U.S. 262, 311 (1932) (Brandeis, J., dissenting).

25. United Nations Declaration on the Rights of Indigenous Peoples, U.N. Doc. A/61/L.67, adopted September 13, 2007 (hereinafter UNDRIP).

26. "Announcement of U.S. Support for the United Nations Declaration on the Rights of Indigenous Peoples," https://2009-2017.state.gov/documents/organization/184099.pdf (accessed August 14, 2023).

27. As one federal court described it, "Courts have consistently held that UNDRIP is a non-binding declaration that does not create a federal cause of action." *Standing Rock Sioux Tribe v. U.S. Army Corps of Engineers*, 301 F.Supp. 3d 50, 60 (2018).

28. For a useful history of the development of UNDRIP and its purposes, see Claire Charters and Rodolfo Stavenhagen, eds., *Making the Declaration Work: The United Nations Declaration on the Rights of Indigenous Peoples* (Copenhagen: International Work Group for Indigenous Affairs, 2009).

29. 25 U.S.C. §1911(b).

30. 25 U.S.C. §1919(a).

31. "Such agreements may be revoked by either party upon one hundred and eighty days' written notice to the other party. Such revocation shall not affect any action or proceeding over which a court has already assumed jurisdiction, unless the agreement provides otherwise." 25 U.S.C. §1919(b).

32. It is worthy of note that one of the most important and prominent pieces of legislation concerning Native America in the twentieth century, the Indian Reorganization Act of 1934 (IRA), was foundationally premised on the concept of consent. Well before the Self-Determination Era, the IRA sought to undo many of the ills done by the Allotment Era and specifically enumerated that it would not apply to tribal nations that voted against it. 48 Stat. 984, Sec. 18 (1934). The legacy of the IRA is mixed, and the tenor of the times in which the statute was passed eventually eroded as the United States transitioned into the Termination Era of federal policy in the mid-twentieth century. Nonetheless, the IRA established a nascent version of the legislation-based exercise of consent that the federal government has more fully embraced in the Self-Determination Era. I have chosen not to highlight the IRA in the main body of the text because I have written about the era before, I am fascinated by the IRA and the time period, and I am afraid that if I put any discussion of it in the main body, I will go on for far too long and disrupt the flow. For a really terrific history of the lead-up to, drafting, and early implementation of the IRA, see Elmer R. Rusco, *A Fateful Time: The Background and Legislative History of the Indian Reorganization Act* (Reno: University of Nevada Press, 2000). And for a look at one tribal nation's decision to adopt a constitution and consideration of the IRA, allow me to humbly (?) point you to a different book that I am awfully fond of. Keith Richotte, Jr., *Claiming Turtle Mountain's Constitution: The History, Legacy, and Future of a Tribal Nation's Founding Documents* (Chapel Hill: University of North Carolina Press, 2017).

33. 33 U.S.C. §1377(e).

34. Deloria and Wilkins have noted that consent is fundamental to this political moment and the relationship between tribal nations and the federal government more generally. "Because Congress in one form or another attempts to secure Indian consent before proceeding with legislation that has an impact on tribal rights, it informally recognizes that hidden deep within the American past is the requirement that Indians give their consent before a congressional act can be considered valid with respect to them." Deloria and Wilkins, *Tribes, Treaties*, 159.

35. "Litigation frequently has not proven the best means to resolve the core uncertainties and distrust between states and tribes. Rather than spending resources and goodwill in court, they may find cooperative arrangements better suited to addressing the inter-sovereign dispute. Such arrangements may be no

less helpful in streamlining law enforcement or other regulatory functions and thereby promoting efficient use of scarce governmental resources." Conference of Western Attorneys General, *American Indian Law Deskbook*, 1158. For a brief description of cooperative agreements and how they operate, see Cohen, *Handbook (2012 ed.)*, §6.05—Tribal-State Cooperative Agreements.

36. Cohen, *Handbook (2012 ed.)*, §6.05—Tribal-State Cooperative Agreements.

37. "Suppose, however, that Congress sought to guarantee the continuation of tribal sovereignty by stating in legislation that governing arrangements could not subsequently be altered without tribal consent." T. Alexander Aleinikoff, "Securing Tribal Sovereignty: A Theory for Overturning Lone Wolf," *Tulsa Law Review* 38, no. 1 (Fall 2002): 64; "Thus, the hallmarks of the federal policy of fostering tribal self-determination are individual and tribal consent. While neither federal law nor federal programs have consistently facilitated the process of choice, the cures for the involuntary aspects of the federal reservation policy must be found in efforts to facilitate informed consent rather than in proposals to involuntarily disestablish the reservations and their governing tribes." Robert N. Clinton, "Isolated in Their Own Country: A Defense of Federal Protection of Indian Autonomy and Self-Government," *Stanford Law Review* 33, no. 6 (July 1981): 1054; "Unlike the vague and even fictional consent espoused by thinkers such as Justice Kennedy, and denigrated by critics who bemoan its limitations, tribal consent theory should be explored and integrated in federal Indian law." Fletcher, "Tribal Consent," 54.

38. According to Vine Deloria Jr., "In virtually rewriting American history, the federal judiciary has become unreliable, antagonistic, and a barrier to the Indian quest for justice." Deloria, "Application," 289.

39. Of this implicit divestiture doctrine, Joseph William Singer wrote, "It is troubling enough that the Court has interpreted the Constitution as granting Congress plenary power over Indian tribes, effectively depriving them of constitutional protections to which they would be entitled if they were non-Indian institutions. It is far more worrisome that the Supreme Court has itself begun to exercise this plenary power in a manner that limits tribal sovereignty." Joseph William Singer, "Canons of Conquest: The Supreme Court's Attack on Tribal Sovereignty," *New England Law Review* 37, no. 3 (2002–3): 644.

40. Boy, I am really letting the purple prose fly, aren't I. Can you tell that I am getting excited at the prospect of completing a full draft of this book?

41. As Thurman Lee Hester Jr. has put it, "The labyrinth of Indian law is necessary to hide the fact that the United States is violating its most fundamental principles." Hester, *Political Principles*, 110.

42. Although John Borrows wrote these words within the Canadian context, they hold equal resonance in the American context. "We do not have to abandon *law* to overcome past injustices. In placing our country on firmer footing, we only have to relinquish those *interpretations of law* that are discrim-

inatory." John Borrows, *Canada's Indigenous Constitution* (Toronto: University of Toronto Press, 2010), 20 (emphasis in original). This is a very good book, and I highly recommend that you read it.

Acknowledgments

1. This is an inside joke that was created and perpetuated to amuse a young child and a dad who often acts like a young child. In truth, I suspect—although cannot confirm—that Uncle Ian and Aunt Michelle have never eaten donkey meat.

2. No, everyone was great; I'm just kidding. Or am I? YOU WILL NEVER KNOW! BWAHAHAHAHAHAHAHAHAHAHAHAHAHAHAHAHAHAHA HAHA!!!!!!!!!!!!!!

3. If we run into each other at a conference and I have some time and I am in the right mood, maybe I will tell you about it.

Bibliography

Books and Articles

Ablavsky, Gregory. "Beyond the Indian Commerce Clause." *Yale Law Journal* 124, no. 4 (January–February 2015): 1012–90.

Adams, David Wallace. *Education for Extinction: American Indians and the Boarding School Experience, 1875–1928*. 2nd ed. rev. and exp. Lawrence: University Press of Kansas, 2020.

Aleinikoff, T. Alexander. "Securing Tribal Sovereignty: A Theory for Overturning Lone Wolf." *Tulsa Law Review* 38, no. 1 (Fall 2002): 57–72.

Aleinikoff, T. Alexander. *Semblances of Sovereignty: The Constitution, the State, and American Citizenship*. Cambridge, MA: Harvard University Press, 2002.

Andrews, Stephen. "In Defense of the Indian Commerce Clause." *American Indian Law Journal* 9, no. 2 (2020–21): 182–212.

Bader, William D., and Frank J. Williams. *Unknown Justices of the United States Supreme Court*. Buffalo, NY: William S. Hein, 2011.

Baker, James W. *Thanksgiving: The Biography of an American Holiday*. Durham: University of New Hampshire Press, 2009.

Ball, Milner S. "Constitution, Court, Indian Tribes." *American Bar Foundation Research Journal* 12, no. 1 (Winter 1987): 1–140.

Barnouw, Victor. *Wisconsin Chippewa Myths & Tales: And Their Relation to Chippewa Life*. Madison: University of Wisconsin Press, 1977.

Barsh, Russel Lawrence, and James Youngblood Henderson. *The Road: Indian Tribes and Political Liberty*. Berkeley: University of California Press, 1980.

Berger, Bethany R. "*United States v. Lara* as a Story of Native Agency." *Tulsa Law Review* 40, no. 1 (Fall 2004): 5–24.

Berkey, Curtis G. "United States—Indian Relations: The Constitutional Basis." In *Exiled in the Land of the Free: Democracy, Indian Nations, and the U.S. Constitution*, edited by John C. Mohawk and Oren R. Lyons, 189–226. Santa Fe, NM: Clear Light Publishers, 1992.

Berman, Howard R. "The Concept of Aboriginal Rights in the Early Legal History of the United States." *Buffalo Law Review* 27, no. 4 (Fall 1978): 637–68.

Blackhawk, Maggie. "Federal Indian Law as Paradigm Within Public Law." *Harvard Law Review* 132, no. 7 (May 2019): 1787–1877.

Bodayla, Stephen D. "'Can An Indian Vote?': *Elk v Wilkins*, a Setback for Indian Citizenship." *Nebraska History* 67 (1986): 372–80.

Bolt, Christine. *American Indian Policy and American Reform*. London: Allen & Unwin, 1987.

Borrows, John. *Canada's Indigenous Constitution*. Toronto: University of Toronto Press, 2010.

Boucher, David. "Invoking a World of Ideas: Theory and Interpretation in the Justification of Colonialism." *Theoria: A Journal of Social and Political Theory* 63, no. 2 (2016): 6–24.

Bruyneel, Kevin. "Challenging American Boundaries: Indigenous People and the 'Gift' of U.S. Citizenship." *Studies in American Political Development* 18, no. 1 (April 2004): 30–43.

Burnett, Donald L., Jr. "An Historical Analysis of the 1968 Indian Civil Rights' Act." *Harvard Journal on Legislation* 9, no. 4 (1971–72): 557–626.

Canby, William C., Jr. *American Indian Law in a Nutshell*. 7th ed. St. Paul, MN: West Academic Publishing, 2020.

Carpenter, Kristen A., Matthew L. M. Fletcher, and Angela R. Riley, eds. *The Indian Civil Rights Act at Forty*. Los Angeles: UCLA American Indian Studies Center, 2012.

Charters, Claire, and Rodolfo Stavenhagen, eds. *Making the Declaration Work: The United Nations Declaration on the Rights of Indigenous Peoples*. Copenhagen: International Work Group for Indigenous Affairs, 2009.

Child, Brenda J. *Boarding School Seasons: American Indian Families, 1900–1940*. Lincoln: University of Nebraska Press, 1998.

Clark, Blue. Lone Wolf v. Hitchcock: *Treaty Rights and Indian Law at the end of the Nineteenth Century*. Lincoln: University of Nebraska Press, 1994.

Cleveland, Sarah H. "Powers Inherent in Sovereignty: Indians, Aliens, Territories, and the Nineteenth Century Origins of Plenary Power over Foreign Affairs." *Texas Law Review* 81, no. 1 (November 2002): 1–284.

Clinton, Robert N. "The Dormant Indian Commerce Clause." *Connecticut Law Review* 27, no. 4 (Summer 1995): 1055–1250.

Clinton, Robert N. "Isolated in Their Own Country: A Defense of Federal

Protection of Indian Autonomy and Self-Government." *Stanford Law Review* 33, no. 6 (July 1981): 979–1068.

Clinton, Robert N. "Redressing the Legacy of Conquest: A Vision Quest for a Decolonized Federal Indian Law." *Arkansas Law Review* 46, no. 1 (1993): 77–160.

Clinton, Robert N. "There Is No Federal Supremacy Clause for Indian Tribes." *Arizona State Law Journal* 34, no. 1 (Spring 2002): 113–260.

Cohen, Felix S. *Handbook of Federal Indian Law*. Washington, DC: USGPO, 1942.

Cohen, Felix S. *Handbook of Federal Indian Law (1982 ed.)*. Charlottesville, VA: Michie Bobbs-Merrill, 1982.

Cohen, Felix S. *Handbook of Federal Indian Law (2012 ed.)*. San Francisco: Lexis-Nexis, 2012.

Collins, Richard B. "Indian Consent to American Government." *Arizona Law Review* 31, no. 2 (1989): 365–88.

Conference of Western Attorneys General. *American Indian Law Deskbook, 2022 edition*. St. Paul, MN: Thomson Reuters, 2022.

Cortner, Richard A. *Civil Rights and Public Accommodations: The* Heart of Atlanta Motel *and* McClung *Cases*. Lawrence: University Press of Kansas, 2001.

Coutin, Susan Bibler, Justin Richland, and Véronique Fortin. "Routine Exceptionality: The Plenary Power Doctrine, Immigrants, and the Indigenous Under U.S. Law." *University of California Irvine Law Review* 4, no. 1 (2014): 97–120.

Crowell, David M. "*Gonzales v. Raich* and the Development of Commerce Clause Jurisprudence: Is the Necessary and Proper Clause the Perfect Drug?" *Rutgers Law Journal* 38, no. 1 (Fall 2006): 251–320.

Cunningham, James K., Teshia A. Solomon, and Myra L. Muramoto. "Alcohol Use Among Native Americans Compared to Whites: Examining the Veracity of the 'Native American Elevated Alcohol Consumption' Belief." *Drug and Alcohol Dependence* 160, no. 1 (March 2016): 65–75.

De La Hunt, Jill. "The Canons of Indian Treaty and Statutory Construction: A Proposal for Codification." *University of Michigan Journal of Law Reform* 17, no. 3 (Spring 1984): 681–712.

Deer, Sarah, Elise Higgins, and Thomas White. "Editorializing ICWA: 40 Years of Colonial Commentary." *Indigenous Peoples' Journal of Law, Culture, and Resistance* 7 (2022): 27–58.

Deloria, Vine, Jr. "The Application of the Constitution to American Indians." In *Exiled in the Land of the Free: Democracy, Indian Nations, and the U.S. Constitution*, edited by John C. Mohawk and Oren R. Lyons, 281–316. Santa Fe, NM: Clear Light Publishers, 1992.

Deloria, Vine, Jr. *Custer Died for Your Sins: An Indian Manifesto*. New York: Macmillan, 1969.

Deloria, Vine, Jr., and Raymond J. DeMallie. *Documents of American Indian Diplomacy, Vols. 1 and 2*. Norman: University of Oklahoma Press, 1999.

Deloria, Vine, Jr., and Clifford M. Lytle. *American Indians, American Justice.* Austin: University of Texas Press, 1983.

Deloria, Vine, Jr., and David E. Wilkins. *The Legal Universe: Observations on the Foundations of American Law.* Golden, CO: Fulcrum Publishing, 2011.

Deloria, Vine, Jr., and David E. Wilkins. *Tribes, Treaties, and Constitutional Tribulations.* Austin: University of Texas Press, 1999.

Densmore, Frances. *Chippewa Customs.* Washington, DC: Smithsonian Institution, 1929; St. Paul: Minnesota Historical Society Press, 1979. Citations are to the Minnesota Historical Society Press edition.

Doran, Michael. "The Equal-Protection Challenge to Federal Indian Law." *University of Pennsylvania Journal of Law and Public Affairs* 6, no. 1 (2020–21): 1–74.

Duthu, N. Bruce. *American Indians and the Law.* New York: Viking, 2008.

Duthu, N. Bruce. *Shadow Nations: Tribal Sovereignty and the Limits of Legal Pluralism.* New York: Oxford University Press, 2013.

Eaglewoman, Angelique Wambdi, and Stacy L. Leeds. *Mastering American Indian Law.* 2nd ed. Durham, NC: Carolina Academic Press, 2019.

Echo-Hawk, Walter R. *In the Light of Justice: The Rise of Human Rights in Native America and the U.S. Declaration of the Rights of Indigenous Peoples.* Golden, CO: Fulcrum Publishing, 2013.

Ennis, Samuel E. "Implicit Divestiture and the Supreme Court's (Re)Construction of the Indian Canons." *Vermont Law Review* 35, no. 3 (Spring 2011): 623–88.

Epps, Garrett. *American Epic: Reading the U.S. Constitution.* Oxford: Oxford University Press, 2013.

Erdoes, Richard, and Alfonso Ortiz. *American Indian Trickster Tales.* New York: Penguin Books, 1999.

Fisher, Louis. "The Staying Power of Erroneous Dicta: From *Curtiss-Wright* to *Zivotofsky.*" *Constitutional Commentary* 31, no. 2 (Summer 2016): 149–220.

Fixico, Donald L. *Termination and Relocation: Federal Indian Policy, 1945–1960.* Albuquerque: University of New Mexico Press, 1986.

Fletcher, Matthew L. M. *The Ghost Road: Anishinaabe Responses to Indian-Hating.* Wheat Ridge, CO: Fulcrum Publishing, 2020.

Fletcher, Matthew L. M. "Preconstitutional Federal Power." *Tulane Law Review* 82, no. 2 (December 2007): 509–66.

Fletcher, Matthew L. M. *Principles of Federal Indian Law.* St. Paul, MN: West Academic Publishing, 2017.

Fletcher, Matthew L. M. "Tribal Consent." *Stanford Journal of Civil Rights & Civil Liberties* 8, no. 1 (April 2012): 45–122.

Frickey, Philip P. "Adjudication and Its Discontents: Coherence and Conciliation in Federal Indian Law." *Harvard Law Review* 110, no. 8 (June 1997): 1754–84.

Frickey, Philip P. "Domesticating Federal Indian Law." *Minnesota Law Review* 81, no. 1 (November 1996): 31–96.

Getches, David H., Charles F. Wilkinson, Robert A. Williams, Matthew L. M. Fletcher, and Kristen A. Carpenter. *Cases and Materials on Federal Indian Law.* 7th ed. St. Paul, MN: West Academic Publishing, 2017.

Goldberg, Carole E., Rebecca Tsosie, Robert N. Clinton, and Angela R. Riley. *American Indian Law: Native Nations and the Federal System, Cases and Materials.* 7th ed. New Providence, NJ: LexisNexis, 2015.

Gonzalez, Vivian M., and Monica C. Skewes. "Belief in the Myth of an American Indian/Alaska Native Biological Vulnerability to Alcohol Problems Among Reservation-Dwelling Participants with a Substance Use Problem." *Alcoholism: Clinical and Experimental Research* 45, no. 11 (November 2021): 2309–21.

Gyory, Andrew. *Closing the Gate: Race, Politics, and the Chinese Exclusion Act.* Chapel Hill: University of North Carolina Press, 1998.

Harring, Sydney L. *Crow Dog's Case: American Indian Sovereignty, Tribal Law, and United States Law in the Nineteenth Century.* New York: Cambridge University Press, 1994.

Harring, Sidney L. "The Distorted History That Gave Rise to the 'So Called' Plenary Power Doctrine: The Story of *United States v. Kagama.*" In *Indian Law Stories*, edited by Carole Goldberg, Kevin K. Washburn, and Philip P. Frickey, 149–88. New York: Thompson Reuters/Foundation Press, 2011.

Harvey, Irene K. "Constitutional Law: Congressional Plenary Power over Indian Affairs: A Doctrine Rooted in Prejudice." *American Indian Law Review* 10, no. 1 (1982): 117–50.

Hathaway, Oona A., Spencer Amdur, Celia Choy, and Samir Deger-Sen. "The Treaty Power: Its History, Scope and Limits." *Cornell Law Review* 98, no. 2 (January 2013): 239–326.

Helbig, Alethea K. *Nanabozhoo: Giver of Life.* Brighton, MI: Green Oak Press, 1987.

Hester, Thurman Lee, Jr. *Political Principles & Indian Sovereignty.* New York: Routledge, 2001.

Hobson, C. F. "The Yazoo Lands Sale Case: *Fletcher v. Peck* (1810)." *Journal of Supreme Court History* 42 (November 2017): 239–55.

Hoxie, Fredrick E. *A Final Promise: The Campaign to Assimilate the Indians, 1880–1920.* Lincoln: University of Nebraska Press, 1984.

Hoxie, Frederick E. "From Prison to Homeland: The Cheyenne River Indian Reservation Before World War I." In *The Plains Indians of the 20th Century*, edited by Peter Iverson, 55–76. Norman: University of Oklahoma Press, 1985.

Hyde, Lewis. *Trickster Makes This World: Mischief, Myth, and Art.* New York: Farrar, Straus & Giroux, 2010.

Hynes, William J., and William G. Doty. "Introducing the Fascinating and Perplexing Trickster Figure." In *Mythical Trickster Figures: Contours, Contexts, and Criticisms,* edited by William J. Hynes and William G. Doty, 1–12. Tuscaloosa: University of Alabama Press, 1993.

Institute for the Development of Indian Law. *Old Problems, Persistent Issues: Nine Essays on American Indian Law.* Washington, DC: Institute for the Development of Indian Law, 1979.

Jacobs, Margaret D. *A Generation Removed: The Fostering and Adoption of Indigenous Children in the Postwar World.* Lincoln: University of Nebraska Press, 2014.

Jacobs, Margaret D. *White Mother to a Dark Race: Settler Colonialism, Maternalism, and the Removal of Indigenous Children in the American West and Australia, 1880–1940.* Lincoln: University of Nebraska Press, 2009.

Johnston, Basil. *The Manitous: The Spiritual World of the Ojibway.* St. Paul: Minnesota Historical Society Press, 2001.

Kidder, Homer H., recorder, and Arthur P. Bourgeois, ed. *Ojibwa Narratives of Charles and Charlotte Kawbawgam and Jacques LePique, 1893–1895.* Detroit, MI: Wayne State University Press, 1994.

Killenbeck, Mark R. "A Prudent Regard to Our Own Good? The Commerce Clause, in Nation and States." *Journal of Supreme Court History* 38, no. 3 (November 2013): 281–308.

Krakoff, Sarah. "Mark the Plumber v. Tribal Empire, or Non-Indian Anxiety v. Tribal Sovereignty? The Story of *Oliphant v. Suquamish Indian Tribe.*" In *Indian Law Stories,* edited by Carole Goldberg, Kevin K. Washburn, and Philip P. Frickey, 261–96. New York: Thompson Reuters/Foundation Press, 2011.

Krakoff, Sarah. "They Were Here First: American Indian Tribes, Race, and the Constitutional Minimum." *Stanford Law Review* 69, no. 2 (February 2017): 491–548.

Ledford, Taylor. "Foundations of Sand: Justice Thomas's Critique of the Indian Plenary Power Doctrine." *American Indian Law Review* 43, no. 1 (2018): 167–202.

Leeds, Stacy, Robert Miller, Kevin Washburn, and Derrick Beetso. "*Oklahoma v. Castro-Huerta*—Rebalancing Federal-State-Tribal Power." *Journal of Appellate Practice and Process* 23, no. 1 (Winter 2023): 47–104.

Lightfoot, Sheryl R. "Decolonizing Self-Determination: Haudenosaunee Passports and Negotiated Sovereignty." *European Journal of International Relations* 27, no. 4 (December 2021): 971–94.

Martin, Jill E. "'The Greatest Evil': Interpretations of Indian Prohibition Laws, 1832–1953." *Great Plains Quarterly* 23, no. 1 (Winter 2003): 35–53.

McKinley, Herald. *Myths of the Native Americans.* New York: Cavendish Square, 2016.

Miller, Robert J. "The Doctrine of Discovery: The International Law of Colonialism." *Indigenous Peoples' Journal of Law, Culture, and Resistance* 5, no. 1 (2019): 35–42.

Musicant, Ivan. *Empire by Default: The Spanish-American War and the Dawn of the American Century*. New York: H. Holt, 1998.

Nelson, Grant S., and Robert J. Pushaw Jr. "Rethinking the Commerce Clause: Applying First Principles to Uphold Federal Commercial Regulations but Preserve State Control over Social Issues." *Iowa Law Review* 85, no. 1 (October 1999): 1–174.

Newton, Nell Jessup. "Federal Power over Indians: Its Sources, Scope, and Limitations." *University of Pennsylvania Law Review* 132, no. 2 (January 1984): 195–288.

Norgren, Jill. *The Cherokee Cases: Two Landmark Federal Decisions in the Fight for Sovereignty*. Norman: University of Oklahoma Press, 2003.

Nunez, D. Carolina. "Dark Matter in the Law." *Boston College Law Review* 62, no. 5 (May 2021): 1555–1620.

Pevar, Stephen L. *The Rights of Indians and Tribes*. 4th ed. New York: Oxford University Press, 2012.

Pommersheim, Frank. *Broken Landscape: Indians, Indian Tribes, and the Constitution*. New York: Oxford University Press, 2009.

Pommersheim, Frank. "Is There a (Little or Not So Little) Constitutional Crisis Developing in Indian Law? A Brief Essay." *University of Pennsylvania Journal of Constitutional Law* 5, no. 2 (January 2003): 271–87.

Ponsa-Kraus, Christina Duffy. "The Insular Cases Run Amok: Against Constitutional Exceptionalism in the Territories." *Yale Law Journal* 131, no. 8 (June 2022): 2449–2541.

Porter, Robert Odawi. "The Inapplicability of American Law to the Indian Nations." *Iowa Law Review* 89, no. 5 (May 2004): 1595–1632.

Prakash, Saikrishna. "Against Tribal Fungibility." *Cornell Law Review* 89, no. 5 (July 2004): 1069–1120.

Pratt, Richard H. "The Advantages of Mingling Indians with Whites." In *Americanizing the American Indian: Writings by the Friends of the Indians, 1880–1900*, edited by Francis Paul Prucha, 260–71. Cambridge, MA: Harvard University Press, 1973.

Prucha, Francis Paul. *American Indian Policy in the Formative Years: The Indian Trade and Intercourse Acts, 1790–1834*. Cambridge, MA: Harvard University Press, 1962.

Pushaw, Robert J., Jr., and Grant S. Nelson. "The Likely Impact of National Federation on Commerce Clause Jurisprudence." *Pepperdine Law Review* 40, no. 4 (2013): 975–1000.

Reese, Michael. "The Indian Civil Rights Act: Conflict Between Constitutional

Assimilation and Tribal Self-Determination." *Southeastern Political Review* 20, no. 1 (June 1992): 29–61.

Richotte, Keith, Jr. *Claiming Turtle Mountain's Constitution: The History, Legacy, and Future of a Tribal Nation's Founding Documents*. Chapel Hill: University of North Carolina Press, 2017.

Richotte, Keith, Jr. *Federal Indian Law and Policy: An Introduction*. St. Paul, MN: West Academic Publishing, 2020.

Richotte, Keith, Jr. "A Legal Pluralist Approach to Tribal Constitutions." *William Mitchell Law Review* 36, no. 2 (2010): 447–502.

Riley, Angela R. "The Apex of Congress' Plenary Power over Indian Affairs: The Story of *Lone Wolf v. Hitchcock*." In *Indian Law Stories*, edited by Carole Goldberg, Kevin K. Washburn, and Philip P. Frickey, 189–228. New York: Thompson Reuters/Foundation Press, 2011.

Robertson, Lindsay G. *Conquest by Law: How the Discovery of America Dispossessed Indigenous Peoples of Their Lands*. New York: Oxford University Press, 2005.

Robertson, Lindsay G. "The Judicial Conquest of Native America: The Story of *Johnson v. M'Intosh*." In *Indian Law Stories*, edited by Carole Goldberg, Kevin K. Washburn, and Philip P. Frickey, 29–59. New York: Thompson Reuters/Foundation Press, 2011.

Roediger, David R. *How Race Survived U.S. History: From Settlement and Slavery to the Obama Phenomenon*. London: Verso, 2008.

Rosen, Deborah A. *American Indians and State Law: Sovereignty, Race, and Citizenship, 1790–1880*. Lincoln: University of Nebraska Press, 2007.

Rusco, Elmer R. *A Fateful Time: The Background and Legislative History of the Indian Reorganization Act*. Reno: University of Nevada Press, 2000.

Saito, Natsu Taylor. *From Chinese Exclusion to Guantánamo Bay: Plenary Power and the Prerogative State*. Boulder: University of Colorado Press, 2007.

Saito, Natsu Taylor. *Settler Colonialism, Race, and the Law: Why Structural Racism Persists*. New York: NYU Press, 2020.

Sejersen, Tanja Brøndsted. "'I Vow to Thee My Countries'—The Expansion of Dual Citizenship in the 21st Century." *International Migration Review* 42, no. 3 (September 2008): 623–49.

Shattuck, Petra A., and Jill Norgren. *Partial Justice: Federal Indian Law in a Liberal Constitutional System*. New York: Berg, distributed exclusively in the United States and Canada by St. Martin's Press, 1991.

Singer, Joseph William. "Canons of Conquest: The Supreme Court's Attack on Tribal Sovereignty." *New England Law Review* 37, no. 3 (2002–3): 641–68.

Silverman, David J. *This Land Is Their Land: The Wampanoag Indians, Plymouth Colony, and the Troubled History of Thanksgiving*. New York: Bloomsbury Publishing, 2019.

Skibine, Alex Tallchief. "Constitutionalism, Federal Common Law, and the Inherent Powers of Indian Tribes." *American Indian Law Review* 39, no. 1 (2014–15): 77–136.

Speed, Nathan. "Examining the Interstate Commerce Clause Through the Lens of the Indian Commerce Clause." *Boston University Law Review* 87, no. 2 (April 2007): 467–90.

Tebben, Carol L. "In Defense of ICWA: The Constitution, Public Policy, and Pragmatism." In *Facing the Future: The Indian Child Welfare Act at 30*, edited by Matthew L. M. Fletcher, Wenona T. Singel, and Kathryn E. Fort, 270–92. East Lansing: Michigan State University Press, 2009.

Thompson, Michael, and Jacob Warrenfeltz. "Rabbit and the Tug-of-War." In *Trickster: Native American Tales, a Graphic Collection*, edited by Matt Dembicki, 63–70. Golden, CO: Fulcrum Publishing, 2010.

Tingle, Tim, and Pat Lewis. "Rabbit's Choctaw Tail Tale." In *Trickster: Native American Tales, a Graphic Collection*, edited by Matt Dembicki, 79–88. Golden, CO: Fulcrum Publishing, 2010.

Toler, Lorianne Updike. "The Missing Indian Affairs Clause." *University of Chicago Law Review* 88, no. 2 (March 2021): 413–86.

Torres, Gerald. "Who Is an Indian? The Story of *United States v. Sandoval*." In *Indian Law Stories*, edited by Carole Goldberg, Kevin K. Washburn, and Philip P. Frickey, 109–45. New York: Thompson Reuters/Foundation Press, 2011.

Tullberg, Steven, and Robert T. Coulter. "The Failure of Indian Rights Advocacy: Are Lawyers to Blame?" In *Rethinking Indian Law*, compiled and edited by National Lawyers Guild, Committee on Native American Struggles, 51–56. New York: National Lawyers Guild, Committee on Native American Struggles, 1982.

Tushnet, Mark. "Willis Van Devanter: The Person." *Journal of Supreme Court History* 45, no. 3 (November 2020): 308–27.

Tweedy, Ann E. "Connecting the Dots Between the Constitution, the Marshall Trilogy, and *United States v. Lara*: Notes Toward a Blueprint for the Next Legislative Restoration of Tribal Sovereignty." *University of Michigan Journal of Law Reform* 42, no. 3 (Spring 2009): 651–718.

Vinzant, John H. *The Supreme Court's Role in American Indian Policy*. El Paso, TX: LFB Scholarly Publishing, 2009.

Watson, Blake A. *Buying America from the Indians:* Johnson v. McIntosh *and the History of Native Land Rights*. Norman: University of Oklahoma Press, 2012.

Wilkins, David E. *American Indian Sovereignty and the U.S. Supreme Court: The Masking of Justice*. Austin: University of Texas Press, 1997.

Wilkins, David E. *Hollow Justice: A History of Indigenous Claims in the United States*. New Haven, CT: Yale University Press, 2013.

Wilkins, David E. "The U.S. Supreme Court's Explication of 'Federal Plenary

Power': An Analysis of Case Law Affecting Tribal Sovereignty, 1886–1914." *American Indian Quarterly* 18, no. 3 (Summer 1994): 349–68.

Wilkins, David E., and K. Tsianina Lomawaima. *Uneven Ground: American Indian Sovereignty and Federal Law*. Norman: University of Oklahoma Press, 2001.

Wilkinson, Charles F., and Eric R. Biggs. "The Evolution of Termination Policy." *American Indian Law Review* 5, no. 1 (1977): 139–84.

Williams, Robert A., Jr. *The American Indian in Western Legal Thought: The Discourses of Conquest*. New York: Oxford University Press, 1990.

Williams, Robert A., Jr. *Like a Loaded Weapon: The Rehnquist Court, Indian Rights, and the Legal History of Racism in America*. Minneapolis: University of Minnesota Press, 2005.

Williams, Robert A., Jr. *Linking Arms Together: American Indian Treaty Visions of Law and Peace, 1600–1800*. New York: Oxford University Press, 1997.

Zug, Marcia. "ICWA's Irony." *American Indian Law Review* 45, no. 1 (2020–21): 1–88.

Cases

Adoptive Couple v. Baby Girl, 570 U.S. 637 (2013).

Balzac v. Porto Rico, 258 U.S. 298, 304–5 (1922).

Beecher v. Wetherby, 95 U.S. 517 (1877).

Board of Com'rs of Creek County v. Seber, 318 U.S. 705 (1943).

Board of Com'rs of Jackson County v. U.S., 308 U.S. 343 (1939).

Brown v. Board of Education, 347 U.S. 483 (1954).

Chae Chan Ping v. United States, 130 U.S. 581 (1889).

Cherokee Nation v. Georgia, 30 U.S. 1 (1831).

Cherokee Nation v. Hitchcock, 187 U.S. 294 (1902).

Cherokee Nation v. Southern Kan. Ry. Co., 135 U.S. 641 (1890).

The Cherokee Tobacco, 78 U.S. 616, 619 (1870).

Choate v. Trapp, 224 U.S. 665, 671 (1912).

Choctaw Nation v. United States, 119 U.S. 1 (1886).

Chouteau v. Molony, 57 U.S. 203, 237–38 (1854).

Conley v. Ballinger, 216 U.S. 84 (1910).

Cramer v. United States, 261 U.S. 219 (1923).

Creek Nation v. United States, 318 U.S. 629 (1943).

Delaware Tribal Business Committee v. Weeks, 430 U.S. 73 (1977).

Dobbs v. Jackson Women's Health Organization, 142 S. Ct. 2228 (2022).

Downes v. Bidwell, 182 U.S. 244, 279 (1901).

Duro v. Reina, 495 U.S. 676 (1990).

Elk v. Wilkins, 112 U.S. 94 (1884).

Ex Parte Crow Dog, 109 U.S. 556 (1883).

Federal Power Commission v. Tuscarora Indian Nation, 262 U.S. 99 (1960).

Fin. Oversight & Mgmt. Bd. for P.R. v. Aurelius Inv., LLC, 140 S. Ct. 1649 (2020).

Fletcher v. Peck, 10 U.S. 87 (1810).
Fong Yue Ting v. United States, 149 U.S. 698, 712 (1893).
Gibbons v. Ogden, 22 U.S. (9 Wheat.) 1 (1824).
Gritts v. Fisher, 224 U.S. 640 (1912).
Haaland v. Brackeen, 599 U.S. ___, 11, 143 S. Ct. 1609 (2023).
Heart of Atlanta Motel v. United States, 379 U.S. 241 (1964).
Heckman v. United States, 224 U.S. 413 (1912).
In re Heff, 197 U.S. 488 (1905).
Johnson v. McIntosh, 21 U.S. 543 (1823).
Jones v. Meehan, 175 U.S. 1 (1899).
Kan. Indians, 72 U.S. 737 (1867).
Katzenbach v. McClung, 379 U.S. 294 (1964).
Lessee of Lattimer v. Poteet, 39 U.S. 4 (1840).
Levindale Lead & Zinc Min. Co. v. Coleman, 241 U.S. 432 (1916).
Lone Wolf v. Hitchcock, 187 U.S. 553 (1903).
McClanahan v. State Tax Commission of Arizona, 441 U.S. 164 (1973).
Merrion v. Jicarilla Apache Tribe, 455 U.S. 130 (1982).
Mescalero Apache Tribe v. Jones, 411 U.S. 145 (1973).
Michigan v. Bay Mills Indian Cmty., 572 U.S. 782 (2014).
Missouri v. Holland, 252 U.S. 416 (1920).
Mitchel v. United States, 34 U.S. 711 (1835).
Montana v. Blackfeet Tribe of Indians, 471 U.S. 759 (1985).
Montana v. United States, 450 U.S. 544 (1981).
Morton v. Mancari, 417 U.S. 535 (1974).
Mountain States Tel. & Tel. Co. v. Pueblo of Santa Ana, 472 U.S. 237 (1985).
Nevada v. Hicks, 533 U.S. 353 (2001).
New State Ice Co. v. Liebmann, 285 U.S. 262 (1932).
Nix v. Hedden, 149 U.S. 304 (1893).
Northwestern Bands of Shoshone Indians v. United States, 324 U.S. 335 (1945).
Oklahoma v. Castro-Huerta, 597 U.S. ___, 142 S. Ct. 2486 (2022).
Oliphant v. Suquamish Indian Tribe, 435 U.S. 191 (1978).
Oneida County, N.Y. v. Oneida Indian Nation of New York State, 470 U.S. 226 (1985).
Parks v. Ross, 52 U.S. 362 (1851).
Perrin v. United States, 232 U.S. 478 (1914).
Plessy v. Ferguson, 163 U.S. 537, 544 (1896).
Ramah Navajo School Bd., Inc. v. Bureau of Revenue of New Mexico, 458 U.S. 832 (1982).
Roe v. Wade, 410 U.S. 113 (1973).
Scott v. Sandford, 60 U.S. 393 (1857).
Seminole Nation v. United States, 316 U.S. 286 (1942).
Seminole Tribe of Florida v. Florida, 517 U.S. 44 (1996).
Shoshone Tribe of Indians v. United States, 299 U.S. 476, 496 (1937).

Sizemore v. Brady, 235 U.S. 441 (1914).
Standing Rock Sioux Tribe v. U.S. Army Corps of Engineers, 301 F.Supp. 3d 50 (2018).
State of Netherlands v. Federal Reserve Bank, 201 F.2d 455, 461 (1953).
Stephens v. Cherokee Nation, 174 U.S. 445 (1899).
Sunderland v. United States, 266 U.S. 226 (1924).
Talton v. Mayes, 163 U.S. 376 (1896).
Tee-Hit-Ton Indians v. United States, 348 U.S. 272 (1955).
Thomas v. Gay, 169 U.S. 264 (1898).
Tiger v. Western Inv. Co., 221 U.S. 286 (1911).
United States Use of Mackey v. Coxe, 59 U.S. 100, 103 (1856).
United States v. Antelope, 430 U.S. 641 (1977).
United States v. Bryant, 579 U.S. 140 (2016).
United States v. Candelaria, 271 U.S. 432 (1926).
United States v. Celestine, 215 U.S. 278 (1909).
United States v. Chavez, 290 U.S. 357 (1933).
United States v. Clapox, 35 F. 575 (1888).
United States v. Curtiss-Wright Export Corp., 299 U.S. 304 (1936).
United States v. Fernandez, 35 U.S. 303 (1836).
United States v. Forty-Three Gallons of Whiskey, 93 U.S. 188 (1876).
United States v. Jackson, 280 U.S. 183 (1930).
United States v. John, 437 U.S. 634 (1978).
United States v. Kagama, 118 U.S. 375 (1886).
United States v. Lara, 541 U.S. 193 (2004).
United States v. Lopez, 514 U.S. 549 (1995).
United States v. McGowan, 302 U.S. 535 (1938).
United States v. Minnesota, 270 U.S. 181 (1926).
United States v. Mitchell, 445 U.S. 535 (1980).
United States v. Mitchell, 463 U.S. 206 (1983).
United States v. Morrison, 529 U.S. 598 (2000).
United States v. Nice, 241 U.S. 591 (1916).
United States v. Noble, 237 U.S. 74 (1915).
United States v. Pelican, 232 U.S. 442 (1914).
United States v. Ramsey, 271 U.S. 467 (1926).
United States v. Rickert, 188 U.S. 432 (1903).
United States v. Rogers, 45 U.S. 567 (1846).
United States v. Rowell, 243 U.S. 464 (1917).
United States v. Sandoval, 231 U.S. 28 (1913).
United States v. Thomas, 151 U.S. 577 (1894).
United States v. Waller, 243 U.S. 452 (1917).
United States v. Wheeler, 435 U.S. 313 (1978).
Upstate Citizens for Equal., Inc. v. United States, 140 S. Ct. 2587 (2017).

Washington v. Confederated Bands and Tribes of Yakima Indian Nation, 439 U.S. 463 (1979).
White Mountain Apache Tribe v. Bracker, 448 U.S. 136 (1980).
Williams v. Lee, 358 U.S. 217 (1959).
Winton v. Amos, 255 U.S. 373 (1921).
Worcester v. Georgia, 31 U.S. 515 (1832).

Laws

1790 Trade and Intercourse Act, *U.S. Statutes at Large*, 1:137–38.
18 U.S.C. § 1161.
1802 Trade and Intercourse Act, *U.S. Statutes at Large*, 2:139–46.
1834 Trade and Intercourse Act, *U.S. Statutes at Large*, 4:729–35.
Allotment Act, *U.S. Statutes at Large*, 24:388–91.
American Indian Religious Freedom Act, 92 Stat. 469.
Appropriations Act of March 3, 1871, 16 Stat. 544, 566 (codified as amended at 25 U.S.C. § 71).
Civil Rights Act of 1964, 78 Stat. 241.
Clean Water Act, 33 U.S.C. Ch. 26, §§ 1251–1389.
"*Duro* Fix," 25 U.S.C.A. § 1301(2).
End of Treaty Making, *U.S. Statutes at Large*, 16:566.
Indian Arts and Crafts Act of 1990, 104 Stat. 4662.
Indian Child Welfare Act, 92 Stat. 3069, 25 U.S.C. § 1901 et seq.
Indian Citizenship Act, *U.S. Statutes at Large*, 43:253.
Indian Civil Rights Act, 25 U.S.C. § 1301 et seq.
Indian Reorganization Act, 48 Stat. 984.
Indian Self-Determination and Education Assistance Act, 25 U.S.C. §§ 5301–5423.
Major Crimes Act, *U.S. Statutes at Large*, 23:385.
Northwest Ordinance, *Journals of the Continental Congress*, 32:340–41.
U.S. Constitution.

Treaties and International Documents

Treaty of Peace Between the United States of America and the Kingdom of Spain, December 10, 1898, 30 Stat. 1754.
Treaty with China, July 28, 1868, 16 Stat. 739.
Treaty with the Miami, November 6, 1838, 7 Stat. 569.
Treaty with the Seminole, March 21, 1866, 14 Stat. 755.
Treaty with the Shawnee, May 10, 1854, 10 Stat. 1053.
Treaty-China, November 17, 1880, 22 Stat. 826.
United Nations Declaration on the Rights of Indigenous Peoples, U.N. Doc. A/61/L.67, adopted September 13, 2007.

Government Publications

American Indian Policy Review Commission. *Final Report, Submitted to Congress, May 17, 1977*. Washington, DC: USGPO, 1977.

Declaration of Independence.

Department of the Interior, Bureau of Indian Affairs. "Indian Child Welfare Act Proceedings; Final Rule." *Federal Register* 81, no. 114 (June 14, 2016): 38778–38876. https://www.govinfo.gov/content/pkg/FR-2016-06-14/pdf/2016-13686.pdf.

U.S. Congress. House. Committee on Indian Affairs. Unpublished Hearings, May 19, 1924.

U.S. Congress. House. Committee on Interior and Insular Affairs, Subcommittee on Indian Affairs. *Rights of Members of Indian Tribes Hearing, Mar. 29, 1968*. 90th Congress, 2d sess. Washington, DC: USGPO, 1968.

U.S. Congress. House. Hearings Before a Subcommittee on Indian Affairs and Public Lands. February 9 and March 9, 1978, 85th Congress, 2nd sess., S. 1214.

U.S. Congress. Senate. Committee on the Judiciary, Hearings Before the Subcommittee on Constitutional Rights. *Constitutional Rights of the American Indian, Aug. 29, 30, 31, and Sep. 1*. 87th Congress, 1st sess. Washington, DC: USGPO, 1962.

U.S. Congress. Senate. Committee on the Judiciary. *Protecting the Rights of the American Indian*. Report No. 841. 90th Congress, 1st sess. Washington, DC: USGPO, 1967.

U.S. Congress. Senate. Committee on the Judiciary, Subcommittee on Constitutional Rights. *Constitutional Rights of the American Indian, Committee Print*. 89th Congress, 2nd sess. Washington, DC: USGPO, 1966.

Supreme Court Briefs

Brief for individual petitioners, *Haaland v. Brackeen*, Nos. 21-376, 21-377, 21-378, 21-380, May 26, 2022, On writs of certiorari to the United States Court of Appeals for the Fifth Circuit, Supreme Court of the United States.

Brief for the States of California, Arizona, Colorado, Connecticut, Idaho, Illinois, Iowa, Maine, Massachusetts, Michigan, Minnesota, Nevada, New Jersey, New Mexico, New York, North Carolina, Oregon, Pennsylvania, Rhode Island, South Dakota, Utah, Washington, and Wisconsin, and the District of Columbia, as *Amici Curiae* in Support of Federal and Tribal Defendants, *Haaland v. Brackeen*, Nos. 21-376, 21-377, 21-378, 21-380, August 19, 2022, On writs of certiorari to the United States Court of Appeals for the Fifth Circuit, Supreme Court of the United States.

Brief for tribal defendants, *Haaland v. Brackeen*, Nos. 21-376, 21-377, 21-378, 21-380, On writs of certiorari to the United States Court of Appeals for the Fifth Circuit, Supreme Court of the United States.

Brief of *Amicus Curiae*, Senator James Abrorezk, in Support of Federal and

Tribal Parties, *Haaland v. Brackeen*, Nos. 21-376, 21-377, 21-378, 21-380, August 18, 2022, On writs of certiorari to the United States Court of Appeals for the Fifth Circuit, Supreme Court of the United States.

Brief of Casey Family Programs and twenty-six other child welfare and adoption organizations as *Amici Curiae* in Support of Federal and Tribal Defendants, *Haaland v. Brackeen*, Nos. 21-376, 21-377, 21-378, 21-380, August 19, 2022, On writs of certiorari to the United States Court of Appeals for the Fifth Circuit, Supreme Court of the United States.

Brief of the American Bar Association as *Amicus Curiae* in Support of Petitioners in 21-376 and 21-377, and in Support of Respondents in 21-378 and 21-380, *Haaland v. Brackeen*, Nos. 21-376, 21-377, 21-378, 21-380, August 18, 2022, On writs of certiorari to the United States Court of Appeals for the Fifth Circuit, Supreme Court of the United States.

Legal Treatises

Gustafson, Jill. 78 Am Jur 2d War § 118.

Online Sources

"Announcement of U.S. Support for the United Nations Declaration on the Rights of Indigenous Peoples." https://2009-2017.state.gov/documents/organization/184099.pdf (accessed August 14, 2023).

Becker, Jo, and Danny Hakim. "Ginni Thomas Urged Arizona Lawmakers to Overturn Election." *New York Times*, May 20, 2022, updated September 29, 2022. https://www.nytimes.com/2022/05/20/us/politics/ginni-thomas-election-trump.html?action=click&module=RelatedLinks&pgtype=Article.

Casey Family Programs. *Child and Family Services Practice Model: A Safe and Permanent Family for Every Youth*. March 2021. https://www.casey.org/media/101-Practice-Model.pdf.

D'Errico, Peter. "Scalia's Death: Will It Affect Indian Country?" ICTNews.org, February 18, 2016, updated September 12, 2018. https://ictnews.org/archive/scalias-death-will-it-affect-indian-country.

Fort, Kathryn. "A Quick Brackeen Opinion Post." Turtle Talk, June 15, 2023. https://turtletalk.blog/2023/06/15/a-quick-brackeen-opinion-post/.

"Frequently Asked Questions." Suquamish Tribe, 2024. https://suquamish.nsn.us/home/about-us/faqs/.

Kaplan, Joshua, Justin Elliott, and Alex Mierjeski. "Billionaire Harlan Crow Bought Property from Clarence Thomas. The Justice Didn't Disclose the Deal." ProPublica, April 13, 2023. https://www.propublica.org/article/clarence-thomas-harlan-crow-real-estate-scotus.

Kaplan, Joshua, Justin Elliott, and Alex Mierjeski. "Clarence Thomas and the Billionaire." ProPublica, April 6, 2023. https://www.propublica.org/article/clarence-thomas-scotus-undisclosed-luxury-travel-gifts-crow.

Kaplan, Joshua, Justin Elliott, and Alex Mierjeski. "Clarence Thomas Had a Child in Private School. Harlan Crow Paid the Tuition." ProPublica, May 4, 2023. https://www.propublica.org/article/clarence-thomas-harlan-crow-private-school-tuition-scotus.

Johnson, Lyndon B. "Special Message to the Congress on the Problems of the American Indian: 'The Forgotten American.'" Online by Gerhard Peters and John T. Woolley, The American Presidency Project, March 6, 1968. https://www.presidency.ucsb.edu/node/237467.

"List of Countries with Highest Military Expenditures." Wikipedia, last edited March 16, 2024. https://en.wikipedia.org/wiki/List_of_countries_by_military_expenditures.

"Military Power of USA and Canada." ArmedForces.eu, 2019. https://armedforces.eu/compare/country_USA_vs_Canada.

Nixon, Richard. "Special Message to the Congress on Indian Affairs." Online by Gerhard Peters and John T. Woolley, The American Presidency Project, July 8, 1970. https://www.presidency.ucsb.edu/node/240040.

"Race and Ethnicity in the United States: 2010 Census and 2020 Census." United States Census, August 12, 2021. https://www.census.gov/library/visualizations/interactive/race-and-ethnicity-in-the-united-state-2010-and-2020-census.html (accessed Aug. 9, 2023).

Index

Ablavsky, Gregory, 227–28n81
Aboriginal title, 55
abortion, 31
Abourezk, James, 143
Adams, David Wallace, 244n34
adoptions, 139
alcohol, 103–5, 106, 113
Aleinikoff, T. Alexander, 201n15, 222n23, 256n37
Allotment Act (1887), 82
Allotment Era, 27–29, 82, 83, 100, 103, 181; destructiveness of, 2–3, 10, 19, 27, 136–37, 143–44; Indian Citizenship Act linked to, 95; liquor laws in, 104; motivations for, 136; plenary power in, 15, 141; Termination Era likened to, 138
American Bar Association, 143
American Indian Law Deskbook, 134
American Indian Religious Freedom Act (1978), 144
American Revolution, 54
Andrews, Stephen, 241–43n29
arguing in the alternative, 179
Articles of Confederation, 104

Baldwin, Henry, 205–6n54
Ball, Milner S., 210–11n103, 241–43n29
Balzac v. Porto Rico (1922), 222n20
Barnouw, Victor, 239n11
Barrett, Amy Coney, 115, 140, 141, 142–43, 181, 234n147
Beecher v. Wetherby (1877), 66
Belgrade, Daniel, 16–17
Berkey, Curtis G., 226n64, 241–43n29
Berman, Howard R., 203nn26, 28, 205n52
Black, Hugo, 60, 82, 106
Blackhawk, Maggie, 201n12
Blackmun, Harry, 112
boarding schools, 2 ,15, 137–38
Board of Com'rs of Creek County v. Seber (1943), 211–14n110

Bolt, Christine, 243n31
Borrows, John, 256–57n42
Bourgeois, Arthur P., 239n11
Brennan, William, 70
Brewer, David J., 208n76
Breyer, Stephen, 22–23, 24, 34, 40, 41, 84, 102, 114
Brown, Biscuit, 18
Brown, Henry B., 85–86, 228–29n87
Brown v. Board of Education (1954), 98
Burger, Warren, 101, 106, 112
Burlingame Treaty (1868), 86–87

Cahuilla Nation, 18
Canada, 73
Canby, William C., Jr., 209n82
canons of construction, 216n120
Cardozo, Benjamin, 60
Chae Chan Ping v. United States (1889), 86–89, 90
Cherokee Nation, 26, 58, 59, 99
Cherokee Nation v. Georgia (1831), 25, 64, 217n122
Cherokee Nation v. Hitchcock (1902), 211–14n110
Cherokee Nation v. Southern Kan. Ry. Co. (1890), 211–14n110
Child Welfare League of America, 138
China, 86
Chinese Exclusion Act (1882), 86
Chippewa Nation, 21
Choate v. Trapp (1912), 217–18n125
Choctaw Nation v. United States (1886), 211–14n110
Choctaw Nation, 99
citizenship, 29, 68, 95–97, 169, 218–19n126
civil law, 3
Civil Rights Act (1964), 107, 108, 109
Civil Rights Act (1968), 108, 110
Civil War Amendments, 11
Clean Water Act (1972), 177, 180
Cleveland, Sarah H., 198n118, 210n96, 229–30n89
Clinton, Robert N., 201n15, 210n101, 229–30n89, 241–43n29, 251n3, 253n13, 256n37
Collins, Richard B., 201n14
colonization, 47
Commerce Clause, 11–12, 91–92, 94, 106–8, 158, 169. *See also* Indian Commerce Clause
concurrent jurisdiction, 177
Conley v. Ballinger (1910), 211–14n110
conquest, 73–74
consent, 44–45, 74–75, 90, 102, 162–74, 177–80, 182–83
constitutional rights, 31–33
cooperative agreements, 177–78
corporate personhood, 44
Cortner, Richard A., 232n131
Coulter, Robert T., 250–51n84
Coutin, Susan Bibler, 241–43n29
Coyote, ix, 154
Cramer v. United States (1923), 211–14n110
Creek Nation, 83
Creek Nation v. United States (1943), 69–70
criminal law, 3–4
Crow Dog, 1–3; appeal by, 4–6; arrest and conviction of, 3–4

Davis, David, 65, 80, 81, 94, 104
Declaration of Independence, 42–43
Delaware Tribal Business Committee v. Weeks (1977), 253n11
Deloria, Vine, Jr., 194n49, 198n103, 200n9, 217n123, 241–43n29, 249n75, 252n6, 255n34, 256n37
Densmore, Frances, 238n7, 239–40n16
Dobbs v. Jackson Women's Health Organization (2022), 32

Doctrine of Discovery, 54–60, 64, 66, 72, 88
Doran, Michael, 241–43n29
Doty, William G., 237nn1, 3
double jeopardy, 19–21, 22
Douglas, William O., 108, 111
Downes v. Bidwell (1901), 85, 89, 90
Dred Scott v. Sandford (1857), 57, 58–59, 65
dual citizenship, 96–97
duress, 44
Duro, Albert, 18, 19
Duro v. Reina (1990), 18, 214–15n111
Duthu, N. Bruce, 195n61, 230n92

Echo-Hawk, Walter R., 251n4
Elk, John, 66
enumerated powers, 8–9, 74, 116–17, 167, 168, 174
environmental regulation, 177
Epps, Garrett, 226n61
Erdoes, Richard, 238n6
Ervin, Sam, 109
Ex parte Crow Dog (1883), 5–6, 16–19

family law, 138–39
federalism, 26–27, 43, 80, 81, 92, 138
Federal Power Commission v. Tuscarora Indian Nation (1960), 211–12n111, 217n122
Field, Stephen Johnson, 65–66, 86, 88–89
5th Amendment, 20
Fletcher, Matthew L. M., 201n13, 201–2n16, 209n80, 216n115, 236–37nn173–74, 250n83, 256n37
Fletcher v. Peck (1810), 50, 60
Fong Yue Ting v. United States (1893), 224n49
foreign affairs, 74–75
Fortin, Véronique, 241–43n29
foster care, 139
14th Amendment, 11, 228–29n87
Frickey, Philip P, 194n51, 202n17, 250n83, 251–52n5
Fuller, Melville, 83

Gila River Pima Maricopa Indian Community, 18
Gray, Horace, 66
Grier, Robert Cooper, 65
Gritts v. Fisher (1912), 211–14n110

Haaland v. Brackeen (2023), 140–41, 143, 147, 181, 234n147
Hamilton, Alexander, 92
Handbook of Federal Indian Law (Cohen), 134, 216n119, 217–18n125
Harvey, Irene K., 217n121, 241–43n29
Heart of Atlanta Motel v. United States (1964), 232–33n132
Heckman v. United States (1912), 211–14n110
Helbig, Alethea K., 238n7
Hester, Thurman Lee, Jr., 200n11, 208n77, 226n61, 234n153, 257n41
Hoxie, Frederick E., 244n32, 245n41
Hyde, Lewis, 237n2, 237–38n4, 239n13, 240n20
Hynes, William J., 237nn1, 3

Iktomi, ix
Illinois Nation, 51
immigration, 86–87
implicit divestiture, 167, 178
Indian Adoption Project, 138
Indian Arts and Crafts Act (1990), 144
Indian Child Welfare Act (ICWA, 1978), 135, 139–41, 144–45, 176–77, 181
Indian Citizenship Act (1924), 95
Indian Civil Rights Act (1968), 20, 108–10, 112, 141

Indian Commerce Clause, 11, 41, 72, 80, 99, 145, 170; original understanding of, 92, 97; plenary power linked to, 23, 24, 40, 48, 76, 84, 90–91, 96, 102–4, 106, 111, 112–14, 134–35, 142, 143, 147, 158–59, 181–82; social contract theory linked to, 95
Indian Gaming Regulatory Act (IGRA), 198–99n108
"Indian liquor laws," 103–4, 106, 113, 158
Indian Reorganization Act (IRA, 1934), 255n32
Indian Self-Determination and Education Assistance Act (1975), 144
Indian title, 55
inherent authority, 74–75
In re Heff (1905), 211–14n110
Insular Cases (1901), 84–85
international law, 160–61, 174–75
Interstate Commerce Clause, 107, 225–26n60
Iyouse, 9

Jackson, Andrew, 26
Jacobs, Margaret D., 244nn35–36, 244–45n37, 245nn43–44
Jefferson, Thomas, 103
Johnson, Lyndon B., 110, 112
Johnson, William, 171, 204n37
Johnson v. McIntosh (1823), 25, 50–57, 61, 65–66
Jones v. Meehan (1899), 211–14n110
judicial review, 9

Kagan, Elena, 234n146
Kavanaugh, Brett, 101
Kennedy, Anthony, 18–19
Kidder, Homer H., 239n11
King, Martin Luther, Jr., 110
Kiowa, xii

Lara, Billy Jo, 21–22, 41
Ledford, Taylor, 235n163
legal fictions, 43–44, 47
Lessee of Lattimer v. Poteet (1840), 205–6n54
Levindale Lead & Zinc Min. Co. v. Coleman (1916), 211–14n110
Lomawaima, K. Tsianina, 242–43n29
Lone Wolf v. Hitchcock (1903), 28, 33, 67, 83, 87, 100, 105
Lytle, Clifford, 249n75

Madison, James, 92
Mahawaha, 9
Major Crimes Act (1885), 8–15, 20, 23, 141, 143–44
Marshall, John, 13–14, 59, 67, 72, 82, 85, 97; Doctrine of Discovery justified by, 53–57, 64, 88; as iconic figure, 57, 63; Native inferiority assumed by, 16; Native and state land claims equated by, 50; plenary power viewed by, 25–26, 81, 92, 94, 95, 104, 141; protection rationale foreshadowed by, 62–64
Marshall, Thurgood, 70, 98, 107, 111, 112, 114
Matthews, Stanley, 5, 6–8, 16, 99–100
McKinley, Herald, 238n5
McClanahan v. Arizona Tax Commission (1973), 98, 107, 111, 114, 217–18n125
McLean, John, 59, 99, 205–6n54
Merrion v. Jiarilla Apache Tribe (1982), 214–15n111
Mescalero Apache Tribe v. Jones (1973), 108, 111, 214–15n111
Miami Nation, 208n78
Michigan v. Bay Mills Indian Cmty. (2014), 214–15n111
Miller, Samuel Freeman, 12–16, 23, 59, 67, 82, 84, 144
Minnesota, 138

Missouri v. Holland (1920), 254n18
Mitchel v. United States (1835), 205–6n54
Montana, 138
Montana v. United States (1981), 214–15n111
Morton v. Mancari (1974), 214–15n111, 217–18n125
Murphy, Frank, 69–70, 100–101

Nanaboozhoo, ix, 36–38, 76–79, 122–32, 148–57
Nevada v. Hicks (2001), 197–98n98, 214–15n111
New Deal, 105
New State Ice Co. v. Liebmann (1932), 254n24
Newton, Nell Jessup, 206–7n64
Nicholson, Jacob, 58
Nixant, ix
Nixon, Richard M., 108, 110, 112
Non-Intercourse Acts (Trade and Intercourse Acts), 92–94, 103
Norgren, Jill, 198n100, 210n101, 241–43n29
Northwestern Bands of Shoshone Indians v. United States (1945), 219–20n129
Northwest Ordinance (1787), 164, 209n81
Nunez, D. Carolina, 225n50

obligation, of U.S. to Native Americans, 164–65, 166, 180
occupancy rights, occupancy title, 55, 60, 64, 66
Oklahoma v. Castro-Huerta (2022), 101
Oliphant, Mark David, 16–17
Oliphant v. Squamish Indian Tribe (1978), 16–19, 60, 69, 166
Ortiz, Alfonso, 238n6

Perrin v. United States (1914), 211–14n110
Pevar, Stephen L., 202n17
Piankashaw Nation, 51
Pilgrims, 49, 76–77
Plenary Power Doctrine, 15–16, 22–31, 33–35, 92, 145; Indian Commerce Clause linked to, 23, 24, 40, 48, 76, 84, 90–91, 96, 102–4, 106, 111, 112–14, 134–35, 142, 143, 147, 158–59, 181–82; land-based rationale for, 48–62; protection-based rationale for, 62–72, 104–5; taxing power likened to, 40, 41, 45
Plessy v. Ferguson (1896), 98
Pommersheim, Frank, 236n167, 241–43n29, 248n74, 252n7, 253–54n16
Ponsa-Kraus, Christina Duffy, 222nn20, 25
Porter, Robert Odawi, 249n75
Powell, Lewis F., Jr., 70, 112
Prakash, Saikrishna, 254n21
Pratt, Richard Henry, 2–3, 136
presidential power, 74
Property Clause (Territory Clause), 61, 72–73, 134
Prucha, Francis Paul, 226–27n72, 227n73

Rabbit, ix–xi
railroads, 86
Ramah Navajo School Bd., Inc. v. Bureau of Revenue of New Mexico (1982), 214–15n111
Raven, ix, xii
Rehnquist, William, 16, 17, 34, 60–61, 69, 106, 234n146
Richland, Justin, 241–43n29
Robertson, Lindsay, 204n34
Roe v. Wade (1973), 32
Rogers, William S., 58
Roosevelt, Franklin D., 108

Saito, Natsu Taylor, 248n68
Salt River Pima Maricopa Indian Community, 18
Sandoval, Filipe, 104–5
Saynday, xii–xiii
segregation, 89, 90, 98
Self-Determination Era, 19, 29–30, 110–13, 139, 144, 148, 160, 177–78
Seminole Nation, 208n78
Seminole Nation v. United States (1942), 69, 214–15n113
Seminole Tribe of Florida v. Florida (1996), 198–99n108
Shattuck, Petra A., 198n100, 210n101, 241–43n29
Shawnee Nation, 208n78
Shiras, George, Jr., 83
Sicangu Lakota Oyate, 1–7
Singer, Joseph William, 256n39
16th Amendment, 40
Skibine, Alex Tallchief, 241–43n29, 253n12
Snyder, Homer P., 228n82
social contract, 43–45, 47, 48, 61, 95, 162
Sonosky, Marvin J., 109
South Dakota, 138
Spanish-American War, 84
Speed, Nathan, 229–30n89
Spirit Lake Reservation, 21
Spotted Tail, 1–2, 5
Squamish Nation, 16
State of Netherlands v. Federal Reserve Bank (1953), 220n130
Stephens v. Cherokee Nation (1899), 83, 211–14n110
Sunderland v. United States (1924), 211–14n110
Supremacy Clause, 31–32
Swayne, Noah Haynes, 59

Taft, William Howard, 100
Talton v. Mayes (1896), 100
Taney, Roger B., 57–59, 61, 65
taxation, 40, 41, 45, 80, 81–82
Tebben, Carol L., 246n49
Tee-Hit-Ton Indians v. United States (1955), 207–8n72, 219–20n129
10th Amendment, 43, 101
Termination Era, 110–11, 138
Territory Clause (Property Clause), 61, 72–73, 134
Thanksgiving, 49
Thomas, Clarence, 116, 146–47, 171
three-fifths clause, 11
Tiger v. Western In. Co. (1912), 211–14n110
Toler, Lorianne Updike, 252n6
Torres Martinez Band, 18
Trade and Intercourse Acts (Non-Intercourse Acts), 92–94, 103
treaties, 28, 61, 71, 93, 160–61, 163, 168–69; statutes in conflict with, 87
Treaty Clause, 72–73, 111, 114, 134, 142, 166, 167–69, 179–80, 182
Treaty of Paris (1898), 84
tribal courts, 177
tribal nationhood, 168
tribal police, 2, 15
trickster stories, 120–28, 132–35, 142–48, 155–65
trust relationship, 62–63, 70
Tweedy, Ann E., 219n127, 241–43n29
Tullberg, Steven, 250–51n84
Turtle Mountain band, 21

United Nations Declaration on the Rights of Indigenous Peoples (UNDRIP), 175–76
U.S. v. Candelaria (1926), 211–14n110
U.S. v. Celestine (1909), 208n76, 217n122
U.S. v. Chavez (1933), 211–14n110
U.S. v. Clapox (1888), 199n113
U.S. v. Fernandez (1836), 205–6n54

U.S. v. Jackson (1930), 211–14n110
U.S. v. Kagama (1886), 17–19, 27, 83, 84, 85, 100–102, 105, 144; constitutional question in, 10–12; disingenuousness of, 90; facts of, 9; Indian Commerce Clause dismissed by, 23, 24, 41, 158; Native dependency asserted by, 13–15, 33, 67, 82, 89; plenary power authority asserted by, 16, 22, 28, 34, 59, 74; racism in, 16, 23; Thomas's criticism of, 147
U.S. v. Lara (2004), 21–24, 40, 74, 84, 102, 114, 141, 145, 158
U.S. v. McGowan (1938), 211–14n110
U.S. v. Minnesota (1926), 211–14n110
U.S. v. Mitchell (1980), 214–15n111
U.S. v. Noble (1915), 211–14n110
U.S. v. Pelican (1914), 211–14n110
U.S. v. Ramsey (1926), 211–14n110
U.S. v. Rickert (1903), 211–14n110
U.S. v. Rogers (1846), 57–59, 61
U.S. v. Rowell (1917), 211–14n110
U.S. v. Sandoval (1913), 29, 33, 67–68, 83, 104–5
U.S. v. Thomas (1894), 211–14n110
U.S. v. Waller (1917), 211–14n110
U.S. v. Wheeler (1978), 214–15n111

Van Devanter, Willis, 67–6, 83, 105–6
Vinzant, John H., 195n57

wardship, 7, 13–15, 33, 66–70, 81–83, 108, 111–12, 159, 164–65
War Power, 134
Washington v. Confederated Bands and Tribes of Yakia Indian Nation (1979), 214–15n111
Wayne, James Moore, 65
White, Edward Douglass, 67, 83, 100
Wilkins, David E., 194n49, 200n9, 207n67, 217n123, 241–43n29, 243n30, 255n34
Williams, Robert A., 194–95n56, 195–96n62, 206n61, 209n87, 251n85, 251–52n5, 252n6
Williams v. Lee (1959), 82, 197–98n98, 217–18n125
Winton v. Amos (1921), 211–14n110
Wisconsin, 138
Worcester v. Georgia (1832), 25–26, 64–65, 80, 82, 94, 95, 104, 217–18n125

Zug, Marcia, 247n56